HOW THE B[...]
ROCKED T[...]

Leslie Woodhead

HOW *the* BEATLES ROCKED *the* KREMLIN

The Untold Story of a Noisy Revolution

LESLIE WOODHEAD

BLOOMSBURY

LONDON · NEW DELHI · NEW YORK · SYDNEY

First published in Great Britain 2013

Copyright © 2013 by Leslie Woodhead

The moral right of the author has been asserted

No part of this book may be used or reproduced in any manner whatsoever
without written permission from the Publisher except in the case of brief
quotations embodied in critical articles or reviews

Bloomsbury Publishing Plc
50 Bedford Square
London
WC1B 3DP

www.bloomsbury.com

Bloomsbury Publishing, London, New Delhi, New York and Sydney

A CIP catalogue record for this book is available from the British Library

ISBN 978 1 4088 4042 9

10 9 8 7 6 5 4 3 2 1

Typeset by Westchester Book Group
Printed and bound in Great Britain by CPI Group (UK) Ltd, Croydon CR0 4YY

To Artemy Troitsky—my indispensable guide
and improbable friend.

PROLOGUE

Moscow, Red Square, May 24, 2003

As the sun slides behind the Kremlin, a hundred thousand people pack into Red Square, into the heart of Russia. The fairy-tale domes of Saint Basil's cathedral and the ancient red walls of the Kremlin seem to be on fire. The vast crowd roars—and many weep—as a familiar figure strikes the first chords. "Back in the U.S.S.R." rolls out across the square—and Paul McCartney is here at last to sing it.

"People cried rivers and waterfalls of tears," says Artemy Troitsky, Russia's celebrity rock guru. "It was like something that sums up your whole life." "Moscow girls make me sing and shout," sings McCartney, and the crowd sings back, laughing, crying, hugging, dancing to an anthem that had once put some of them in jail, lost them their jobs and their education, turned them into outcasts. Now the Soviet Beatles generation, the kids of the 1960s and the decades of stagnation, are gathered to welcome a real live Beatle. "It was as if the mystical body of the Beatles came to the middle of Moscow," says Sasha Lipnitsky, who has been waiting for more than forty years.

The story of how that Red Square spectacular—unimaginable for decades—finally came to pass is an extraordinary, untold tale. It's the story of how the Beatles changed everything back in the U.S.S.R. and turned a world upside down. It is also the dramatic and troubled history of popular music in the Soviet Union. During seventy years of totalitarian rule in a society where culture always had the power to drive change, exotic Western imports—jazz, dance music, bards with a message, rock 'n' roll—had a seditious force. For decades before the Beatles became a catalyst for change, popular musicians and their music had alarmed Soviet leaders, triggering bizarre wars between guardians of official culture and the generations of musical rebels who insisted on dancing to a different tune.

Unrecorded in accounts of the collapse of the Soviet Union, the impact of the Beatles—and the musical revolution they inspired—were crucial in washing away the vast totalitarian edifice. Their music, their style, their spirit were the keys. They were forbidden, never allowed to play in the U.S.S.R. But their music was irresistible. It blasted open the door to Western culture, fomenting a cultural revolution that helped to destroy the Soviet Union.

Now, the Soviet Union was gone and a Beatle was playing in Red Square. Down in the front row of the audience were Putin and Gorbachev and the bosses of the new Russia, inheritors of the men who once ran the KGB and the vast Soviet empire, the men who had called rock 'n' roll "cultural AIDS" and banned the Beatles. Now the heirs of those repressive old men who had stood on Lenin's tomb gazing out on the armies and the missiles parading through this same Red Square were tapping their feet to "Can't Buy Me Love."

Stalin and Brezhnev and all the others buried in the Kremlin walls could never have imagined this night. They were men whose mission was to turn culture into politics, and create Soviet culture. "The Party couldn't give the kids anything," said Art Troitsky. "There was nothing that reminded me of my dreams." Official culture meant men with bad haircuts belting out patriotic anthems at beefy matrons in cardigans, dancing bears, and massed choirs of soldiers.

It had been in the mid-1960s that the music first reached the Beatles generation, gathered now in Red Square. By stealth, by way of gossip and whispers, through the illicit late-night broadcasts on Radio Luxembourg, the BBC, and Voice of America, the kids tuned in. "Bitles," they whispered. "Yeah, yeah, yeah."

As a generation of Soviet kids dared to sing along, they gave up on "building Socialism" and abandoned the beliefs of their parents. "The Cold War was won by the West," says Troitsky, "not by nuclear missiles, but by the Beatles."

Sitting near Artemy Troitsky to hear Paul McCartney in Red Square was Kolya Vasin. The bear-shaped Vasin is Russia's ultimate Beatles fan, a man who insists his soul was saved by finding the Beatles. "My soul flew to the light," he says, recalling the first time he heard them, "flying with the Beatles." Like so many Soviet kids who defected into their own world, he found a private refuge of peace and love and music. Exiling himself in his own tiny apartment from the repressive realities of the Soviet state, Vasin had created "the John Lennon Temple"—"the only place where I could feel like a free man." Today he dreams of expanding his temple into a vast tower on the edge of Saint Petersburg.

Vova Katzman had made the pilgrimage from Kiev to be here. As a boy, he had defied police and parents to keep the faith with the Beatles. Now he ran Kiev's Kavern Club, a bar crammed with Beatles memorabilia where devotees from across Ukraine and beyond gathered to swap stories of old battles under the banner of the Fab Four. Being here in Red Square, Vova said, "was like a fable—something fantastic." He struggled to find words. "I was shivering deep inside."

Andrei Makarevich was here, too. At school thirty years earlier he had decorated his books with Beatles drawings, and dreamed of starting a band. "Just get a guitar, play like the Beatles, and the world would be smashed." For Makarevich, the dream came true. His band, Time Machine, became the biggest group in the U.S.S.R.—and eventually they were to record at the Beatles' Abbey Road Studio in London.

The Beatles generation were gathered that day in Red Square, many of them grandpas and babushkas now, many who had waited decades, from the very first whispers of the names John, Paul, George, and Ringo—from that moment when they knew there was something else.

Kolya Vasin told me that he had first seen moving pictures of the Beatles forty years ago in a black-and-white clip filmed in Liverpool's Cavern Club, a grainy piece of ancient history. I told him I made that little film, and his face glowed. "You are great man!" he roared.

For me, it all started with that film. Back in August 1962 I made a two-minute cameo of four unknown kids bashing out rock 'n' roll in a Liverpool cellar. Soon the Beatles were conquering the world. But it wasn't until twenty-five years later in Russia that I began to hear stories—incredible at first—about how those lads I first heard in the cellar had undermined the Cold War enemy.

Over more than two decades of traveling and filmmaking as the Soviet Union collapsed and the new Russia was born, I pursued stories of how the Beatles rocked the Kremlin. Everywhere, I found traces of an improbable but unstoppable epidemic, spawned by the Beatles and their music, which swept through the Soviet Union and helped to destroy Communism. Along the way, I came upon the story of how a superpower struggled for seventy years to control Soviet music; and how finally the state lost its hold on millions of kids who escaped into their own world to dance to the music of four irreverent rockers from England.

I found confirmation of the Beatles' impact in unexpected places. An academic at the austere Institute of Russian History insisted that "Beatlemania washed away the foundations of Soviet society," adding, "They helped a generation of free people to grow up in the Soviet Union."

As I got deeper into my journey, I wondered from time to time why I was so obsessed with the Soviet Beatles revolution. Why did it feel so haunting, so personal? There was that little film, of course, and there were my first encounters with the Fab Four long ago. There was the fact that I learned some Russian during my military service as a junior spy back in the 1950s. But underlying all that, for me—a child of the Cold War—the pull was that the story felt like an essential narrative of my times. The standoff between East and West split the world, and nuclear oblivion seemed a real possibility. I remember wondering one night in October 1962 during the depths of the Cuban Missile Crisis if I would wake up the next morning. But somehow the Cold War didn't boil over, and the austerities of the postwar world began to relax. Better times were driving change everywhere across the West; and the soundtrack was rock 'n' roll.

From the early 1980s, I began to work in the Soviet Union and the Soviet satellites of Eastern Europe, spending time in Czechoslovakia, Poland, and Yugoslavia—as well as in Russia—all still under strict authoritarian control. As I came and went—often unofficially—I met up with those kids who made the Soviet Beatles revolution. In the mid-eighties I hung out with nervy rock dissidents in Leningrad and Moscow; in the nineties I journeyed through the messy liberations of post-Communist Russia where the Beatles music was legal at last in a gangster state. Over the past decade, I followed the story to the outer edges of Russia, seven time zones east of Moscow in the once-closed city of Vladivostok. I tracked down Beatles true believers in the chaotic new states of Ukraine and Belarus, where fourteen-year-olds and their grandparents still insisted "All you need is love."

Their stories of how it was for them back in the U.S.S.R. are wild and funny, scary and farcical, and foolishly brave. Their memories of doing battle with the crazed repressions of official culture also chart the final acts of the huge Soviet epic.

I

Four men in kilts stood outside "Lennon's bar," downing pints of beer on a warm summer's afternoon. They sniggered as a busker took a stab at "Day Tripper," and a drunk grabbed a pretty girl, jigging her to the music. Her boyfriend looked on, uncertain. "If you say the wrong thing," the busker told the boy, "he'll knock you out." It came to me that the little drama could be a vignette from "Penny Lane." It was always my favorite Beatles song, and now it played in my head: "In Penny Lane the barber shaves another customer . . ."

I was in Mathew Street in the heart of Liverpool, where it all began for me and the Beatles more than fifty years ago. The narrow alleyway, no more than a gash between looming Victorian warehouses, still held hints of the tough backstreet I remembered. But now I had come back to a Liverpool refashioning itself in 2008 as "European City of Culture." The city I used to know in the early sixties would, I reckon, have had some caustic things to say about that lofty label hung around the neck of their raunchy old town. Still, there was something reassuring about the stories that had swirled around the culture carnival in the city—tales of twenty-million-pound debt scandals, of squabbling politicians, of last-minute panics. A local culture supremo caught the spirit. "Like a fractious family wedding," he said.

On Mathew Street, it was obvious that "culture" meant the Beatles. I was adrift in a Beatles theme park. I wandered into the Cavern Walks mall, past the Lucy in the Sky snack bar, and found myself in the From Me to You Beatles Superstore. A couple of deaf matrons with backpacks were having an excited discussion in sign language about a Yellow Submarine photo frame.

At the Beatles shop, they were playing "I Want to Hold Your Hand"—in German. I was drowning in Beatle stuff: an Abbey Road lunch tin; a facsimile of Paul McCartney's stamp collection; a red plastic Beatles guitar, 1963 vintage, "offers over £900." I needed some air.

And then, just down the street, the Cavern Club. I felt my own ghost, twenty-four years old with everything still ahead of me, looking over my shoulder. On a black metal door a sign proclaimed, THE ORIGINAL ENTRANCE TO THE CAVERN CLUB. I knew this was the place, but that featureless door seemed determined to seal up my memories.

A plastic-covered information sheet told me that the Cavern had been shut down in 1973 to make way for the ventilation shaft of an underground railway that was never built. There was more about the sad story of the site, filled in with rubble, used as a car park, exhumed in the early 1980s and then buried again. It read like a routine for a local comedian, a chronicle of Liverpool's hard times over the past thirty years, laced with droll mishaps.

But it seemed Liverpool resilience had saved the day. The sheet on the door told me there was a new Cavern Club just up the street, built from the reclaimed bricks of the original. Maybe I would find a whiff there of 1962 and my own Beatles epiphany.

Down the steep stairs, and for a moment a mirage of the old Cavern hung in the gloom. The low brick archways, like the crypt of an abandoned church, looked convincingly Cavernous. There was the tiny bandstand jammed against the back wall. But then the illusion collapsed. Geezers in sports jackets sipped lagers, tourists grabbed snaps with their digital phones. In the immaculate loo, the man peeing next to me said, "It's full of history here."

Back on Mathew Street, a fat man with a head borrowed from Nikita Krushchev rolled up to me. "Izvenite—excuse," he said, confirming my Russian hunch, "where I can get Dzohn and Yoko record?" I suggested the Beatles hypermarket just down the street, but I wanted to hear more from this Beatles nut from the former Evil Empire.

This was, after all, why I was back in Liverpool: on the lookout for hints and memories to refuel my search for Russia's "Beatles Generation." Now here was Anatoly from Saint Petersburg, summoned to transport me, like a herald from Beatlestan.

"So what brings you here?" I asked him. It was like opening my door to a Mormon missionary. "Bitles, for me were like Jesus Christ second coming," Anatoly said, "like Heaven." His big face was radiant. "They were flame of freedom," he crooned, "most important legend for my generation." I started to ask him something about how he first heard the Beatles, but he was like the Ancient Mariner, unstoppable. He grabbed my sleeve, and he had one more thing he needed me to understand. "Bitles killed Communism," he said. "Come to Saint Petersburg and I show you!" He rolled off in search of relics.

And then I saw something that took me back to the beginning of my own Beatles story. I spotted a little photograph stuck on a corner of the Cavern door. Black-and-white and grainy, it looked like a snapshot from an old family album. I would have recognized it anywhere: the Cavern, August 22, 1962. It was a still from my film, and the people in the photo were the Beatles.

"It must be dead glamorous being in TV," said the man in the pub.

The setting was a Liverpool drinking den near to closing time, a summer's night in 1962. My drinking companion was a jaunty young man with the eyes of a spaniel, implacably confident of its charm. He was keen to hear about television, I was more interested in what he did. His name, I gathered, was Paul McCartney.

I had been working at Granada Television in Manchester for just a few months. As a very raw researcher on a local TV show, I felt underequipped with evidence of TV glamour. It struck me that the startling performance by Paul and his chums that evening in a nearby cellar was easily the most exotic thing I'd come across in my brief and unspectacular showbiz career. I was still feeling a bit stunned by the banquet of noise the four unknowns had served up in that cellar.

I was aware that the sharp one called John would probably have a withering put-down, ready to pounce if I tried to impersonate a media fast-tracker. I mumbled something humble in reply to Paul's inquiry about my glamorous life, and bought the embryonic Fab Four some more beers.

My regular research beat involved persuading worthies and eccentrics, local officials or champion knitters to come into the studio for the early evening magazine show *People and Places*. My greatest coup to date had been managing to borrow the waxwork head of a recently executed murderer for the program, but the producer got cold feet and insisted that I return it.

Recently things had begun looking up a bit. I had been teamed with a bright young director and assigned to make a series of little films—three or four minutes at most—featuring the old and the new in our region of Northern England under the stolid title *Know Your North*. The notion was, I suppose, a faint hint of the stampede of change that was soon to invade the Britain of the early sixties. I was sent off to track down a crusty old cobbler who still made traditional clogs in a damp shed, and then pair him with a man building a chain of electricity pylons across the Pennine Moors. There had been other odd couplings: an old-style toffee maker and a gay young man designing frocks in a terraced house.

Along the way, I discovered a passion that changed my life and still crowds my dreams: the curious and obsessive trade of filmmaking. Somehow, the pleasures of recording bits of reality on celluloid, and then ordering them on an editing machine, grabbed me. Maybe it had the same appeal for me as assembling those plastic galleons and bombers that had sailed across the sideboards and touched down on the coffee tables of my parents' house in the 1950s. Maybe my passion for filmmaking also had something to do with the need of an only child of the Cold War to impose an order on an unpredictable world.

Filming was a primitive business back then, involving clockwork cameras and vast hair-frying lights. But charging around the North West of England in my pale blue Mini in pursuit of those little films with my mentor—a documentary-film obsessive himself—gave me a running seminar on the magical mechanisms of filmmaking. I was instantly hooked.

It had been decided that our series needed a musical contrast. In a village hall smelling of beer and potted meat sandwiches, I arranged to shoot with the Brighouse and Rastrick Brass Band. We filmed a rousing march, a rich blast of traditional Northern music making, returning to Manchester well satisfied that our music film was half done. But what about the other half? I cast around for something to contrast with the men of brass. Rock 'n' roll was an obvious candidate, but that was happening in London with Cliff Richard and Tommy Steele or in America with Elvis. Where would I find it in the orbit of Manchester?

"There are these kids making a lot of noise in some cellar in Liverpool," a fellow researcher told me. Dick Fontaine was the coolest human I had ever met, effortlessly in touch with trends beginning to stir in the early sixties. I was in particular awe of his jacket—a striped job with narrow lapels, obviously imported from London. It was rumored that Dick had been to America, and had even got to know some black people. Of course he would know about those kids in Liverpool. "They haven't made any records yet," he said, "but they're supposed to be a hit with the local teenagers. Why don't you ring up a man called Brian Epstein?"

A few days later I was sitting with Dick in the grand foyer of the Adelphi Hotel in Liverpool, waiting for Epstein. It was the poshest place in town, a palace of civic pride where self-made businessmen would gather to carve out a deal over a brandy and a cigar. It seemed an unlikely hangout for a rock impresario. This evening the vast lobby was almost deserted. After a while, I began to wonder if our man would turn up. I looked across again at the dapper businessman in a three-piece suit who also seemed to be waiting for someone. This was hardly my idea of a rock 'n' roll manager. "Mr. Epstein?" I inquired. "Let me take you to see the boys," he said.

As Epstein led me down the dungeon stairs into the Cavern Club, a visceral noise surged up to meet me. Tangled up with a woozy cocktail of disinfectant and sweat, it felt physical, dangerous, like an assault. Now, decades after rock 'n' roll became the default soundtrack for generations of kids and their rock-marinated parents, it's hard to recapture the raw shock of my first contact with the Beatles. I stood behind the crowd of kids packed in front of the tiny stage, and the sound came up through the soles of my feet, into my guts. Through a fug of smoke and bodies, I saw four lads crammed against the end wall under an arch of bricks. Their natty waistcoats, white shirts, and ties—and those odd, floppy hairstyles—seemed to be mocking the music that was roaring out of them. It was exhilarating, unsettling. I felt sick.

This was not my music. I was—and am—a modern jazz fanatic. My parents had a music shop in Yorkshire, and since my early teens I had been excavating their treasure trove of jazz albums. Seduced by those cover pictures of well-groomed jazz folk creating cool sounds in Californian Shangri-las, I had discovered a special passion for West Coast jazz. The velvety blending of French horns and oboes with the little-boy-lost trumpet of Chet Baker had become my musical drug of choice. From the mid-fifties, I had been horrified by the first rock 'n' roll upstarts to invade my parents' little record shop. The raucous gang led by Bill Haley and his honking Comets had elbowed aside the bland crooners—the Dickie Valentines and Guy Mitchells, and Ruby Murrays—who had ruled the British turntables. I fumed about Elvis and Cliff, deploying the sneering disdain and portentousness of the teenage jazz convert. I loathed rock 'n' roll.

And now I was stuck in a cellar with the Beatles. "Roll Over Beethoven," "Kansas City," "Money"; the kids in the waistcoats and floppy hair belted out a rock 'n' roll assault. For some reason, I found myself taken with the chugging strut of a song called "Some Other Guy." Their connection with the teenagers packed into the Cavern crypt was electric. Singing those American songs in their thick Liverpool accents made the music fresh, gave it a seditious hint of music hall. They chatted with the audience, trading jokes and cheerful insults. They were charged up with sexual juice. Faces glowed, sweaty and adoring. For sure, something was happening here. Despite myself, I was caught up in the noise and the energy, and the arrogant, fearless confidence of these four young men.

When it was over and the audience had yelled itself hoarse, Epstein led me behind the stage to meet "the boys." In a tiny space not much bigger than a cupboard, they were smoking and joking. "This is John," Epstein said, pointing me at a Beatle who was wringing out his sweat-soaked shirt into a bucket. John said "Hi" and continued wringing. "Why don't we have a drink," I offered.

So I found myself in that Liverpool pub with the fledgling Beatles. They were funny and approachable, but I had no doubt they were sizing me up for my potential as a gatekeeper into TV. We chatted for a while, and Paul told me, "We've written all these songs, but nobody really wants to hear them." I felt he was sure they soon would. John said they had been down to London a few weeks earlier for an audition with Decca records. Now they were waiting to see if anything would come of it. A spot on TV would clearly help. I made encouraging noises.

A couple of weeks later I fumbled my way down the steps into the Cavern Club, with a film crew trailing behind me. With Dick I had lobbied a dubious producer into accepting the Beatles as the second half of our film with the brass band. We were there to shoot a couple of numbers during a lunchtime session.

Hundreds of fans were already queuing down the street, a parade of beehive hairdos, duffel coats, and black stockings. Epstein had clearly made sure to spread the news of the Beatles' first TV appearance. I spotted the poster on a wall in Mathew Street:

AT THE CAVERN CLUB, WEDNESDAY LUNCHTIME
THE SHOW WILL BE FILMED BY GRANADA TV CAMERAS
FEATURING THE NORTH'S TOP GROUP:
THE BEATLES

Filming in the Cavern was going to stretch our primitive capacities. The lead brick of a camera, powered by a car battery and anchored on a big wooden tripod, could only peer at the stage, through a lens with optics that might have failed to impress Galileo. The sound was to be recorded via a single microphone onto a magnetic stripe welded to the black-and-white film. The heat from the lights turned the Cavern into a sauna. The crew, more used to shooting local news items with sheep farmers, were ill at ease.

I had chosen a couple of songs for the filming: the raw, loping "Kansas City" and the song that had caught my fancy a few weeks earlier, "Some Other Guy." With the crowd packed around us, we filmed as the Beatles belted out the two numbers. Unfazed by the looming camera and the harsh lights, they were stunning. I was surprised to see that they had a new drummer, a humorous looking lad with a big nose who seemed a bit out of place. A boy next to me in the crowd told me they'd just dumped their drummer, Pete. The new Beatle was called Ringo, and he'd joined the group just four days earlier. "We hate him," the boy said, gazing ferociously at the drummer, and spitting out, "They dumped Pete Best." Then he yelled, "Pete forever, Ringo never!"

After the band finished playing "Some Other Guy," John shouted, "I suppose we'll have to do it again!" The kids screamed, and they did. The sweaty cellar was stifling now under our lights. We filmed the second song, a searing version of "Kansas City," and then our cameraman climbed onto the stage with a handheld clockwork camera to shoot silent pictures of the band in close-up: faces, guitars, those trendy Cuban-heeled boots. The close-ups would have to be edited somehow into the songs to try and capture something of the atmosphere. In less than an hour, we had shot the first film with the Beatles.

But we were not finished yet. As we wrapped up our equipment and the kids dashed back to their jobs, a gang of burly men took over the stairway to the street. "You should hang on a bit," said the head bouncer. "There's some scallys up there who fancy their chances. They want to rough somebody up about Pete Best and Ringo, and you could be in the firing line." Somebody said George had already been given a black eye by a furious fan. It was an abrupt lesson in the passions of Merseybeat in the early sixties, and in the fierce loyalties the Beatles were already stirring. After a while, I saw a couple of the bouncers slipping iron bars into their sleeves and heading up the stairs. Soon, we heard a shout. "OK, you can come up now."

Driving back to Manchester down the East Lancashire road, I felt glutted with the overload of stuff the Beatles had served up in the Cavern. Abruptly, I had to stop the car and be sick in a ditch.

Then I hit a big problem. I had forgotten about the Musicians' Union. I discovered that the union minimum was twelve guineas—around twenty dollars back then—for each musician. That wasn't a huge issue with the Beatles, and Brian Epstein quickly returned their signed contracts. But the sixteen men of brass would cost our little local program more than two hundred pounds—a budget-wrecking prospect. We were stuck with half a film.

To add to my confusion, I was now an obsessed Beatles fan, trailing after the lads as they played a dismal assortment of Northern clubs, village halls, and a dance promoted by a local horticultural society. The Oasis club in Manchester was a rare classy venue. But a couple of weeks after our filming in the Cavern, in early September 1962 the Beatles recorded a session in Abbey Road Studios in London and met a producer called George Martin. Things were moving, and the posters were getting more excited: THE SENSATIONAL BEATLES, THEY'RE TERRIFIC, YOU MUST SEE THEM! My failure to give Epstein a date for the film to appear on TV was becoming acutely embarrassing.

At the beginning of October, Brian Epstein mounted his most ambitious promotion to date—at the Tower Ballroom, New Brighton, just across the river Mersey from Liverpool—a five-and-a-half-hour rock 'n' roll spectacular, headed by Little Richard and featuring the Beatles. I wandered along the dispiriting Mersey waterfront, gazing out at the mudbanks and wondering what I could say to Brian.

I sweated through Little Richard's screaming rock 'n' roll assault, and then witnessed the Beatles bringing the house down. As they left the stage, Epstein found me and pinned me in a corner. "When are you going to put the boys on TV?" he hissed, switching on the intimidating patrician glare that would help to propel his boys to global stardom. "Just a few days now, Brian," I promised. I had no idea how to make that happen.

With the Cavern film still marooned by the unaffordable brass band, there was only one way out. I had to persuade the producer of the nightly magazine show to let them do a live spot in the studio. He was a kindly Australian eccentric, given to commissioning bizarre items such as sketches performed by political fish puppets, or mounting competitions to find the most attractive big toe in the North West. After sustained lobbying by Dick Fontaine and me, he yielded. "OK kiddos," he sighed, "next Wednesday."

On October 17, 1962, the Beatles appeared on live TV for the first time. Between the usual mix of gardening tips and an interview with a local bell ringer, they performed two numbers: my old favorite "Some Other Guy" and their brand-new record "Love Me Do." To me, they seemed to be a bit muted by the studio atmosphere, and I wished we'd been able to show the film from the Cavern that had captured the raw energy I saw that day. Nobody seemed much interested in the young rockers from Liverpool. As I escorted the boys out of the studio, Ringo said, "Thanks for getting us this gig." I bought myself a pair of Cuban-heeled boots.

Within two weeks, the Beatles were back in Granada's little Studio Four, and they returned again and again over the next few months. By the time they came to do "Please Please Me" in January 1963, there were ten thousand kids trying to break through the studio gates. Days later, they were Number One.

The little film in the Cavern Club was finally aired, more than a year after we shot it, in November 1963. By then the Beatles had four number-one hits, starred at the Royal Variety Performance, and Beatlemania was spreading around the world.

Only the Iron Curtain resisted the invasion. In the Soviet Union, the Communist leadership were determined to block the Beatles virus. Every hint of the Beatles' seditious music was to be stifled. Radios were jammed, censors were equipped with record scratchers, sneering anti-Beatles campaigns were mounted. They were lampooned as "the Bugs," and a cartoon showed insect poison being shaken over the scuttling Beatles.

The mop-top epidemic was perfectly timed to put the four lads from Liverpool in the front line of the standoff between East and West. As the Cold War threatened to explode, the Soviet president, Nikita Krushchev, declared that the electric guitar was "an enemy of the Soviet people"; and the Fab Four's first TV spot in the Granada studio came just five days before the Cuban Missile Crisis brought the world to the brink of nuclear war. Twenty years later, General Secretary Konstantin Chernenko was still shaking his fist: "Rock music is part of an arsenal of subversive weapons, aimed at undermining the commitment of young Russians to Communist ideology."

The Soviet campaigns against the Beatles were skirmishes in the long battle between the cultural commissars in the Kremlin and those Soviet citizens whose music refused to obey the rules.

2

Moscow 1988

"The Beatles more or less melted the hearts and brains of millions of Russian youngsters, and prepared them for the end of the Soviet Union." Artemy Troitsky's casual declaration about the impact of the Fab Four on his generation when I met him in London in 1987 was for me the ultimate seduction. He insisted the Beatles were more decisive than nuclear missiles in winning the Cold War for the West. I was riveted.

Troitsky was to become my unpredictable guide, skeptical prophet, and unlikely friend over those extraordinary years as the world I had always known—the world where East and West growled at each other and pawed the frozen ground, and the Berlin Wall split the planet—cracked and shifted. I became a regular visitor and fascinated witness as the curtain began to tumble down on the vast drama of the U.S.S.R.

Troitsky was in many ways an improbable friend. Handsome in a stubbled, thrown-together Hollywood way, arrogant—he sometimes called himself "the Jesus of cool"—ultra-skeptical, ultra-bright, he moved effortlessly through the gathering Soviet counterculture.

Artemy Troitsky, my essential guide to the Soviet Beatles generation.

A star in his own right, he was a celebrity in Russia, when "celebrity" was an unfamiliar label. He was a fearless impresario of Soviet rock when that could be costly, exploring and promoting the scattered, chaotic rock scene from the Baltic states to Georgia and Siberia.

In 1985, Troitsky had been exiled from the official state press— what he called "the comfortable swamp of the Soviet cultural elite." Soon after Mikhail Gorbachev became the Soviet leader, his cultural commissars had announced an official "Rock club" in Moscow. It seemed an encouraging sign, but Troitsky was immediately suspicious. "The club was arranged by the usual impeccably official organizations," he said, "the Communist Youth organization Komsomol, along with the Moscow city cultural department and the trades unions—so I didn't have much hope." Art was duly ejected from the door of the Orwellian "House of People's Creativity." For Moscow's rock community, it was not an encouraging introduction to Gorbachev's new Russia.

Troitsky responded by mounting a huge benefit rock concert in

May 1986 for the victims of Chernobyl, bulldozing through the opposition of nervous officials at a time when mega rock charity was unknown in Russia. The concert for Chernobyl was a serious embarrassment for the unseasoned Gorbachev regime, which was still trying to manage information about the disaster with a defensive spasm of evasion and denial. The Kremlin had remained silent until the radioactive plume from Chernobyl triggered sensors in Sweden, and the government had failed to warn people in the area to protect themselves. The Soviet state now found itself upstaged in supporting victims by Troitsky's rock benefit. Inspired by Live Aid, the Moscow concert attracted a crowd of thirty thousand to hear seven top Soviet bands. It was an unprecedented demonstration of enterprise beyond the control of the state, and it was months before Soviet TV broadcast selected highlights.

I had met Art Troitsky when he came briefly to London, allowed to travel through the Iron Curtain at last in the early days of Gorbachev—though Art's wife was made to stay in Moscow for fear the couple might defect. He said he was sorry that he hadn't escaped in a hot air balloon. He came to promote his book about rock music in Russia, inevitably entitled *Back in the USSR*. It had an eye-catching cover parodying the Soviet hammer and sickle: the hammer had been replaced by a guitar. It was, Troitsky emphasized, with a confidence that brushed aside his slight stammer, "the very first book on Soviet rock." He introduced me to an alternative universe of Latvian gypsy rock organists and Estonian rockabilly groups with homemade synthesizers, of bands called Hairy Glass and Russo-Turkish War and Purple Catastrophe. It was a rock culture where groups were hedged in by state regulations and required to compete before judges in a kind of Soviet *Pop Idol* for official prizes. Somehow, the music continued to flourish in a thousand exotic shapes—the "curious epidemic," as Troitsky diagnosed it, of Russian rock.

Troitsky had no doubt about the source of that epidemic. "Every Soviet rock band," he insisted, "caught the rock virus from the Beatles." He first heard the Fab Four when he was nine years old in 1964. He still recalled that moment. "For us the Beatles hit the bull's-eye. They had everything—joy, rhythm, beauty, spontaneity." Art said he would introduce me to some of the Soviet Beatles generation, and in the winter of 1988 I traveled to Moscow, hungry to hear more.

I had been in Moscow just once before, a couple of years earlier, as part of a delegation of British TV folk. We had arrived in the uncertain dawn of a new era for the Soviet Union. Mikhail Gorbachev had been the Soviet leader for just a few months, and his citizens were struggling to get to grips with his new policies, known as *glasnost* and *perestroika*. The words meant "openness" and "reconstruction," and there was talk of bold initiatives to overturn the stagnation of the past twenty years, as well as allowing more free speech and a degree of cultural freedom. But people were all too familiar with empty slogans, and there was a brooding suspicion about what the new policies might mean, beyond a clampdown on alcoholism. Still, long-banned books, plays, and movies had been released, and it seemed that our invitation to screen films and share ideas with Soviet Television movers and shakers was aimed at opening doors to the West.

But Moscow was still a grim place, confirming all my stereotypes of the Evil Empire. There were as rumored no bath plugs, and all the restaurants seemed to close for lunch. Endless queues waited, hoping for a delivery of plastic shoes. The lives of young people were still largely organized by the Komsomol, the Communist Youth organization which had forty million members—a mobile pool of cheap labor and political activism. Komsomol youth knew that obedience to the official line would be rewarded with privileges and promotion. Glasnost promised to alert the leadership to the concerns of Soviet youngsters; but it also reignited old debates about whether rock music was a Western import aiming to weaken the nation's fiber and should be banned. Continuing "Revolutionary vigilance" was urged.

Fun seemed in short supply, and the music I watched on Soviet TV was an unvarying diet of folk songs and balalaika music. The only hint of rock 'n' roll I encountered was when I overheard one of our interpreters saying good-bye to a colleague with a solemn "see you later, alligator."

That first visit was an uneasy few days. As a former Cold War eavesdropper with a history of snooping on Soviet pilots in Berlin thirty years earlier, I couldn't shed a paranoid fantasy that some heavy would come and tap me on the shoulder. Hadn't I heard that there were as many as ten KGB watchers for every foreign visitor? I had after all signed Britain's Official Secrets Act. Maybe I'd be hauled off for interrogation at the huge yellow-brick KGB headquarters near my hotel. The fearsome Lubyanka—the prison in the bowels of the building—had been dragging confessions from enemies of the people since Stalin's time; surely they would be licking their lips at the prospect of a Western infiltrator? My uneasiness hadn't been helped by the fact that in recent years I had made several clandestine trips through the Iron Curtain in pursuit of TV films. In Poland and Czechoslovakia and Yugoslavia I had tracked down off-limits locations and held whispered conversations with dissident troublemakers who insisted that we meet in remote parks, away from bugs and prying eyes.

But Moscow felt different on my second visit in 1988. A few days before I arrived, Gorbachev had dared to use the word *democracy*, and there was some evidence to support Gorby's recent declaration that "what is not forbidden is allowed." He had suggested that there might perhaps be no need for a party line on everything from ballet to scientific experiments. There was a huge cultural blossoming fueled by an openness unknown for six decades. Dave Brubeck's "Take Five" was playing in the hotel lobby, and the reception desk accepted American Express. I found myself inspecting everything—shops, buildings, people—for signs of change.

Still, three years after Gorbachev began his campaign against decades of stagnation and lethargy, the ice floes of inertia were slow to melt. The more than forty-year-old decrees of culture chief Andrei Zhdanov demanding that artists devote their energies to rallying the people around the Socialist cause had not been revoked. Glasnost was defined as "openness in the interest of Socialism," and eighteen million bosses commanding countless bureaucrats continued to govern the daily lives of ordinary citizens. The doorman at my foreigners-only hotel still looked like Brezhnev in a cardigan, and ruled his little domain with an apparatchik's casual brutality, turning away most Soviet visitors. Only the fact that Art Troitsky and his fashion journalist wife, Svetlana, were confident and stylishly dressed, he in black, she in a pink Italian jacket and miniskirt, allowed them to breeze past the doorman.

We ate in the hotel's dining room, taking in a stupendous view of Red Square through the ruched net curtains while an orchestra got up as Cossacks played Viennese waltzes. Snow swirled around the Kremlin towers, creating a cinematic tableau as Art talked about how the first rumors of the Beatles had reached the Soviet Union.

"Their music arrived here at exactly the right time in the mid-sixties," he said. "A couple of years earlier, the Beatles might have landed on far less fertile ground. We had our own heroes then—Yuri Gagarin, the first man in space, and Fidel Castro with his romantic bearded revolutionaries in Cuba, plus of course our charismatic leader Nikita Khrushchev, who promised to bury the United States. And we believed it. I remember as a kid it was cool to be a Soviet." Troitsky's father, a Soviet journalist specializing in relations with Latin America, had known Che Guevara. "My dad idolized Che," he told me.

Khrushchev called Yuri Gagarin "the new Columbus" and Gagarin's pioneering space flight inspired an explosion of heroic songs. "We had many very popular patriotic songs about our victories in space," Art recalled, and he sang me a little of a ballad by Shostakovich: "The motherland knows how her son is flying in orbit." "It was the last splash of genuine popular enthusiasm for the Soviet Union," he said. A song cycle called the "Constellation of Gagarin" with soaring lyrics celebrating "the heavenly dome aflame with the dawn of a Gagarin Spring" sold millions of records. I recalled Krushchev's welcome to Gagarin when the space hero returned to Moscow. He kissed Gagarin on both cheeks, and delirious crowds danced in Red Square.

Troitsky's father was based with the family in Prague from 1963, just before the first echoes of the Beatles reached the Soviet Union. Art grew up in the Czech capital, where Western radio was more accessible than in Moscow. There he discovered rock 'n' roll as an eleven-year-old, and it soon got him into trouble.

"I played Beatles and Stones, Beach Boys and Kinks tracks over the school radio during break times. The other kids loved it, but the school head didn't."

Troitsky was ordered to stop, but he protested that this was the music of progressive youth, music against the Vietnam War, the music of love and peace.

"The head was unmoved and told me I must repent. When I refused, I was called 'uncorrectable' and expelled from the Young Pioneers youth organization."

In the spring of 1968, the Troitsky family were recalled to Moscow. Art kept quiet about his rock'n' roll sins, and got hold of a red scarf so he could look like a Young Pioneer. But when the Soviet tanks rolled into Prague that summer to stamp out "Socialism with human face" in Czechoslovakia, Art told his classmates the truth about the invasion.

"I said that Soviet propaganda about how the soldiers were welcomed by cheering crowds was a lie."

His shocked parents were hauled into the school to hear young Artemy being rebuked—and once again expelled from the Young Pioneers. His life as a cultural dissident was launched.

By the time the Troitsky family had returned to Moscow, the

heady days of Krushchev's heroic Socialism when it was "cool to be a Soviet" were long gone. But then, as Art put it, reducing titanic Kremlin power struggles to a hip shorthand, "in 1964, Mr. Khrushchev was kicked out and replaced by a bunch of much more boring guys. And this was exactly the moment when the Beatles' music started to infiltrate our hearts and brains."

We went upstairs to the smoky little bar where hard-currency hookers in angora sweaters stuffed themselves from a box of chocolate-covered cherries and clawed at German businessmen. The bar seemed poised on the edge of the new Russia, Pepsi-Cola cans displayed in a glass case like precious icons, while an ancient babushka with a broom snoozed in a corner. Troitsky talked about the irresistible appeal of Beatles music for Soviet kids. "American rock 'n'roll like Little Richard was way too fast, too violent, too weird. When the Beatles arrived with their beautiful melodies, it was completely different. And they had the 'something else' factor—the electric sound, long hair, the spirit of freedom."

Troitsky's wife, Svetlana, had her own early memories of the Beatles. "At the beginning, they looked very unthreatening, like Russian men who live with their mums till they're forty, wearing nice little suits and white shirts." She glanced at the hookers and their German targets, and it seemed to spark a recollection of a more innocent time. "I remember at school I could buy a very bad copy of a Beatles photo for fifty kopeks—it was a choice either to have breakfast or the picture."

Art chatted with a British journalist friend, Martin Walker from the *Guardian*, who was feasting on stories of Gorby's new Moscow, where Soviet rock and the new privatized lavatories jostled for his attention. Walker had dubbed Russia "Upper Volta with rockets"—like an impoverished African state, equipped with nukes—but it was nirvana for a young reporter. He had been Art's best man at his wedding, and as they huddled to talk about some new story, Svetlana explained how she had improvised her own style by copying items from Western magazines and hunting down vintage dresses in antique markets. She recalled the early impact of the Beatles with a fashion writer's eye. "We cut the lapels off old jackets to make a collarless Beatles-style copy we called a 'Bitlovka.'" Lennon's rimless glasses came from second-hand shops, and Armenian shoemakers improvised Cuban-heeled boots from old army castoffs. "So it was like a fairy tale," she said, "thousands of kids grabbing this window from the West to change their image just a little."

We headed off into the Metro, on our way to meet up with a Soviet rock pioneer Troitsky had found for me. In the gorgeous Stalinist palace of Mayakovsky station, a couple of American tourists with guidebooks were gaping at this workers' paradise of gray marble and mosaics celebrating the "Soviet Sky." On the spot where Stalin had addressed the Communist Party faithful at the opening of the station just fifty years earlier, Art began a tirade about the oppressive horrors of Soviet culture when he was growing up. "I just hated it all," he growled, "because it was all totally square, totally uncool, the singers had awful haircuts and sang like Brezhnev at the Party Congress. It was totally unsexy, totally rigid." I could hear the train approaching, but Troitsky was on a roll. "There was nothing bright and free and funky and funny about it. And those were exactly the vitamins we needed back then in the sixties, so we grabbed them from the Beatles." The train swept away the rest of Troitsky's dazzling rant.

In Gorky Park, crackling loudspeakers were belting out "The Skaters Waltz," and skaters were twirling on a frozen pond. They looked effortless, as if freed for a moment from the oppressive heaviness of their daily lives.

The paths were frozen, too, and skaters regularly swished past us as we teetered along in the darkness. Art was talking now about Russian rock. "The real wave started in the mid-sixties," he said, "and without exception they were all inspired by the Beatles." Another skater hurtled past, and Art picked up his story. "Listening wasn't enough—they wanted to do it themselves. They played cover versions of Beatles songs, trying to copy the English words, but most of them had no idea what they were singing about." In Gorky Park, we were headed to meet one of the first of those Soviet Beatles.

We came to a building near the Moscow River, where a wheezy old guy was minding the door. Along a shabby corridor the sound of assorted rock guitars rattled the flimsy walls, mingled with the smell of cooking. There seemed to be a warren of rehearsal rooms, and somewhere a kitchen. Album sleeves lined the walls, all featuring a hairy tribe led by a chubby guy with a tangle of black hair.

"This is Stas Namin's place," Troitsky announced.

I knew something about Namin. The grandson of Anastas Mikoyan, a former premier of the Soviet Union, he had been raised in a house of privilege and music. Shostakovich, Rostropovich, and a parade of famous musicians were regular visitors. At a top military cadet school in the early sixties, Namin marched in Red Square parades—and fell in love with the music of the Beatles. He got permission to form a rock band at the military school, playing to officers and fellow cadets. When he left the military, Namin grew his hair and deployed his impressive political pedigree to establish a rock group of his own called Tsvety—"Flowers." A quarter of a century before Gorbachev's liberations, the band pioneered official rock in the Soviet Union; they were invited to join the fusty Composers' Union and were allowed to make nationwide tours.

I had a memory that things had not always gone well for Namin, and while we waited for him to show up I asked Art to fill me in. "What happened to him is what happened to lots of people when rock music got mixed up with big shit called Communism." Art sounded as bitter as I had ever known him. "Stas was great at using his contacts, and he managed to make the first Soviet rock records on the state label Melodiya." Troitsky made "Melodiya" sound like a dirty word. "Then the press called Stas's group 'the Soviet Beatles,' so the Ministry of Culture banned them and their name 'Flowers' for making Western propaganda and pushing hippie ideas."

I looked at the faded photos on the album covers around the walls, and now the faces had a feeling of condemned men. There seemed to be a kind of watchful insecurity in the shifting kaleidoscope of styles. Here they looked as well drilled as Socialist Young Pioneers, there they leaped in the air with the abandon of sixties flower children, sometimes they were Europopsters with shining white T-shirts, sometimes they were big-city funk stars with satin pants and greasy hair. Surviving through it all, Namin was a rock star for all seasons. Troitsky carried on with his story. "Stas took a two-year break, and then re-formed his band with a safe, boring name—the Stas Namin Group. It was even more popular, but of course it was banned again—forbidden to appear on TV or radio, never mentioned in the press."

Another political mood swing in the early eighties allowed the group to surface once more, but following an enthusiastic review in *Time* magazine—a bourgeois endorsement that made them politically suspect—they were targeted by the KGB. By 1983, Stas Namin had had enough. He switched to film and video, and became a successful photographer. The head-spinning contortions of official policy made me understand how Namin and his generation of Soviet musicians had often simply given up on fighting the system.

"But that wasn't the end of the story," Troitsky said. "Like lots of us, he was rescued by Gorbachev. Stas and his band were the first Soviet rock group to tour America, and they went around the world."

And now Namin had a new focus for his unstoppable energies. Art said this down-at-heel hangout in Gorky Park was the Stas Namin Center—one of Russia's first enterprises not controlled by the state. "The idea," Troitsky said, "is to give a chance to young artists, poets, designers, and musicians." It was hard to see this ramshackle place with its food smells, flimsy walls, and candles in Chianti bottles as a hub of creativity, but I guessed if anyone could pull it off, Stas Namin might be the man.

And here he was at last, looking much like the hairy troll on those album covers. Art said he had given me a big buildup as a guy who had made films with the Beatles and the Stones, and I was hit by a tide of charm and affability that must have been a key asset in Namin's long battles with the state. We sat down at a little table with a pink check tablecloth, and Stas talked about the Beatles.

"They changed everything," he said, "our music, our way of dressing, our way of living." He laughed, a genial rumble that strained at his tight T-shirt. "Officially the Beatles were called things like 'Long-haired bastards,' very rude and unpleasant. But at that time everything that came from the West was forbidden." Namin's group were regularly accused of smuggling "Western-style music" to subvert their audiences, and his family connections with Soviet power gave him an understanding of how authority felt about the Fab Four. "They were very dangerous for the regime, because [the leaders] knew the Beatles gave Russian kids some kind of freedom inside." It seemed extraordinary that the drab apparatchiks who ruled over Soviet culture would have been aware of a threat from these boys far away in Liverpool. "Did the people at the top really understand this threat?" I asked him. "They felt it," Namin said. "They didn't really understand, because that would be too smart for them." I could see Troitsky nodding. "But they always hate everything not under their control"—his hands mimicked pushing something away—"they were scared by anything that has power and might influence people. Their music, their energy was not under control. That's why the Beatles were dangerous."

Namin's insight into how four kids from the backstreets of the Cold War enemy had alarmed the all-powerful men in the Kremlin was fascinating. But it was also puzzling. How could this seemingly artless music, free of any obvious political message, sung in a foreign language with regional accents, have provided a catalyst for changing an entire generation? It felt almost like a chemical reaction, as though something at the heart of Soviet culture had been touched and altered by the Beatles and their music. I wanted to track down how that had happened, and what it meant for millions of the children of Socialism.

Abruptly, the cunning Stas Namin became very Russian. "The Beatles were a strange mystical phenomenon," he murmured, "way beyond a rock group." His command of English seemed to be running out of oxygen, and he wanted to talk about something else. "What do you think of this?" he said. He walked across the room and slipped a tape into a cassette player. Thunderous rock music flooded over us. "My new band," Stas said, "Gorky Park." He was already on to his next adventure.

3

Stas Namin's stories of negotiating the whims of the Soviet cultural commissars were wild and illuminating. They gave me a glimpse of the surreal relationship between popular music and the state, and I wanted to know more. If it had been tough for Namin over the past twenty years, how was it for musicians back in the 1930s trying to stay out of Stalin's gulags? How could they keep up with the ever-shifting rules and borderlines? And what—in the name of Vladimir Ilyich Lenin—was the Kremlin's idea of an acceptable pop song?

Art Troitsky was my guide as I began to excavate the tragicomic drama of Soviet pop from jazz to rock in the shadow of what he called his "monster state."

"There's a favorite story of mine from the early thirties," he began. "It will give you a flavor of how the Kremlin has always tried to hijack popular music. So Stalin had gathered a group of comrades from the Central Committee for a party at his dacha. How would you have liked to be at that party? Stalin used to go on about how 'music is an excellent thing since it reduces the beast in men.'" Troitsky shook his head. "How would he know? The old ghoul apparently had a 'sweet voice,' and he liked to sing peasant folk songs,

Georgian laments, Cossack ballads—even hymns, if you can believe it." At the end of the evening, Art's story continued, Stalin took control of a gramophone, imported from America, and began to play dance music. As the nervous comrades tried to guess their leader's whim, he urged them onto the floor. Art pictured the scene: the gray apparatchiks of the politburo required to dance with one another while Stalin roared with laughter. "Then of course he relished tormenting his Kremlin creatures with insults and menacing suggestions about how clumsy dancing might indicate a lack of Socialist commitment."

Art suggested the grisly charade could be a metaphor for the turbulent history of popular music in the Soviet Union, as fearful apparatchiks struggled to interpret the deadly mood swings of the leadership. As he laid out the story over seven decades of the relationship between the Kremlin and popular music, it was clear how the ebb and flow of politics—domestic and international—was always crucial in dictating the authorized musical line. As a consequence, the official Soviet attitude to popular music was unpredictable and hazardous, swerving dangerously from approval to suppression and back in repeated waves of state paranoia.

I told Troitsky a story of my own. In the depths of the Cold War, I had found myself at the top of a shaky watchtower just yards from a battalion of Soviet soldiers. I was a teenage intelligence spook, recently graduated from a secret spy school in Scotland where I'd been taught Russian by the Royal Air Force along with hundreds of other Cold War conscripts. I could see Art was already intrigued, and I went on with my story.

After months of training in military Russian, clamped inside headphones and bombarded daily by messages such as "my undercarriage is down and locked," I was posted to Berlin in the fall of 1957. In the depths of the Cold War, I arrived at a former Luftwaffe base, where some buildings were still decorated with swastika carvings. My assignment was to listen in on Soviet pilots flying over

Communist East Germany, and scribble down their routine communications. The purpose of this was unclear to me or any of my fellow linguists. Scared and bored in the middle of endless night duties, I regularly defected from my routine espionage trawl to indulge in a private passion. I tuned my radios to the American Forces Network and found the *Jazz Hour*.

My chilly outpost on the edge of the Iron Curtain was suddenly flooded with the delectable noise of the Modern Jazz Quartet, and the richly reassuring voice of the deejay, Willis Conover. The Cold War melted for those few—highly unauthorized—minutes. What I didn't know then was that for some of those Soviet soldiers just over the fence, Willis Conover and his jazz programs were even more precious. From the mid-1950s for a quarter of a century, Conover brought Jazz to the U.S.S.R. and Eastern Europe. Although his program *Music U.S.A.* was inevitably launched as part of America's Cold War propaganda arsenal, Conover's relaxed and undogmatic style somehow survived the blizzards of Soviet jamming, and allowed the music to speak for itself. *Music U.S.A.* became an essential ingredient in the story of how popular music from the West found its way into the ears and hearts of Soviet citizens who resisted the culture imposed by their leaders, and chose "the sound of surprise."

"I remember my father talked about those Voice of America broadcasts," Troitsky said, "but of course he was a Socialist true believer so he thought that was all enemy propaganda. For my father's generation the broadcasts and the music were Capitalist weapons, aiming to undermine our revolution." That feeling of being besieged, of needing to stay on guard against outsiders, especially the West and its ceaseless efforts to subvert the U.S.S.R., was fundamental to the worldview of millions of Soviet citizens. It was of course the flip side of the paranoia about Communism that shaped the worldview of millions of Americans. What fascinated me was the role of popular music in fueling and maintaining that standoff over seventy years.

Most of all, I wanted to find out how, in the end, the music had changed the U.S.S.R. and the world.

During visits to the Soviet Union from the late 1980s, I talked to Art Troitsky and to other people who helped me to understand and negotiate the obsessive entanglement of culture, politics, and state paranoia that had shaped Soviet ideas about music in the decades before the Beatles. I came to see how that stew of belief, ideology, and fear had also shaped the response to the lads from Liverpool, who never played here, but who made the music that challenged everything.

From the beginning, the aim of the Russian Revolution had been to create "the new Soviet man." As the state set about reshaping millions of Soviet citizens, culture was to be a key weapon—and official culture was to reach into every citizen's life. Inspired by Soviet artists, the people's energies would be harnessed in a collective spasm of shared labor to create the perfect society. The leaders of the revolution believed that exposure to Socialist art would transform selfish citizens into selfless builders of Socialism. The defining slogan was delivered by Stalin in 1932 when he declared that the writer—and, by extension, the artist—was "the engineer of the human soul."

But at the beginning of the revolution of 1917, a very different cultural revolution—messy and uncontrollable—was erupting on the other side of the planet as jazz spilled out of New Orleans and across the world. The chasm between those visions of culture—the utopian dictatorship of the Kremlin and freewheeling Western capitalism—was to shape the battles between musicians and the state over the seven decades of the Soviet Union.

Even before the Soviet revolution, a fierce debate over music had begun. Hard-line Socialists demanded cultural engineering, by a state organization known as Proletkult, to produce a proletarian music that would reject all influences from the West such as European opera or popular songs. They were opposed by traditionalists who recommended that peasants and workers be exposed to the best of established classical music—symphonies, operas, and ballet music.

After the early years of the revolution, Lenin rejected the hard-liners of Proletkult in his determination to stamp out all potential rivals. After 1920, he established a centralized bureaucracy to control and supervise music in line with the Communist Party's program to regulate every area of life in the new society. Traditional peasant choirs were reshaped as factory workers' collectives and military ensembles, while central authorities exercised tight control over their repertoires. Folk songs were reworked as political propaganda, and cultural commissars ensured the ideological correctness of all musical material. Artistic Control Commissions in Moscow and other big cities issued permits for all concerts, establishing a system of controls that, over the next seventy years, would work to supervise and regularly intimidate musicians and every kind of music.

But musicians and their music proved to be unruly subjects; and as the Communist Party shifted its line to match the whims of its leadership, the story of popular music in the U.S.S.R. was always more unpredictable and surprising than the official version planned by the political masters in the Kremlin.

By the early 1920s, the leaders of Russia's proletarian revolution found themselves having to respond to the cultural assault of Western jazz and dance music. The coming of jazz to the Soviet Union prefigured in many ways the conflicts and struggles that would torment the state and its rulers when the rock 'n' roll virus arrived forty years later.

A craze for American-style dances—ragtime and the cakewalk—had linked Russian bourgeoisie and the United States since the beginning of the twentieth century. The foxtrot had reached Saint Petersburg by the eve of the revolution. Prince Felix Yusupov reported that as he poisoned Rasputin, "the gramophone was playing 'Yankee Doodle Went to Town.'"

For the new revolutionary authorities, jazz presented a confusing challenge. It came from the decadent United States, it was rough and unprofessional and hard to discipline—unacceptable in the new workers' paradise that sought to control every aspect of life. At the same time, jazz was "proletarian music," which was approved by the cultural commissars—and the people were fascinated. Lenin was not a jazz fan; he had a passion for Beethoven, and few in the new Soviet leadership had any great enthusiasm for the folk music of the peasant masses.

In the chaotic period after the revolution, an assault on American popular music was launched. A "proletarian cultural movement" campaigned furiously against the Western intruder, and in an attempt to provide a wholesome Soviet music, the Commissariat of Public Enlightenment organized concerts of operatic classics for the masses. The vast bureaucracy of the Artistic Control Commissions proliferated in the cities, shutting off the new nation from the music that was sweeping through the West. A famine of musical instruments, particularly the saxophone—which was virtually unavailable across the Soviet Union—stifled any stirrings of musical dissidence. For the next sixty years, the dreaded sax was to be a weathervane for the volatile climate of popular music in the U.S.S.R.

I wonder how my father would have dealt with those stifling controls and regulations as he dreamed of trying to build a musician's life. In the 1920s he was a working-class boy in the North of England, studying the violin and saxophone, and listening to records of the new dance bands bringing the wild music from America. It must have been hard enough to face the disapproval of godly parents and curtain-twitching neighbors. But my father didn't also have to confront the fierce denunciations of an all-powerful state. And of course he could get hold of a saxophone without feeling like a criminal.

In the hothouse of fledgling revolution, massive social dislocation, and bureaucratic mania, Russia's first jazz band took root as a freakish outcrop of Soviet culture. In July 1921, Russian émigré Valentin Parnakh, a Dadaist poet, surrealist and dancer, became fascinated by American jazz bands he heard in Paris. Parnakh was to become a central figure in the burgeoning Soviet arts of the early 1920s, promoting the films of Charlie Chaplin, writing regularly about contemporary Western music, and even having his portrait painted by Picasso. In Paris, Parnakh was electrified by the potential he saw in jazz to destroy the decadence of classical ballet. In his essay "The Jazz Band," he enthused about "a music of dissonances, syncopations, crashes, soaring brasses, howls and alarm sirens." For him, the band was itself part of a wild dance.

In the summer of 1922, Parnakh returned to Moscow with a collection of jazz instruments. He mounted a press campaign, insisting that jazz was the essence of modern movement and extolling the "eccentricity" of the new music. His timing was perfect. Faced with huge resistance to forced collectivization in the countryside and the factories, Lenin had recently announced a New Economic Plan. He dismantled the state monopoly of agriculture and allowed individual enterprises, while maintaining tight central control. After years of repression, Russia's artists embraced the new freedoms, and Parnakh was ready.

On October 1, 1922, his First Eccentric Orchestra of the Russian State Federation and Socialist Republic gave its opening concert at the State Institute for Theatrical Art in Moscow. With a band made up of piano, banjo, two violins, xylophone, and drums, the music would surely have been unrecognizable to the originators of jazz in New Orleans. But the audience in Moscow was enthusiastic, and at a second concert Parnakh read jazz poetry and demonstrated new dance steps, while his band performed alongside a "noise orchestra" of bottles, sheet metal, and machines. It all sounds oddly reminiscent of a hippie "happening" fifty years later in San Francisco. But with no radio or recording outlets, the audience for Parnakh's jazz orchestra remained limited to a small elite in Moscow.

Those early encounters between the ponderous institutions of the state and the new music sound as improbable and comic as an elephant dancing with the Bolshoi ballet. However, the commissar for public enlightenment, Anatoly Lunacharsky, was intrigued by reports of Parnakh's jazz band. In November 1922 the orchestra was hired to play at a Congress on the Fifth Anniversary of the Bolshevik Revolution. The commissar of agriculture was also impressed, hiring the band to play at the first All-Union Exhibition of Agriculture and Cottage Industries in May 1923. A Soviet press report boasted: "For the first time jazz music was performed at an official state function, something which has never happened in the West." Only half a dozen years after the revolution, "new Soviet man" was embracing the decadent music from the West—and claiming to be taking a lead in promoting jazz.

While Parnakh prospered, official efforts to attract Communist youth with a concert of *agitmuzyk*, dour propaganda songs calculated to arouse support for the revolution, failed to win much enthusiasm. A campaign by the Association of Proletarian Musicians to promote ideologically committed music was finding proletarian audiences hard to seduce. Meanwhile Parnakh's band claimed the film and theater directors Sergei Eisenstein and Vsevolod Meyerhold as fans. For the next half-dozen years of the New Economic Plan, jazz and Parnakh flourished in the Soviet Union—while in the West, jazz was often reviled and sometimes censored. The isolation of revolutionary Russia insulated the new state from the campaigns against jazz in the outside world. In America, the music was called "the path of degredation," while in Britain anti-jazz curfews were imposed.

It was at about this time that my father quit his solid job as a printer in Yorkshire to take to the road as a dance band musician. I look at the yellowed photographs of the studious young man, bashfully cradling his tenor sax, and try to imagine what it must have taken to break away from a conventional life in a provincial town for a career playing the disreputable new music. I always thought it must have been a step as bold as abandoning a career as a high-flying lawyer forty years later to join a rock band.

Lenin died in January 1924, after warning against the ambitions of Josef Stalin. In a secret testament, Lenin recommended that Stalin be removed from the Soviet leadership; but Stalin schemed to block the release of the testament and quickly moved to execute or exile all opponents. Soon he was establishing his unchallenged dictatorship over the Soviet Union, building a personality cult around his leadership. For the next quarter century, Stalin would rule over every aspect of the lives of more than one hundred fifty million Soviet citizens. But the first years of his leadership gave few hints of what was to come.

Lenin's death had released an explosion of bourgeois excess. In February 1926 an advance brigade of the international jazz revolution came to Russia. A group of thirty-five black American dancers, singers, and jazzmen arrived in Moscow for a three-month tour of the Soviet Union. Sam Wooding and his Chocolate Kiddies were warmly received and handsomely paid, and they were an immediate sensation with Russian artists and urban audiences.

The Chocolate Kiddies introduced the Charleston, and exotic spectaculars flooded the popular theaters. Despite his success, Sam Wooding's insistence on playing a hybrid symphonic jazz limited his appeal to Soviet youth who were reminded of the bland music their parents listened to. The arrival from America in the mid-twenties of an authentic jazz band, Benny Peyton's Jazz Kings, thrilled audiences from Moscow to Kiev. Their star clarinet and saxophone soloist, Sidney Bechet, electrified Soviet fans with his searing solos and wild, vodka-fueled lifestyle. Bechet, born in New Orleans, exuded the raw energies of the real thing. Even the forbidding Commissar Lunacharsky would drop in to hear the band at the Malaya Dmitrovka theater—no doubt trying to avert his gaze from the couples indulging in the decadent Charleston. But when Peyton and Bechet left the U.S.S.R. in 1926, the door closed behind them. It was to be more than thirty years before another band from the West would be permitted to play in the Soviet Union.

The huge popular success of the American visitors impressed the music commissars, who were desperate to try and reach a popular audience with Soviet musicians. Early in 1926, Soviet cultural leaders embarked on an extraordinary initiative. Lunacharsky dispatched a jazz ambassador to America. Leopold Teplitsky, a pianist from Leningrad, was given a mission to master American techniques, buy American instruments and arrangements, and then establish a jazz band back in his home city. He tracked down America's leading jazz impresario and conductor, Paul Whiteman, recently celebrated as the patron of George Gershwin's "Rhapsody in Blue." Teplitsky returned to Leningrad laden with recordings, arrangements, and a stock of instruments.

In April 1927, Teplitsky's new jazz group played an opening concert that mirrored the continuing tensions between popular and classical music as Soviet commissars and musicians grappled to absorb the curious American import. The concert featured a bewildering mix of material from "Fascinating Rhythm" and "Yes Sir, That's My Baby" to jazz versions of Liszt, Gounod, and Rimsky-Korsakov. There was withering criticism from Rimsky-Korsakov's son, who savaged the group's "barbarous harmonies" and "senseless parody of melody and chords." But Teplitsky's band went on to deliver a series of successful concerts in the provinces, delighting an audience of steel workers with "the latest American music."

But a half-dozen years after Valentin Parnakh had pioneered jazz in the Soviet Union, it remained an elite taste. Musicians and audiences were drawn almost entirely from the educated upper classes. While the peasant masses and the commissars of high culture remained untouched by jazz, the upstart music fashioned by impoverished blacks on the other side of the world had somehow defied every obstacle to find a place—if not a mass audience—in revolutionary Russia.

By 1928, the limited freedoms of the New Economic Plan were in retreat. Soon, the first of the cyclic repressions that were to convulse the Soviet Union over the next six decades would focus its deadly gaze on jazz. Stalin's first Five Year Plan, dedicated to rolling back the liberations introduced since the death of Lenin, swept through every corner of the vast country, devastating the lives of millions of people with ferocious campaigns demanding forced collectivization and rapid industrialization. Culture was to be a key weapon in Stalin's new revolution, and jazz was an obvious target for attack. All foreign influences were to be exiled, smashed aside by the imposition of Russian peasant culture. It was an assault that was to have echoes in official denunciations of the Beatles more than thirty years later.

Despite eleven years of diktats about Soviet culture, music for the masses remained much as it had been before the revolution. According to Lunacharsky, Soviet music was still failing completely to reflect the revolutionary objectives of society, while he insisted culture's task was "the organizing of human consciousness." All music and art should be dictated and controlled by Communist Party commissars. The Party's cultural puritans, more fundamentalist even than the government, called Tchaikovsky a "feudal lord" and Chopin a "bourgeois aesthete." There was the first of many campaigns to ban the devilish saxophone. The saxophone, with its power to arouse unruly passions through the sexual wailing and screaming it could produce, had always generated hostility among revolutionary puritans. For decades, the instrument remained a rarity in the Soviet Union, where they were neither produced nor imported.

The writer Maxim Gorky led the backlash against jazz. In April 1928, his furious assault was published in *Pravda* with the title "On the Music of the Gross." Gorky's essay was to define the Soviet contempt for jazz and imported Western music for years to come. "It is like the clamor of a metal pig," he wrote, "the amorous croaking of a monstrous frog." The cultural commissar Anatoly Lunacharsky— the same Lunacharsky who, just two years earlier, had dispatched a jazz ambassador to America—now savaged the music, calling it "sonic

idiocy of the bourgeois Capitalist world." The Russian Union of
Proletariat Musicians attacked syncopation, claiming that it would
cause youngsters to show less enthusiasm for social work and calling
for a proletarian popular music. Foreign records were banned.

From December 9, 1930, all amateur musicians were subordinated
to "official organs"—state-certified regulators—stifling any basis
for popular initiative. Lunacharsky connected jazz with dancing
and degradation, dismissing the music as a symbol of blatant erot-
icism. Jazz and foxtrot, it was claimed, were being manipulated by
Capitalists to spread their power and destroy the U.S.S.R. from
within. They should be countered by untainted proletarian dances.
The struggle to devise politically acceptable dance steps produced a
string of farcical hybrids over decades. A quarter of a century later, a
Soviet cultural magazine was still championing eleven new Socialist
dances including the Moskvichka, the Terrikon, and the Herringbone. They were declared "certain to attract the attention of youth":
inevitably dancers fled the floor whenever the new routines were
introduced.

Leopold Teplitsky, the ambassador of jazz, was arrested and exiled. Children were compelled to confess to a love of jazz before
their classes, and girls were expelled from an international school for
listening to "alien music." Anyone caught importing or playing American jazz records could be fined or imprisoned. Soviet cultural commissars wrestled with a dilemma that was to baffle and torment
them for the next half-century. Jazz was popular precisely because
its rhythms implied a personal liberation that challenged the puritanical orthodoxy of the state.

But the imported Western music had taken root in the cities of
the U.S.S.R.

Party theorists conceded that jazz was a product of suppressed
blacks and Jews—the music of the proletariat. At the same time,
Party idealogues feared that it might arouse passions and behavior
that could be hard to control. By 1930, jazz was beginning to win

converts among workers in the big cities—increasing the alarm of cultural supervisors. Meanwhile, the Communist Party's official propaganda songs were colorless and dogmatic, winning few working-class fans.

In the early 1930s, the Soviet cultural engineers were instructed to foment a black revolution in the United States. And it was jazz that would oil its wheels. But not just any jazz. Stalin decreed that true proletarian jazz, the only kind suitable for the revolutionary masses, existed exclusively among poor blacks of the Deep South. Jazz in American's northern cities was deemed bourgeois; and Stalin didn't much care that it had been taken there by black musicians migrating from the South. Propaganda was the point, and Soviet cultural crusaders dreamed of a separate black American republic. To raise the consciousness of the black American proletariat and to propel a revolution, what could be better than a major motion picture?

The film project, *Red and Black*, began in confusion and ended in farce. The Sixth Congress of the Comintern—the Communist International—in Moscow had declared that the negroes of America's Southern states were a separate nation, and instructed the American Communist Party to campaign for their independence. To further the campaign, a movie was proposed by theorists in Moscow. The subject would be an attempt by black steelworkers to organize a strike, and the film would also feature black music—spirituals, work songs, and jazz. The Marxist ideologues conceived of a film so powerful and radical that it would stir the black Americans who saw it to rise in rebellion. Since Stalin himself had backed the project, it had to be pursued.

Twenty-two black Americans were recruited by the American Communist Party in New York and shipped off to Russia. The group of middle-class teachers, students, office workers, and aspiring actors who arrived in Moscow in the spring of 1932 dismayed their Soviet hosts. It was immediately clear that they lacked the required gnarled workers' hands; they rebelled at a Soviet worker's diet; worst of all, these "toiling negroes" couldn't sing or dance. The bewildered cast were sent off on a tour of southern Russia while the project languished and died in Moscow.

In the end, President Franklin D. Roosevelt unwittingly came to the rescue when he recognized the Soviet Union in late 1933. The scheme to create a black republic in America, dreamed up by functionaries in Moscow, was never close to a reality, and there were no further delusional schemes to foment revolution in the States. Stalin's cultural engineers turned their energies to the challenging task of devising a popular music that might be popular with the people.

The success of Stalin's Five Year Plan after 1932 shifted the cultural climate yet again. The plan drove through rapid industrialization, delivering unprecedented prosperity for millions of workers in the cities. For the next three years as Stalin gathered himself for another, more terrible purge, a period of genuine public euphoria rolled out from cities to villages. The word *Jazz* was everywhere, in theaters, in dance halls, and even in the circus. Balalaikas were abandoned in favor of trumpets. A "red era of jazz" blossomed with Soviet bands broadcasting and recording, as German and Czech bands toured the Soviet Union. The lugubrious Association of Proletarian Musicians was abolished, and a *New York Times* correspondent reported that "Jazz is staging a remarkable comeback in the Soviet Union after years of virtual prohibition." He found that Western visitors yearning for a taste of authentic folk music were assailed by jazz wherever they went. After the years of puritan repression, Western dances were also wildly popular. By 1934, workers could get free lessons in the foxtrot at the end of a day of churning out tractors.

Stalin spoke of the need for a new Soviet culture that would be an "upbeat, joyous art full of fun and laughter." In 1933, the Communist Party Central Committee called a conference at which they advanced the slogans "Give us Comedy" and "Laughter is the Brother of Strength." The country's leading filmmakers were directed to produce comedies. A breezy statement from Stalin adorned many factories and offices: "Life has become better, comrades! Life has become more cheerful!"

But despite popular enthusiasm in the fast-growing cities for Western music and dancing, the U.S.S.R. remained isolated, largely cut off from the recorded music that was by now the soundtrack of young people across the Western world. Only a privileged handful of trusted individuals—approved artists, Communist officials, businessmen, wealthy traders—were permitted to travel abroad. Even they often had to leave behind a wife or a child who could be used as a hostage if the traveler upset the Kremlin in some way. The envied few who were allowed to escape the shackles of the state for a brief trip provided a channel for Western luxuries, which were the stuff of dreams for most Soviet citizens. There was a special appetite for the few records brought back by those temporary travelers to another world—a hunger that would be echoed by millions of Beatles fans in the 1960s.

Across the Soviet Union in the mid-1930s, a new elite was being born, managers and professionals whose life was rapidly improving and whose loyalty was secured by the leadership with better pay and housing and the vision of a better future. Jazz became something of a symbol for the generation who were being groomed to be in the vanguard of building Socialism. And the new managers could even take their wives dancing to a jazz band.

For that special evening out in Moscow, the young couple would perhaps have made their way to a dance where Alexander Tsfasman's band was playing. I like to think of them, Oleg and Irina, he a manger of a state machine tool factory, she a secretary in the planning agency, flushed with their new prosperity, heading off in their smartest clothes to the Casino Restaurant on Mayakovsky Square where Tsfasman's Moscow Guys band is resident. Oleg and Irina have seen Tsfasman's band in a recent hit film, *The Whole World Is Dancing*, and now they're looking forward to seeing him in the flesh. The impeccable "Bob" Tsfasman in his tailored blue suit and silk cravat leads a swing band that rattles the restaurant's chandeliers. They play the latest American hits, and Irina especially enjoys smooching with her husband to "Smoke Gets in Your Eyes." Tsfasman is unapologetic about his enthusiasm for American music, and a highlight of the young couple's evening out is the American negro called Scott who performs dazzling tap dances with the band. Oleg knows that the Moscow Guys have a raffish reputation as late-night gamblers and wild drinkers, but he also knows that powerful fans in high places seem to be able to give them protection.

Tsfasman had recorded the U.S.S.R.'s first jazz record as early as 1930, and he was to remain the Soviet Union's most durable popular musician, surviving political purges and wartime devastations until he lost his band in 1947. But he was rehabilitated after Stalin's death, when he was revered as an Honored Artist of the Russian Republic and recognized as the iconic figure in Soviet jazz. As late as the 1960s, he remained a defiant original, condemning the Beatles as "out of date."

I came across a photograph from the mid-1930s that gave me a jolt of familiarity. A line of Soviet musicians, sax players I think, jaunty and confident, march in step, each with his hand on the shoulder of the man in front, legs raised like chorus girls. And suddenly I'm looking at my father eighty years ago with his band, Syd Seymour and His Mad Hatters. They're fooling around on some English seaside promenade, and it's exactly the same chorus-girl pose. The smiles are the same, too, untroubled, sure of good times to come. For my father, those days on the road before I was born always glowed in his memory, a carefree kaleidoscope of summer seasons, mirror balls spinning over crowded ballrooms, and freedom. He told me a dancer once stuffed five pounds in the bell of his saxophone, and the story stayed with me in the depths of Cold War Britain, a message from a vanished nirvana. Looking at that old Soviet photograph, and imagining what had probably come next for those jaunty young men, I found myself investing it with that same feeling of lost happiness.

From the summer of 1936, Stalin's Great Terror began to consume the U.S.S.R. A vast purge of alleged oppositionists, saboteurs, political rivals, and anyone suspected of dissent was to result in the deaths of as many as a million people over the next two years. More than a hundred thousand officers in the Red Army were shot. Jazz and popular music were inevitable targets, victims of their own success during the boom of the mid-thirties. Hundreds of musicians were rounded up and vanished into labor camps. Valentin Parnakh, the leader of the pioneering Eccentric Jazz Orchestra, was just one victim. Fans and record collectors disappeared. Musicians with foreign contacts were especially vulnerable, and alien foreign elements in music were banned. Classical musicians, the singers of patriotic ballads, and the gypsy bands who had been humiliated and sidelined by the jazz boom were back in favor. Cultural commissars emphasized the ideological purity of peasant folk music and denounced jazz as bourgeois decadence and "ape music." The Jewish origins of some musicians aroused particular resentment among puritanical nationalists.

On November 21, 1936, the newspaper *Izvestia* published a long letter under the heading "Jazz or a Symphony." Written by two classical musicians, the letter protested that the mania for jazz had driven serious classical music from concert stages and from the popular resorts of the Black Sea coast. The letter triggered a ferocious struggle between the two leading official newspapers: *Pravda*, which supported jazz, and *Izvestia*, which condemned the music. While thousands were being tortured and murdered in Stalin's prisons and gulags, the debate raged on over two months and nineteen articles. Bizarrely, *Pravda* accused its rival paper of "bourgeois fanaticism" and flouting the Communist Party line. The musical spat had become savagely political, and in the hysterical climate of the Great

Terror, defeat was fatal for the losers. *Izvestia*'s entire editorial board was purged and many members were executed.

Terror had spread to every area of Soviet society, and now even the enemies of jazz were targets.

Throughout the years of the Terror, jazz and popular music continued to play on, providing a ghoulish counterpoint to the horrors that were sweeping across the country. Thousands of "mass songs" hailing the glorious future were published, wrapped in covers featuring peasants, workers, and children striding out with radiant faces toward a new dawn.

The jarring contrast between popular culture and the Great Terror found its ultimate expression in a film that reached Soviet cinemas in April 1938. As Stalin's purge was murdering hundreds of thousands, and imprisoning another two hundred thousand for telling jokes seen as critical of authority, an upbeat film musical titled *Volga-Volga*—a kind of Socialist *Showboat*—became hugely popular. The movie's songs were played in dance halls everywhere. "This free life will never end," sang the joyful peasants in the closing scene. "Spring has come to our motherland." Throughout the country long lines queued to see the film, and among its most devoted fans was Stalin himself. He had the film screened so often that he would recite many jokes before they came up on the soundtrack. He even sent a copy to President Roosevelt for his education.

The official line called now for a "proletarian" jazz, and in 1938 a GosJazz ("People's Jazz") Orchestra was unveiled. A bloated assembly of more than forty musicians, it was yet another attempt by the bewildered captains of Soviet culture to win the hearts of their citizens. But the bland official offerings of the GosJazz Orchestra, mixing pop versions of Tchaikovsky with light jazz renditions of "Tea for Two," were no more popular than the other music manufactured on the conveyor belt of official culture. Concerts were drowned out by the hisses and boos of unappreciative workers. But since the only important audience was the father of the nation, and Stalin had nodded his approval during a concert in the Kremlin, totalitarian jazz became a fixture for many state ensembles across the U.S.S.R.

As the Great Terror raged on, jazz maintained powerful supporters. Stalin's minister of railways and heavy industry, the fearsome Lazar Kaganovich, who had orchestrated a genocidal famine in the Ukraine, hailed jazz as "above all the friend of the jolly, the musical organizer of high-spirited youth." While it is unclear what the murderous Kaganovich understood as "jazz," he wrote a "jazz guide leaflet" entitled "How to Organize a Railway Ensemble of Song and Dance and Jazz Orchestras." Kaganovich insisted: "There should be a 'dzhaz band' at every Soviet station." Another Soviet leader who combined a taste for popular music with a talent for arranging executions was Marshal Kliment Voroshilov, who took dancing lessons with his wife. It's not hard to imagine Stalin and his inner circle dancing the foxtrot and tapping their feet as they commissioned mass murder—a terrible vignette of the entanglement of music and politics in the Soviet Union. But the vast country would soon be engulfed in a catastrophe that would transcend Stalin's worst nightmare.

Hitler's invasion of the Soviet Union in June 1941 pitched the nation into the horrors of the "Great Patriotic War." Popular music was immediately mobilized as a key weapon in lifting the morale of Stalin's hard-pressed armies. Alexander Tsfasman led an orchestra that played a hundred concerts at the front lines. The Red Army and Soviet Navy put together many swing bands, echoing the exploits of Major Glenn Miller in delivering an uplifting soundtrack for the Second World War.

For me, growing up in wartime Glasgow where the shipyards were a regular target of Nazi bombers, I still remember nights in an air-raid shelter with my Mickey Mouse gas mask, followed by exciting mornings hunting on the street for the shrapnel fragments of bombs. One of our neighbors was an ardent Communist, who had imbued his children with a reverence for the great war hero, Josef Stalin. I recall street games where the "red" kids from next door faced off against ardent Churchill worshippers. Looking back now on the naïve choreography of those childish wartime battles, I'm reminded of the heroic tableaux of the floats trundling through Red Square with pyramids of athletes balancing on slogans to celebrate the triumphs of the Soviet army. I like to imagine the story of popular music in the Soviet Union during the Second World War as a similar parade of heroic tableaux through the heart of Moscow.

The most dramatic float would be in celebration of the nine-hundred-day Siege of Leningrad by Hitler's armies. The siege caused the deaths of at least one and a half million people by bombardment and starvation. The human losses at Leningrad dwarfed the casualties from the destructions of Hiroshima and Nagasaki. But while the desperate population were reduced to cannibalism, the Baltic Fleet Jazz Orchestra played at halls throughout the city, sometimes within sight of the German guns.

Music was a vital part of the city's defenses. On August 9, 1942, the *Leningrad Symphony* by Dmitri Shostakovich was played by the Radio Orchestra of Leningrad, and the concert was broadcast on loudspeakers placed across the city and aimed toward the enemy lines. For many, the concert came to symbolize the turning of the tide in favor of the Soviet army.

Other tableaux in that Red Square parade of heroic music would feature folk groups playing sentimental ballads for the troops as a reminder of home. As the war continued, there was a gathering official backlash against foreign influences in music and a focus on nationalistic themes. By October 1944, *Pravda* was insisting that "popular music is called upon to fulfill serious social and political tasks." Now at last, fueled by a wild enthusiasm for patriotic anthems and sentimental ballads about lovers at the front, there was a genuine connection between the state's musical decrees and popular taste.

But the years of exposure during the war to jazz and popular

Western music in dance halls, in concerts, and on the radio had left a lasting impression on Soviet soldiers from the big cities. In wartime, the contagion reached the countless peasant soldiers, giving them a glimpse of a new postwar society. The music hinted at better times and a prospect of liberation.

In the desperate years of the struggle against Hitler, the Soviet government supported the influx of music from their Western allies. American wartime hits such as "Over there!" and "Honeysuckle Rose" were given new lyrics extolling the Red Army. But the ban on short-wave radios meant that most civilians had no chance of hearing the imported music.

An unforgettable float in that imaginary Red Square parade of music that won the war would have to feature a Hollywood movie widely seen in the Soviet Union. *Sun Valley Serenade*, an escapist musical extravaganza starring the skater Sonja Henie, also featured performances by the Glenn Miller Orchestra. The film offered a glimpse of a glamorous American nirvana, where skating spectaculars were accompanied by Miller's "Moonlight Serenade" and "Chattanooga Choo Choo." The film was a huge hit with Soviet audiences in grip of wartime austerity. Red Army bands celebrated the liberations of Prague and Krakow with repeated performances of "Chattanooga Choo Choo" to ecstatic audiences. Soviet musicians were still playing versions of the score twenty years later.

The wartime alliance with the Western powers gave an opportunity for the closest involvement with Western-style popular music since the Russian Revolution. The allied collaboration also saw the rise of the Soviet Union's most successful and authentic jazzman.

My final imaginary float would have to feature a dapper jazz cornet virtuoso and band leader in a white tuxedo, Eddie Rosner. Rosner was the ultimate music star of the war years, and beyond question the most accomplished jazz man in the Soviet Union up to that time. Uniquely, he was admired both by Stalin and by Louis Armstrong— who called him "the white Armstrong." Rosner blazed through his life with the intensity of one of his solos, skipping across borders and fearlessly reinventing himself to become a mythic figure from Minsk to Moscow and beyond.

Born Adolf Rosner in Berlin in 1910, he was the son of a Polish-Jewish shoemaker. After studying at the Berlin Conservatory he joined a top German jazz band, Stefan Weintraub's Syncopators. From that point, Rosner's story unfolds like a film noir thriller. Rosner was beaten up by a gang of stormtroopers, and after Hitler came to power, he left Germany to settle in Poland. He jammed with Armstrong in Italy, got to know some top American musicians, and learned to speak English. In the late thirties, as Stalin's Terror devastated the Soviet Union, Rosner toured Europe with his band, starring with Maurice Chevalier in Paris before returning to top the bill in Warsaw nightclubs. When Hitler marched into Poland, Rosner headed for the only available refuge—the Soviet Union.

In Minsk, he got lucky, as Frederick Starr records in his book *Red and Hot*. The local Communist Party boss, Comrade Panteleimon Ponomarenko, was a huge jazz fan and burst in on Rosner's dressing room to offer him the job of heading the State Jazz Orchestra of the Byelorussian Republic. So, as hundreds of jazz musicians were being shipped off to gulags, Rosner found himself feted as an honored artist, lavishly paid and given an apartment near the Kremlin with Afghan carpets, silk curtains, and a grand piano.

Eddie Rosner's ultimate command performance came early in 1941. He was summoned with his band to a theater in the Black Sea resort of Sochi, where he was expecting to play for Stalin. He found a completely empty auditorium, but he was ordered to play a two-hour concert, complete with comedy sketches and songs. Only the next morning was he informed that the Father of the Nation had been listening from behind a curtain and had approved of the concert. It was an endorsement that guaranteed Rosner's position throughout the war. For the next four years, he traveled the Soviet Union, sometimes under fire, performing in scores of remote and dangerous locations. The wartime openness to Western music, and of course Stalin's endorsement, guaranteed that until the war was won, Rosner—a German Jew—was an honored ambassador. He was helping to ensure that the music born in America was accepted as a part of the Soviet culture for which the nation was battling. But the ending of the Second World War would signal more troubled times for Eddie Rosner.

4

The endless military parade that rolled through Red Square in the rain on June 24, 1945, to begin the victory celebration for the end of the Second World War was a disturbing preview of what was to come. Stalin watched from the reviewing stand on top of the Lenin Mausoleum, unsmiling, as gray as his greatcoat. Marshal Georgy Zhukov rode past on a white horse at the head of fearsomely drilled battalions and interminable displays of military might. Captured Nazi banners were thrown on the cobbles in front of Stalin as drums thundered. A gun salute echoed over Moscow, like the opening salvo in a new war.

The crowds of Soviet citizens watched from far away, pushed to the margins of the square. But for more than a year, they could hang on to a feeling that better times would come. Eddie Rosner and his band were playing at the stylish Metropole Hotel, and Alexander Tsfasman's orchestra made weekly radio broadcasts. Restaurants, such as the Cocktail on Gorky Street, featured jazz-tinged bands, and the war-weary crowds flooded in.

But toward the end of 1946, a rapid chill descended over the Soviet Union. Every area of cultural life was frozen, and all foreign influences were fiercely repressed. Winston Churchill had given the postwar world its defining headline when, in a speech delivered on March 5, he said that an "Iron Curtain" had descended across the continent of Europe. The phrase also described with grim precision the retreat of the Soviet Union from the outside world.

The intensity of the cultural assault was more vicious than at any time since the Russian Revolution in 1917. All modern artistic trends were declared "bourgeois decadence" and "spiritual destitution." America and all things American were particular targets. Soviet officials feared their state was in danger of being swamped by American influences, especially by American music. Voice of America radio broadcasts of live jazz from New York fueled the paranoia, and cultural commissars were convinced the broadcasts were part of a plot to pollute Soviet minds. An exhausted population, too weary to care, retreated into their own world.

Eddie Rosner and his musicians were early victims of the inquisitions. With his wife, he was arrested and hauled off to the Lubyanka prison in Moscow, where he was interrogated and tortured. Following a brief trial, he was shipped to a Siberian gulag. "Bob" Tsfasman lost his job and his band, while the State Jazz Orchestra was instructed to stop playing jazz. The very word *dzhaz* was banned.

But in his remote prison camp Rosner survived and prospered. Once again, he was rescued by a jazz fan. The camp commandant had heard Rosner play, and decided to build his own band. Rosner was able to gather musicians from other camps and was allowed to travel with his gulag orchestra to other prisons where he entertained guards and officials. His reward was improved food and freedom from the murderous work that killed many thousands of others.

His music soon won him an even bigger sponsor. The director of the prison network in the Soviet Far East, who had built a personal empire in Magadan, recruited Rosner to join his "court" of artists, jesters, and musicians. As there was a rich supply of skilled musicians in the camps, Rosner was soon able to assemble an impressive orchestra to play the arrangements he reconstructed from memory. Safe from the inquisitors far away in Moscow, Rosner enjoyed unique musical freedom in his remote gulag.

Thousands of miles away in the Soviet heartlands, the campaigns against Western music blended terror and whimsical absurdity. The very elements of jazz were dismantled and scrutinized; "blue notes" were banned, vibratos were proscribed, valved trumpets were denounced as "artistic perversion." Most dangerous of all, as ever, were saxophones. All the saxes in Moscow were called in and confiscated. Sax players were refashioned as oboists and bassoonists. Fanatical youth vigilantes from the Komsomol patrolled theaters, bars, and cafés to enforce the bans and to make sure that only "approved" songs were being played, and only acceptable dance styles such as polkas and waltzes were being danced. The campaigns rivaled the grotesque excesses of Chairman Mao's Great Cultural Revolution in China some twenty years later when one campaign ordered millions of people to catch flies.

As the Cold War intensified in the late 1940s, Andrei Zhdanov, the man who had commanded the defense of Leningrad during the three-year siege by the Nazis, was instructed by Stalin to lead a campaign for the purification of Soviet society from Western influences. He applied his ruthless talents to a fearsome crackdown on the Western contagion of Soviet arts. Zhdanov criticized the "disharmony and atonality" of popular music and scorned the lack of Russian traditional elements. He scourged the Soviet peoples' "servility to the West," denouncing jazz as "a tool of U.S. Imperialism" that was aiming to turn Soviet youths into cannon fodder.

The first All-Union Congress of Soviet Composers in April 1948 confirmed the subjugation of music to the Socialist state with greater harshness than ever before. Leading composers such as Khachaturian and Prokofiev, former winners of the Stalin Prize, were denounced for their dissonant music and failure to use folk songs conforming with Socialist Realism. Zhdanov demanded an oath of loyalty from musicians and composers. Borders were slammed shut, radio was jammed, mail was censored. The threat from the West was ceaselessly emphasized in an effort to revive the national spirit that had defeated Hitler. The Iron Curtain seemed impregnable.

The totalitarian attack on Western music, especially jazz, was so determined and prolonged, and the doors to other voices were so firmly closed, that it was bound to have its impact—at least for a while. The problem for the cultural tyrants remained as it had always been. What could they put in its place?

In the years after the war, the leaders of the Party worked to convince an exhausted population that the cultural invasion from the West threatened to "poison the consciousness of the masses" and must be reversed. It was a time when the possibility that four lads from Liverpool might one day be embraced by those Soviet masses seems unimaginable.

Stalin's death on March 5, 1953, shifted the foundations of the Soviet Union. It was a national trauma for a people who had come to feel that their leader was immortal. Locomotives moaned their whistles, cranes bowed their jibs; it seemed that even the machines were in mourning.

The passing of the tyrant who had shaped the lives of millions of citizens for thirty years began to melt the permafrost that had imprisoned Soviet culture. Trumpeter Eddie Rosner was released from his gulag exile in 1953, but his enthusiasm for the Soviet paradise was exhausted. Rosner made scores of requests to emigrate, which were always refused. It wasn't until almost twenty years later, during Richard Nixon's détente with Moscow in 1972, that Rosner was at last allowed to leave the U.S.S.R. He settled in Berlin, where he died in 1976.

The death of Stalin released the pent-up frustrations of a new generation yearning for change. A tide of alienation swept through urban youths, who began to rally around their determination to reject

the Soviet mass culture of their parents in a search to find new ways
to focus on their personal lives. Dropout rates in city schools soared,
and many youngsters, accustomed to the support of the state and
heavily subsidized prices, defected from joining the workforce. The
emergence of Russia's first hipsters in the early 1950s announced a
youth rebellion that within ten years would tune in to Beatlemania.

The Stilyagi—the "Style Hunters"—were a scandalous youth cult,
the first group aiming to separate themselves from the gray multi-
tudes of Cold War Russia. Spurning the official ideal of "the new
Soviet man," the Stilyagi tried to model themselves on American
heroes such as James Dean and, with their greasy Tarzan-style hair,
Johnny Weissmuller. The film *Tarzan's New York Adventure* must
have seemed too exotic to trouble the Russian censors in 1951, but with
its story of a free spirit in the big city, it made a huge impression on
the Stilyagi.

With so little information to go on, the Stilyagi versions of Western icons evolved into bizarre hybrids. They dressed to outrage: narrow short pants, big shoes, long check jackets, long bright ties with
palm trees, monkeys, girls in bathing suits. Their musical idols were
Louis Armstrong, Duke Ellington, and Glenn Miller, and their anthem was "Chatanoogoo Choo Choo." Stilyagi women were derided
for their "dresses stretched tightly over their figures to the point of
indecency."

The Stilyagi's bohemian deviance was calculated to offend every
Stalin-era father. They called themselves "Bob" and "Peter" and held
"cocktail hours." Dance was the center of their existence, displayed
in strange novelty steps they called "the Atomic," "the Canadian,"
and "the Triple Hamburg." The men played billiards for money;
dabbled in black-market nylons, cigarettes, and American jazz records; and shunned work. Their main hangout was Moscow's Gorky
Street, which they called "Broadway."

The Stilyagi's isolation from the Soviet masses was played out at
their favorite winter hangout, the Dynamo skating rink, where jazz

was played on the loudspeakers, possible again after the death of Stalin. Sweeping through the drab crowds in their outrageous costumes, they skated in a pack to defy the insults of furious citizens. Their separation was compounded by the fact that travel restrictions meant there could be no contact with Stilyagi in other cities. As a result, weird variations of dress and dancing styles blossomed in big cities across the country. In smaller places, and in the countryside where conformity was rigidly enforced, the provocations of the Stilyagi were unthinkable.

The Stilyagi's most outrageous challenge was the flaunting of their idleness in a society where work was obligatory. With prices fixed by the state, and the ambitions of earlier generations rejected, thousands of youngsters in the big cities bailed out of work and concentrated on doing as little as possible. Spasmodic trials of work-shy youngsters did little to energize the gatherings of kids hanging around in cafés and on the streets. The stagnation of the Komsomol Communist Youth Organization with its dreary meetings and tired slogans left a void for a disaffected generation.

In the early 1950s the younger Stilyagi embraced modern jazz, particularly bebop, whose furious tempos and complex harmonies repelled outsiders from joining the cult. They were unconsciously echoing one of the aims of the music invented half a world away in New York by black pioneers Charlie Parker and Dizzy Gillespie—a style that often seemed to be determined to exclude Whitey. To complement their new musical passion, the Stilyagi found a new style. Gerry Mulligan's "cool" look—flat-top haircuts, sober suits—became the fashion to imitate.

Ah!—Gerry Mulligan. The name transports me to my own discovery of modern jazz. In the early 1950s, Mulligan and his quartet became my escape from a drab boyhood in an English industrial town. Austerity Britain was still struggling out of the deprivations of the Second World War, locked in shortages and rationing. With the handful of candies my ration coupons allowed, I shut myself into my bedroom with my Dansette record player and those first seven-inch albums, discovered in my parents' record store. The delectable sound of Mulligan and Chet Baker, gruff baritone sax and feathery trumpet, soaring and harmonizing and intertwining, took me away from the damp monochrome rooftops outside my window to a Technicolor Californian paradise where the music was cool and the sun was always shining. Looking back now at that boy and his new obsession, I feel a connection with those Stilyagi who were finding— at the same moment, in the same music—an escape from a colorless and regulated life. I find myself wondering at their courage in finding a way to insist on flaunting the style of an American jazzman on the Moscow streets.

The Stilyagi's limited rebellion was ultimately a yearning for information about the world beyond the Iron Curtain. Starved of real news about the lives and concerns of their generation in New York or London, they devised their own curious culture from the scraps that reached them. Their devotion to Tarzan hints at their other driving motivation. The spectacle of the bare-chested action hero swinging through the trees was embraced as an emblem of freedom, and of a life lived beyond the bounds of any state or regulation. Striding down their "Broadway" or skating in Gorky Park, they could feel for a moment something of that freedom they had found in the jungle fantasies of Tarzan movies.

The Stilyagi remained a tiny fringe group, but in a society obsessed with narrow conformity, the Soviet mainstream reacted with outrage. Concerned citizens abused Stilyagi on the streets of Moscow and Leningrad as monkeys; they were declared "a tumor on the social organism," expelled from colleges, and shunned by conventional society. Vigilantes prowled the streets, cutting hair and trouser legs. But the Stilyagi were finally overtaken not by the vigilantes and commissars, but by the improbable conspiracy of a new record from America and a new man in the Kremlin.

5

Nikita Krushchev, the new Soviet leader, was an unlikely figure to shake the Kremlin. With a peasant's cunning and toughness, he had carried out and survived many purges under the old regime. After Stalin's death, he had beaten off a gang of rivals to grab the top job. He soon set about dismantling Stalin's legacy. In February 1956, Krushchev delivered a secret speech to the Twentieth Congress of the Communist Party, denouncing Stalin's purges and declaring that the lives of millions of Soviet citizens must improve. Soon, thousands were released from the gulags, and books appeared that provided the first accounts of Stalin's crimes. Krushchev also hinted at a more open relationship with the West, and in July 1957 he ordered a spectacular parting of the Iron Curtain.

Krushchev's World Youth Festival unleashed a torrent of youngsters from the West, flooding into Moscow for a vast international jamboree. It was the most dramatic relaxation of the Soviet borders since the Revolution forty years earlier. Thirty thousand delegates arrived from around the world, including a large group from America. In the U.S. delegation, progressive Socialist true believers mingled with F.B.I. snoops. Ecstatic crowds thronged the streets, teams of smiling youths on motorcycles roared down the boulevards streaming flags of welcome. Beatnik poets and contemporary artists, dancers, and athletes socialized with local youngsters, so long starved of contact with the outside world. The visitors also brought their music.

Bill Haley's "Rock Around the Clock" was an instant sensation. There's a short film of the World Youth Festival that captures the euphoria of the moment. Hundreds of dancers pack a hall, waving little American and Soviet flags and dancing to "Rock Around the Clock" in an ecstasy of international togetherness. The festival only lasted two weeks, but the Soviet Union was never quite the same after the delegates went home. Soviet authorities were compelled to break out of the cultural straitjacket that had confined the U.S.S.R. for decades, and tentative links with the West opened up. An exhibition of abstract paintings by European artists and visits by European jazz groups made a lasting impression.

A few months later, I was in my watchtower during my military service in Berlin—and Elvis Presley was starting life as a soldier not far away in West Germany. A personal memory from that time suggests how irresistible rock 'n' roll had become. While I fretted that the Soviet tanks might be about to smash through the fence alongside my watchtower to invade Berlin, a more seditious force was working in the opposite direction. One night, just as we were putting the lights out, a pair of bedraggled and frightened Russian soldiers arrived at my barracks. It was a scary moment. With the other junior spies in my billet, I crowded round the soldiers, trying to work out if they were the vanguard of an invasion. Then we saw how vulnerable they looked, just boys in ill-fitting uniforms, bewildered by the barrage of questions we fired at them. We struggled to understand what on earth could have driven them to cross the Iron Curtain. They mumbled a disjointed story about how they had climbed over the fence from the Soviet Zone of Berlin, and wanted to defect. "Why do you want to take this risk?" I asked them, pushing the limits of my military Russian. "Because," said one of the shivering boy soldiers, "our officer won't let us listen to Elvis Presley."

That officer should perhaps have saved his patriotic energies for guarding the musical frontiers of the Iron Curtain. Soon, another rock invader was infiltrating the motherland. It's not easy now to understand the extraordinary impact of a cheery two-minute novelty, Chubby Checker's "Let's Twist Again." Across the Soviet Union it was a sensation, spawning local copies with titles like "Hey Sailor You've Been Sailing Too Long." Twisting couples filled the dance halls, and popular films featured the new phenomenon. Perhaps it was the simple joy of the thing, which seemed to chime with a new optimism and confidence in Soviet citizens, charged up by Yuri Gagarin's pioneering space flight and the promise of better times.

Despite his liberalizations, Nikita Krushchev was not a fan of Chubby Checker. In the fall of 1962, he expressed "a feeling of distaste for these so-called modern dances brought into our country from the West. They are something unseemly, mad." Officials compared rock with earthquakes and tornadoes, blaming this "ape music" for delinquency, alcoholism, vandalism, and rape. Krushchev's prime target was the electric shock delivered to Soviet youth by "Let's Twist Again." But the twist proved stubbornly resilient. As late as 1967, a crowd of kids celebrating May Day in Red Square with a twisting party had to be dispersed by police.

"Let's Twist Again" also fueled the explosion of a curious phenomenon: "records on bones." Since the mid-1950s, ingenious music fans and hustlers with an eye on a new market had been exploring ways of making illicit records. One answer was to inscribe music taped from Western radio stations onto medical X-ray films. The simple technology available in streetcorner booths where homesick soldiers could record messages to their mothers was hijacked to produce millions of cheap copies of "Rock Around the Clock" and other early hits. "Records on bones" mushroomed from individual copies made after hours in the street booths to major bootleg operations in underground facilities. Chubby Checker's hit became a huge X-ray success, defying Krushchev as well as the Komsomol vigilante patrols that tried to confiscate disks, targeting private profiteering rather than the music itself. The sound quality was terrible, but the X-ray records felt like the real thing to rock-starved kids who could hear "See You Later, alligator" on a shadowy image of some babushka's lungs.

Vladimir Matietsky, a veteran Russian rock musician, told me about daring teenage expeditions to a department store in central Moscow where musical instruments were sold. "On the sidewalk outside, 'sharks' would sell you an X-ray disk. You never knew what you might get, and it was risky with the vigilantes watching out." Forty years later, Matietsky could still recall the excitement of those illicit exchanges. Sliding into the hustler's voice, he spoke from the corner of his mouth. "You want 'shakes'?" he said. "You want some rock 'n' roll flexis? Three rubles—it's good rock 'n' roll." He mimed how the rolled flexible disk would be quickly slipped into his coat sleeve before anyone spotted what was going on. "But it was danger-ous. Some guys who were mass-producing the flexis in Leningrad were sent to a gulag for seven years."

A Soviet legal journal raged that the flexi industry was fueling crime and even murder. War was declared on the X-ray records. Millions of counterfeits flooded the streets containing nothing but scratchy noise and a message: "You like rock 'n' roll? Fuck you, anti-Soviet slime!" But the anti-rock puritans failed to plug a more sig-nificant leak in the dike holding back the rock tide.

From 1960, Soviet-made reel-to-reel tape recorders became avail-able. The Astra, the Yauza 5, the Chaika, and the Nota were the weap-ons that would power the Beatles Revolution. For the first time, a mass audience would be able to take control away from the state. Dramatically expanding the spread of the X-ray disks, the availability of tape recorders made it feasible for ordinary citizens to distribute their tapes across the country. By the time the official brigades of censors, gaggers, and music vigilantes had caught up with the tape menace, the thirty-year running battle between popular taste and authority had been lost.

The arrival in Moscow of the first American band in more than thirty years signaled the relaxation—for a while, at least—of Soviet resistance to Western musical imports. Despite Krushchev's distaste for jazz, the five-city tour by the Benny Goodman Orchestra in the summer of 1962, after years of nervous negotiation, was a huge success with Soviet audiences. Krushchev even turned up at the Moscow concert and joined in the applause.

But Krushchev was warned repeatedly by his advisers that too much cultural freedom could trigger dangerous political consequences. In the vacuum of political activity beyond the control of the Communist Party, culture was always one of the key vehicles for the expression of new—and potentially seditious—ideas. The underlying unease about Western popular music and its capacity to win the hearts and minds of Soviet citizens continued to trouble the Kremlin and its cultural supervisors. Ever since the 1920s, periods of comparative openness were always limited, and the fundamental mistrust of Western influences was always ready to resurface. The volatility of Soviet leaders and their shifting cultural campaigns inevitably compounded public uncertainty, particularly as the majority of the population remained as conservative as their rulers. Over the years, official campaigns were enforced by a range of state authorities—from the top leadership, through local Communist Party officials, down to police and Komsomol vigilantes. For the musicians and their audiences on the receiving end of this unpredictable barrage, the sanctions swerved from mere verbal abuse and censorship to imprisonment and death.

Following Khrushchev's humiliation in the Cuban Missile Crisis of October 1962, the thaw he had initiated began to ice over once again. Attacks by Chairman Mao on Krushchev's openness to the

West pushed the Kremlin toward a renewed isolation. The Soviet leader retreated into outspoken attacks on modern art and jazz, but his regime was fatally wounded.

The coming to power of Leonid Brezhnev in October 1964 marked an end to the freedoms of the Krushchev era. Yet again, the Kremlin's repressive mood swings and capricious edicts began to bear down on popular music and on many other areas of life. For Soviet citizens who had lived through the dangerous and unpredictable policy shifts of the past forty years—from repression to openness and back again as ideology, political infighting, and Stalin's murderous whims dictated—there was a terrible inevitability about the latest crackdown. For a young generation who had tasted the heady possibilities of a more open life, the new regime threatened a return to the deprivations of totalitarian rule, and the isolation of the Cold War.

It was in this climate of frustration and disappointment that the first rumors of the Beatles arrived in the Soviet Union.

6

This had to be the place. A yellow submarine sailed across a wall under a sea of blue where winged Beatles angels fluttered. A sign for JOHN LENNON STREET pointed to the sky. An archway was decorated in relief with sculpted heads of the Fab Four. Through the arch, down a gloomy corridor, I found myself at a metal door. A plaque announced:

> *In the name of John Lennon*
> *The Temple*
> *of Love, Peace*
> *and Music*

Then the door was wrenched open and a huge man, as bearded and hairy as Chewbacca in *Star Wars*, roared a greeting and spread his arms to hug me. "Welcome, welcome, Beatles forever," Kolya Vasin bellowed as he folded me in his furry embrace. Art Troitsky had insisted that I meet Kolya in Leningrad, "a good soul and the beating heart of all things Beatly in Russia." Russia's ultimate Beatles fan did not disappoint.

*Yellow submarine patrols the approach to Kolya Vasin's
temple in Saint Petersburg.*

But Troitsky had hardly prepared me for the gale-force presence
of Vasin, this tornado of hair and beard and affability, yelling snatches
of Beatle chat and greetings in an unstoppable torrent of Russian
laced with free-form English. And nothing could have prepared me
for Vasin's temple. It was as though the man's obsession, pent up
over decades of official hostility, had exploded and scattered all his
dreams and longings into this magical cave. It put me in mind of
another magic grotto. Lenin's tomb had only one exhibit, the em-

Angel Beatles watch over Kolya Vasin's courtyard.

balmed body of the man who made the Soviet Revolution. For Kolya his shrine clearly had something of the same mystical importance.

There was Beatle stuff everywhere: life-size photos of all four Beatles and Liverpool street signs and yellow submarines hanging from the ceiling, scrapbooks and videos and CDs and constellations of Beatle buttons crammed into every space. In the center of it all, crowding out everything else, was a huge circular table loaded with wonders. As I tried to take in the overload of Vasin's hoard, the sheer profusion of objects overwhelmed me: a little ceramic replica of Paul's bass guitar, a Beatles teapot, heart-shaped cups, a STRAW-BERRY FIELDS street sign, a Lennon statue, Russian eggs—I got lost in the layers and byways. Bowls of fruit, plants, and lighted candles suggested a hippie ashram, but then my attention was snagged by other things. A sign announced LIVERPOOL 2,510 KILOMETERS and another pointed to New York. A stained-glass window glowed with a big red heart under an arch proclaiming ALL YOU NEED IS LOVE. Beatles music poured unceasingly from every direction.

Sprawled in a vast leather armchair, the monarch of Beatleland, Kolya Vasin surveyed his domain. "Beatles gave me adventures all my life," he announced. "I fell in love with the Beatles. They became my friends, my spiritual brothers, my fathers, my guides." Looking out at the collection that was the center of his life, he became very

Russian. "I felt as though I was on a dark forest path, and I didn't know where to go or why. And suddenly my soul found a guide—the fire of the music, deep in the forest. And my soul led me like a hunter's dog on a leash. I followed my soul—it led me to the Beatles." The mystical tsunami seemed unstoppable. Vasin launched into a final burst. "I came to a clearing full of strawberries. It was a revelation, and I realized this was the only place I could live like a free man." For all the dreamy intoxication, it was clear that something life-changing had touched this big, smiling man more than twenty years earlier. I wanted to hear his story.

"It was in 1964, spring, and my friends told me about this strange group from England. I heard a tape of their album *With the Beatles*—'All My loving,' 'You Really Got a Hold on Me,' 'It Won't Be Long.' They excited me. It was colossal. It's as though a whole new life began!"

Vasin waved his hand over his treasures. "I started to collect every little thing to do with them. I cut out every article, got hold of every picture. I exchanged things for them, begged for them. People got to know me in the 'Peter' black market"—he used the prerevolutionary nickname for Leningrad. "As a little boy I was already rushing round, getting phone numbers of dealers. I knew the times and places they would meet with records and magazines from the West." The language and the obsessiveness had the intensity of an addict. For Kolya, that's how it felt. "My mother used to say, 'Kolya, you aren't evolving at all. You don't go anywhere, you don't go to the cinema, you don't go to concerts, you're doing badly at school. You should be evolving." He smiled with the memory. " 'Evolving' was the thing back then. And the Beatles evolved me."

I pictured young Kolya, a chubby outsider, desperate to find a place in the harshly ordained world of Brezhnev's Soviet Union. "Soviet culture was shit," he said, "but they managed to get the entire country with their moronic stuff which made slaves of everyone." I recalled Art Troitsky saying there was nothing that reminded him of his dreams. For a boy like Kolya, already a dreamer, not a son of privilege and with no access to those treasures brought back from trips to the West, the monolith of the state must have been stifling. He gave me a powerful sense of the frustrations that had hemmed in millions of kids in those years. But Vasin found an escape. "Thanks to the Beatles, we understood a lot. For me, the world was divided into two parts—the bad world of Soviet propaganda and the Beatles paradise." He glowed at the memory. "Strawberry Fields and Pepperland," he said.

Kolya also found a community. "I got new friends, and gradually a club began to form around me—maybe the first Beatles club in the U.S.S.R. I had some kind of status. I wasn't just another teenager. After the Beatles came into my life, I had some sort of place in society." I had the sense I was listening to a born-again convert, and then Kolya said, "When I got to know the Beatles, I started to believe in God."

It must have been a heady combination: God and the Beatles. At the same moment in 1966, John Lennon had just outraged the American Bible belt by suggesting the Beatles were bigger than Jesus. For Kolya there was no competition. They were on the same side. "I understood I should live my life with music and with God."

A pretty cat, tabby and white, rubbed against Kolya's legs. He leaned down and scooped it up. "This is 'Hey Jude,'" he said. "I call her Judy." Kolya folded the cat into a smothering hug and began to croon softly: "Hey Jude, don't make it bad, take a sad song and make it better . . ." Watching this huge man hugging his little cat, I saw how he had embraced the idea of the Beatles over the years, for comfort and to wrap himself in his special community.

"The Beatles were like an integrity test," he said. "When anyone said anything against them, we knew just what that person was worth. The authorities, our teachers, even our parents became idiots to us. I was ashamed of the country I lived in." Vasin lit up with the memories. "I was ashamed of my parents. In my room I'd listen to

*Fab Four keep watch outside Kolya Vasin's
apartment in Saint Petersburg.*

the Beatles full blast, morning till night. They always told me to turn
it down." He could have been any teenager, making his small rebellion against the world. But for Soviet kids there was a difference. That
teenage rebellion could cost your education, your job, your future.

"I was really afraid. During the Soviet era, all my life was lived in
fear," he told me. Vasin's account of the endless harassment he expe-
rienced gave me a new understanding of the hard realities of being a
Beatles fan in the 1960s and '70s. "I was told 'don't stick out from

Kolya Vasin, Beatles superfan, in his John Lennon Temple.

the crowd.' When I did stick out by arranging concerts or running around the black market, it was really dangerous. I had problems with the police."

After leaving school, like every Soviet citizen, Kolya Vasin had to get a job. He was employed decorating plates and bowls in a state ceramic factory. But the police tracked him down, asking questions about his unofficial concerts. "A lady from the personnel department came to me and said, 'What's all this about? We're getting phone calls from the police. They told us you've been involved with an unofficial activity. You've been shaming our exemplary factory.' I got away with it that time, but my friend went to prison. The police accused him of making money from our concerts."

Vasin's daily life became a ceaseless round of trying to stay ahead of the police. "I was arrested many times, accused of 'breaching social order.' They said anyone who listened to the Beatles was spreading Western propaganda. They said I had no right to organize concerts or print tickets, or arrange places to play." He pointed to a photo on his wall of a bearded man, incongruous amid the Beatles

A few items from Kolya Vasin's John Lennon Temple.

memorabilia. "My hero, the great Russian writer Aleksandr Solzhenitsyn. He said, 'In Russia, freedom means maneuvering,'" and
that's how I had to live. I used to play the fool when they took me in
for questioning—that was how I saved myself. There would always
be the hope that I could get out of that office full of uniforms and
go home to the Beatles. If I'd told them what I really thought of
them I could have been sent to a penal colony, or even to prison."

Vasin hauled himself out of his chair and dragged a huge book
from a shelf, tottering under the weight. With his wild hair and
prophet's beard, he put me in mind of Moses and his tablets. He
started turning pages, excavating the geological layers of his obsession.
"This is my sixties book," he murmured, and the smell of old news-
print wafted from the pages. There were Merseybeat articles from
Liverpool in the early 1960s, concert programs from long-forgotten
Beatles gigs in grimy English clubs, faded fan photos, newspaper articles copied and recopied until they were mere smudges. And there
were Kolya's paintings, beautifully rendered projections of his passion
and frustration. In one picture, a vast green door was sealed by a for-

Kolya Vasin celebrates John Lennon's birthday.

bidding lock. On the door was the shadow of a man. "That's me," Kolya said, "shut in behind the Iron Curtain." A badge hung on the door with the words GET BACK! He turned the page. Now the door was ripped by a gash, and the word BEATLES shone through the tear. Another picture showed an idyllic rural scene in a picture frame, hanging from a gallows, dripping blood, with the title POOR RUSSIA.

A few pages later, Kolya pointed at a black-and-white photo and lit up. "This is from Leslie's film," and it was—a still frame from my filming long ago in the Cavern Club. I couldn't imagine how the thing had found its way through the Iron Curtain to reach him, but Kolya just waved his hand. "After the Beatles, the Iron Curtain was like a fence with holes. That was our secret. We breathed through these holes." He knew far more about that day in August 1962 than I did, and he poured out details I had long forgotten.

He showed me a Soviet flexi disk, printed with the faces of the Fab Four. Then at last he found what he was looking for. He stared at an ancient newspaper cutting and sighed. "This is a bad article, very bad, with bad words—Communist, Communist." He wrinkled up his nose, trembling with anger. "You see here how we were abused." The feature was headed DUNG BEATLES and it radiated disgust. A crude cartoon featured four men, jigging like monkeys. "Kolya looked up from the book. "When I read this I knew the Soviet Union is a bad state. I decided to emigrate to 'free territory' of Russia. In 1964 I said to myself, 'I will live without the Soviets, in my room with the Beatles.' I knew this was important for me."

It was, I thought, an extraordinary declaration. Millions of kids across the Soviet Union must have shared something of Vasin's despair about their society, "strangers in their own country," as Art Troitsky put it. Few of them would have retreated to a temple built in their own apartment. But the impulse of a whole generation to defect from a world that had always been built on the assumption that its people shared collective values, hopes, and beliefs slowly gathered the force of an unstated revolution.

7

Andrei Makarevich opened his school book. As he turned the pages they crackled, releasing the fusty smell of a Soviet classroom a quarter-century ago, and triggering memories of his boyhood obsession with the Beatles. There were pages of elaborate calligraphy and intertwined song titles, painstaking acts of homage inscribed by the young Makarevich. They reminded me of illuminated manuscripts labored over by monks, and they seemed inspired by an almost religious devotion. SERGEANT PEPPER'S LONELY HEARTS CLUB BAND curled into SHE'S LEAVING HOME, A LITTLE HELP FROM MY FRIENDS tangled up with LUCY IN THE SKY WITH DIAMONDS. Russia's most famous rock star gazed at his doodlings, looking wistful. "This was more than a bible for me. I'm sure I did it during a maths lesson or something I hated. My hand did it by itself." On the corner of the first page, he had adapted his name, another Beatles homage: MCCAREVICH

I had asked Art Troitsky to fix for me to meet some of the pioneers of Soviet rock—the generation that had been been galvanized by the Beatles. During visits to the Soviet Union in the late eighties in pursuit of various film projects, I seized the chance to pursue my gathering fascination with the Soviet "Beatles Generation." "You absolutely must talk to Andrei Makarevich," Troitsky had said. "His band, Time Machine, have been the biggest Russian rock outfit for years. And they were so soaked in the Beatles, I always think they sound like a tribute band."

I met up with Makarevich in the lobby of a Moscow hotel, where he arrived after taking part in an animal rights demonstration outside the parliament building. He said he was chilled after standing in the street and ordered a scotch. A comfortable-looking man in a tweedy English sports jacket, Makarevich was soft-spoken, more like an academic than a rock superstar. He sipped his scotch and said he had been in Liverpool recently on a Beatles pilgrimage, and it had been a shock. I recalled how Russian Beatles fans believed that the Fab Four lived in an opulent nirvana, so I could imagine that dirty old Liverpool wasn't what Makarevich had expected. "I couldn't believe how small and poor the city was," he said. "I hadn't realized that when they began, the Beatles were as hard up as Soviet rock bands." It reminded me how the starvation of information about the Fab Four in Russia had turned them into mythical beings, set apart from the mundane realities of grimy working-class Liverpool. Makarevich finished his scotch and said he had brought something to show me. I suggested we go upstairs where we could find a place to talk.

In a room just off Red Square, with the fantastic domes of Saint Basil's cathedral peeping through the window, Makarevich unwrapped his old schoolbook. As he turned the pages where he had transcribed the Beatles' lyrics, he talked about how he had shared the yearnings of his generation. "Every guy who tried to be a Beatle had a book like this—with the words of the songs as we tried to hear them on our terrible tape-recorded copies. I listened ten, twenty, thirty times, trying to write it just as it sounds, without looking for any sense in the words."

I asked Makarevich about the first time he heard the Beatles. "I was twelve or thirteen. My father was an architect and he was allowed to travel abroad. He brought back two albums, *A Hard Day's Night* and a collection of early Beatles songs. I remember I came home from school, and I heard something absolutely extraordinary." As he talked, he seemed to recover the electricity of that first encounter. "It was like lightning. I began to listen twenty-four hours a day. I got crazy."

Andrei's father had lost a leg in the Second World War, and he was an architect trusted by officials, permitted to travel beyond the Soviet Bloc. "Until his final years, he believed that the Soviet way was right, but he struggled all his life with the stupidities of Soviet power, constructing propaganda pavilions for international trade exhibitions."

It was becoming apparent as I met the founders of Russian rock— Art Troitsky, who grew up in Prague with his journalist father; Stas Namin with his illustrious grandfather; and now Andrei Makarevich— that the Soviet rock revolution was shaped by the children of privilege. In the Capitalist West, rock 'n' roll had been bred among the underclasses of Memphis or Detroit or Liverpool, but in Moscow— and later in Leningrad—I was finding a different story.

Troitsky had told me that Western rock music had sent a tremor across the Soviet Union. "Rock 'n' roll meant a lot to absolutely every Soviet kid," he said, "even redneck peasants who lived in a village." I didn't get the impression that Art spent a lot of time trudging through peasant villages, but he had no doubt about why the Beatles mattered, even to those peasants out there in the mud and misery of Mother Russia. "This was the music that made them free, that made them feel slightly different from their parents, who of course didn't understand this noise."

In Moscow, Andrei Makarevich pestered his father about the Beatles: who were this Lennon and McCartney? Who composed these songs? When he was told they were the guys who played and sang, who did it themselves, he had to try to copy them. He started

Time Machine, the essential Soviet Beatles band, 1960s.

scribbling songs, writing the lyrics in English. He tried to find out more, but all he could discover was a scathing article in *Pravda* that said the Beatles sat on the toilet in their raincoats to perform. With his friends, Makarevich hunted for photos of his new heroes. "Which was John, was that Paul or George or Ringo?" He saw a picture of Paul with his watch on his right hand. "I didn't know he was left-handed, so I have always worn my watch like Paul." Searching for any information, he saw a sports film that had two seconds of the Beatles, and went to see it again and again, day after day. "It got shorter every day as the projectionists kept snipping out frames to preserve them."

"We were so crazy," he said. "I had a dream several times that the Beatles come and I show them Moscow, and bring them to school. And the teachers are really worried. They say 'Who are these guys? Where are they from? Why the long hair?' So there's a big scandal. I woke up in a cold sweat."

One of Makarevich's friends was determined to make his fantasies come true. "He heard that John Lennon was secretly in Mos-

cow, so he went to the Rossiya Hotel to wait for him"—he pointed
to the window at the gargantuan building. I had my own memories
of the Rossiya, a dismal citadel where forbidding matriarchs kept
watch from their desks on every floor, monitoring every coming and
going, making disapproving notes. I recalled the cockroaches patrolling the walls of my room, and the echoing restaurants where gangs
of waiters stared without interest at the acres of uncleared tables and
picked their teeth with discarded forks. It didn't seem a likely hangout for John Lennon, but Andrei's friend had the stoicism of the true
fan. "He hid for two days in the bushes outside the hotel without
food or water." Makarevich sucked in his cheeks and became the
starving fan. "Then my friend came back and told us, 'I saw John
Lennon.' We had to believe." Andrei's face shone.

But the ultimate dream was to become a Beatle. "Of course I had
to try to make myself an electric guitar. There were none in the
shops, so I tried to copy from a photo of Lennon's guitar. I made the
body from a piece of wood and painted it red, but then I couldn't
find a pickup." A friend told him you could make one from a telephone handset in a public call box. Makarevich raided the nearest
box, and soon telephones across the Soviet Union had been disabled
by kids scavenging pickups for homemade guitars. The harvesting of
guitar pickups from call boxes was a story I was to hear time and
again, so that it began to feel like a refrain from a Beatles song: "In
Penny Lane a rock kid raids another telephone . . ."

Talking to Makarevich, I could feel his passion to beat the system,
to follow the Beatles and make a rock 'n' roll band. "It looked easy to
play like they did, but of course it wasn't at all. We thought we could
just get a guitar, grow our hair, get a Beatle jacket and we were them.
And if you walked down Gorky Street with a guitar case you were a
hero. So everybody forgot mathematics and sport and literature, and
became Beatles."

Most of Moscow's wannabe Beatles gave up on their dreams
and made their peace with the drab realities of Leonid Brezhnev's

1960s rock star hopeful Andrei Makarevich.

stagnating Soviet Union. It was a time when millions retreated to the sour jokes coined as a kind of sullen rebellion: "They pretend to pay us, we pretend to work"; "Why were Adam and Eve the first Communists? Because they had nothing to wear and only an apple to eat—but they thought they were in Paradise."

Makarevich was different. The music he had discovered on those albums his father brought from the West had changed his life. "I can't say we made music for the first couple of years. We just tried to look like the Beatles and sound like the Beatles. I knew a few chords. We had a drum from the Communist Party Young Pioneers. We stayed at home and just played. We listened and played, listened and played. We tried to sing." He gave a small sigh, and for a moment he seemed lost in those years of trying to make music. "And then," he said, "we moved on."

It sounded like the story of any rock hopefuls anywhere—until I remembered that homemade guitar, and that Young Pioneer drum, and the inevitable cultural commissars, watching, disapproving, controlling. As Makarevich led me through the long journey of Time

Russian rock superstar Andrei Makarevich.

Machine—the band that would become an icon across the Soviet Union—I was swept up in a very Russian adventure.

In the late 1960s, Makarevich and his friends fumbled through "Ticket to Ride" and "Hey Jude," trying to sing in English. "For three years, nobody knew about us. Then we were asked to play before movie screenings, to try and get the crowds, and we began to get known." I had seen a photo of Time Machine from those years. Four cheerful boys in velvet-collared jackets, clones of early Beatles photo shoots, smiled out at me with the undentable confidence of their youth. The tipping point for Time Machine came on a Soviet holiday in November 1970. "They decided we should do a concert to introduce a free screening. It was a big mistake. The entire Moscow hippie community came and broke down the doors. The police arrived, and the crowd threw a motorcycle in the Moscow River. It was a big scandal." Makarevich and his band were hauled off to face an official grilling. The questioning captures the bewilderment of

Soviet authority faced with the gathering rock revolution. "Are you Soviets or what? Why don't you sing our Soviet songs? Do you want to look like English or American boys? Why the long hair? We were stuck in prison for the night, and we were scared," Andrei said. "Then nothing happened. But from that time the Soviet authorities began to pay serious attention to everything we did."

It was the start of years of playing cat and mouse with Soviet cultural commissars for Makarevich and Time Machine. As he talked about his adventures, I got a sense of what fun it must have been to seize the role of rock outlaw against the plodding sheriffs of the state. "It was difficult to catch us, because we were always invited to play in different places. The gigs were absolutely secret; only the people who'd been invited knew where it was happening. So the police usually arrived too late." The occasional night in jail only added to the thrill of youthful rebellion, and as Time Machine were never paid, they could never be charged with "economic crimes"—and they never drifted away from their fans.

It was a defiantly Soviet version of the rock 'n' roll hero, detached in every way from the life of the mega-buck, mega-stadium, Western rock star. Time Machine's regular standoffs with authority lent them a renegade "Easy Rider-ish" profile that would have been the envy of many a Western band. You couldn't buy that authentic renegade stuff on Abbey Road or in Beverly Hills. Hearing about Makarevich's life on the edge of the Soviet mainstream, I thought about how, before the Beatles retreated to the haven of the recording studio, they had become rock hermits, huddling in anonymous hotels, their music drowned by the screams of the crowds. I wondered if Andrei or Paul and John would have been happy to trade places.

By the late 1970s, Time Machine's music was circulating across the Soviet Union on millions of cassettes, commanding big prices for the hustlers who sold them on the black market. The group wrote their own songs, and sang them in Russian. Makarevich wrote all the lyrics, which explored the despair, conformism, and passivity of a generation growing up under the geriatric regime of Leonid Brezhnev. But Time Machine were still totally unofficial, with no possibility of becoming a professional group. "Soviet officials understood that something was happening," Andrei said, "but they didn't know what to do about it."

Makarevich was still playing a watchful game with authority. He avoided direct attacks on Communist ideology and powerful forces in the Party, smuggling his comments in hints and allusions. With no official information published about Time Machine, the fevered imaginations of their fans created wild stories about the band, reminiscent of the fantasies that had circled around the Beatles years earlier. They were rumored to travel under the protection of a squad of karate heavies and a pack of Alsatian dogs. Concerts became wilder and harder to control.

In 1979, weary of the endless battles and angry that the band still had no income while profiteers and forgers fed on proceeds from their cassettes, Makarevich signed up with the state promotion agency, Rosconcert. After a decade of surviving on the edge, Time Machine became legitimate. It meant they could rely on national publicity and a steady income. But it also meant a degree of supervision and control—and it undercut their renegade image.

The Moscow Olympics in the summer of 1980 compelled the state to relax its cultural straitjacket—at least for a while. "They understood they had to open the doors, just a little," Makarevich told me. Time Machine was getting a lot of attention by now, but their real breakthrough came at the Spring Rhythms rock festival in the Georgian city of Tbilisi in March 1980. Competing against bands from across the U.S.S.R., Time Machine won the top prize. Inevitably, some of their fans who had stayed loyal through their long years on the margins felt betrayed. It encapsulated the dilemma of Soviet rock musicians: keep the rebel image of free-spirited opposition and stay unofficial and poor; or join the official mainstream where the state would provide concert bookings and support, but risk losing

credibility and loyal fans. Art Troitsky reported a famous confrontation he had with Makarevich, during which he accused Andrei of
being "a bourgeois sellout." "But we haven't become any worse or
more stupid," Makarevich told Troitsky. "The way I see it, the state
has moved toward us." In a way, I thought, they were both right; in
embracing a rock 'n' roll supergroup, the cultural bureaucrats were
inviting a Trojan horse into the citadel of the state. In due course,
the Beatles generation would break out and begin to shift the foundations of the system that believed it had co-opted and neutralized
the threat.

In the early 1980s, while the U.S.S.R. decayed under the leadership of sick old men, Time Machine flourished. They were an official
supergroup, starring in movies and on TV, traveling their vast country for months with a crew of roadies and piles of stage equipment.
Their song "Povorot" stayed on the top of the Soviet hit list for eighteen months. They were attracting international attention now, and
Time magazine reported that their concerts were "like a return to the
early days of the Beatles."

In 1982, though, during yet another swerve in the Kremlin under
Yuri Andropov, Time Machine were denounced with words that
could have been coined under Stalin: they were dubbed "un-Russian"
and "advocates of indifference." But when they were briefly compelled to wind up the band, protests from thousands of fans earned a
reprieve. Even the Kremlin could no longer ignore the clamor of
a generation. Then Gorbachev arrived, and everything began to
change. Makarevich told me at our meeting in 2007 that he was due
to head off with the band for a tour of Europe and America.

Makarevich turned a page in the old schoolbook and found a
drawing he had done one afternoon, back when the U.S.S.R. had
seemed stuck in time. His fuzzy sketch of four youngsters who were
going to change his life, his generation, and his country looked back
at him, as if he had made it only the previous day. As he was leaving
he glanced through the window at the Kremlin.

"Every time I see Gorbachev," he said, "I say thank you for what you did."

I met Vladimir Matietsky in a Moscow rock club on an afternoon when only the cleaners were performing, vacuuming acres of sticky carpet after the mess of the night before. Art Troitsky had told me that Matietsky was a veteran of the Moscow scene, a bass guitarist and all-around rock survivor. He was a striking figure, well over six feet tall with a bouffant mane of silver hair, louche good looks, and a faintly intimidating self-assurance. He also spoke the excellent English of yet another son of privilege.

We sat down in a cavernous upstairs room, hemmed in by six snooker tables. On the walls I saw that the club had a gallery of exquisite black-and-white photographs of jazz musicians, taken by a hero of mine, Herman Leonard. As we began to talk, I had the sense that Charlie Parker and Miles Davis were listening in.

"It was 1964, and I was twelve years old when I found the Beatles on my short-wave radio. My first thought was 'wow—they sing so high.' But the whole sound was cool, different. Then we made recordings on reel-to-reel tape recorders from LPs parents brought from abroad." It was more evidence how the Beatles revolution was made by bourgeois kids in the Soviet Union, the ones with parents who could travel and had tape recorders—and cameras. "There was a guy in our class," Matietsky recalled, "who started to copy Beatles photos with his camera, and sell them. It was a big business. I got known as an expert, and other guys called me in to check out the photos—to weed out the Stones or the Kinks."

Matietsky recounted a strange fable that had blossomed around the Beatles. The acute shortage of real information bred a tangle of speculations and fantasies about the Fab Four, but his story struck me as especially poignant. "Some fans believed that the Beatles loved Soviet pop music," Matietsky said. "The legend insisted that the band would gather in Lennon's attic to try and listen to Russian radio, hunting for Time Machine and any other groups they could find through the static of British secret-service jamming." The fans also said that the Beatles secretly recorded Russian pop songs on X-ray film, but that they were banned from singing in Russian. "Some kids really built a complete alternative world with this stuff," Matietsky said. "They told stories of how British kids who tried to dance like Russians would be deported to the Falkland Islands."

Soon, like millions of other fans, Matietsky had to do it himself. "Everybody who had a guitar and a mop-top hairstyle was a Russian Beatle. I was." The memory lit him up and he smiled. "I was skinny, big hair, guitar—Paul McCartney playing bass!"

Like everybody I met, Matietsky had his own story about a Beatle in Moscow. "I knew guys who convinced everyone that they saw John Lennon on Gorky Street. 'I definitely saw him buying bread,' one kid told me." I thought it seemed a disappointingly mundane sighting of a rock hero, but then I guess the real point was that the great Lennon might be moving among them, a prophet with his people. Matietsky made me understand how the prophets could be disappointing. "When we got to see *Hard Day's Night,* it was a big surprise that the Beatles were so funny. I thought they were serious, because for us their music was serious. So it was a big shock." It made sense, of course. In a place where people had gone to jail not so long ago for telling jokes, your heroes should not be fooling around. The Beatles' lyrics were a disappointment as well, Matietsky said. "We thought they must be about important stuff, but when we managed to work them out, they seemed mostly about girls and having fun."

But in the end, nothing dimmed the magic. "The Beatles were like fresh air," Matietsky said. "In Russia they had this amazing power, because they had this free spirit. And all the young people started to imitate them, and so they started to feel more free as well." There must have been an acute shortage of attractive role models. I thought of the stodgy middle-aged politicians and bossy officials, the dusty saints Marx and Lenin, the state-approved entertainers with their cardboard suits and military haircuts. Inevitably the Beatles—impulsive, exuberant, fearless—were irresistible.

Matietsky glanced around the club at the jazz photos. "The culture bosses were so stupid they couldn't tell the difference between jazz like this and rock. The Party's youth paper talked about 'the Beatles or some other jazz king.' So the kids had absolutely no respect for anything they said." He shook his head and smiled. "Of course we're living in a completely different world now. But the Beatles are still in the hearts of people who are fifty and kids of ten. No one knows how long it will last." He tossed back his hair that was like a memento from the sixties. "But I think it will."

Matietsky's affair with the Beatles was to have a fairy-tale conclusion. In 2007, as a producer, he arranged for Andrei Makarevich and Time Machine to record an album in the Beatles' legendary Abbey Road Studio in London. They rode around the city in an open-top bus and trooped in single file across the inevitable Abbey Road crossing. In the studio, they gazed at the master tapes for *Sgt. Pepper*, like pilgrims at a holy shrine. Then, just as their recording session was ending, the door opened and Sir George Martin, the "Fifth Beatle," the man who had shaped all the iconic albums, came to say hello. There's a photograph of the moment when, more than forty years after the Beatles' music first reached the Soviet Union, a band from the generation they transformed comes back to where it all began. Andrei Makarevich looks radiant.

8

White on black, snow was sprinkling Sasha Lipnitsky's beret as we talked in a deserted café near the bandstand in Moscow's Hermitage Park. I recalled that this was the place where many of the Soviet Union's first jazz concerts had been held fifty years earlier. Now the pale green pavilions had an abandoned feel, as though a cheery crowd of Young Pioneers had faded into the snow. With his neatly trimmed beard and the world-weary eyes of a character from Chekhov, Lipnitsky seemed a visitor from an earlier time. He was one of Art Troitsky's best friends, and I liked him immediately. Art had told me Sasha was a bass guitarist with one of Moscow's most adventurous bands, Zvuki Mu. I had seen a video of the band in action, and it was hard to match up the dervish contortions of the band's lead singer, Peter Mamonov, with this quiet, aristocratic man in the park.

Lipnitsky was a survivor of the battles between rock and authority, and he told me he owed everything to the Beatles. "Just two songs on a little record, "All My Loving" together with "And I Love Her"—this record changed my life. I was twelve years old." Like almost everyone I was meeting from the Beatles generation, he was a son of privilege. His grandfather interpreted at meetings between Kennedy and Krushchev, and his connections brought him the Beatles long before most Russian kids had tuned into them. "My grandmother was a big movie star, and she brought me that first record from a trip to India. Like a lot of people, I can't explain why I loved the Beatles with all my heart and soul." I was startled by the force of Lipnitsky's declaration. His feeling for the music felt like a confession of faith. "Nobody even tried to understand the words of the songs," he said. "We were trying to understand the feeling behind the music."

"What do you think that was?" I asked him.

"I think freedom, the wind of freedom."

It was said simply, unself-consciously. As so often in Russia, the direct statement of feeling caught me off guard, made me feel jaded, a cynical tourist from a place where that kind of thing was almost an embarrassment. But then Lipnitsky startled me again by insisting that the Beatles and their music were about spiritual liberation. "Russian pop music was very organized; there was no place for improvization." Then he said, "The Beatles brought us the idea of democracy. For many of us, it was the first hole in the Iron Curtain. We were the Beatles generation."

We sheltered under the roof of the café, looking across at the bandstand, blurring now through the falling snow. "This was where Vladimir Vysotsky used to play in the seventies. He was a huge figure for us. He sang his songs about the mess of daily life, about drunks and losers, about real things—about standing in line for everything, about the struggle to find somewhere to live. He was funny and tough and impossible for the system to control, and he was a hero for everyone."

I asked Sasha to tell me more about Vysotsky. "He had a demonic energy, and his life was a nonstop drama of wild drinking, car smashes, and rebellion." Even the headlines of the man's ungovernable life helped me to understand how frustrating it must have been for the bureaucrats to rein him in; and his story also told me something fundamental about how the decades of trying to dictate music according to an official template were ultimately a delusion.

"Vysotsky had two careers, really," Lipnitsky went on. "He was a very successful actor at the Moscow Art Theater, where he was a celebrated Hamlet. If that wasn't enough, Vysotsky also starred in dozens of films. Then he married a French film star; for the fans that only made his legend even greater. But in the early 1970s, the authorities decided to crack down on him." As Sasha told me the story he spoke more quietly and for him it seemed the campaign against Vysotsky summed up the capricious stupidity of state bureaucrats over the years in harassing musicians. "They suddenly announced he didn't have permission to perform as a soloist, and his list of songs at a recent concert had not been approved." The idea of a famous singer needing official approval for a playlist of his own songs was so bizarre that for a moment I wondered if I had misheard Lipnitsky's story.

Vysotsky died in July 1980 at the age of forty-two, unmentioned by official Soviet media. But thirty thousand people turned up on the day of his funeral, and mourners still hold vigils at his graveside every year. "Of course his records were never released," Sasha said, "until after he died, and Gorbachev came to power."

We walked around the snow-covered bandstand where Vysotsky used to play, and Sasha came to a halt. "There's something you should understand," he said. "For many years, we were told that the West was an enemy—nothing more. Not our neighbors on the planet, just 'the Enemy.' The Beatles were the first to show us that there was something wrong with what we had always been taught by our Soviet rulers."

"Do you think that scared them?"

"I think they understood that this idea about the Beatles will change something inside us."

It was snowing steadily now, gathering in little drifts against the bandstand. "Let's go up to my flat," Lipnitsky said.

The apartment overlooking the park was crammed with a tangle of electronic bits and pieces—big old mixers, dead microphones, abandoned amplifiers. For a moment, I thought someone was watching us. Then I realized that the somber faces gazing through the piles of rock castoffs in the gray winter light, were saints—a gallery of icons hung around the walls. "I collect them, and sell some as well," Lipnitsky said. Somehow the collision of rock and Orthodox icons was transcendently Russian, but I found it a bit unsettling.

"Zvuki Mu was born in this apartment," Lipnitsky said, "and we did all our rehearsing here." Art had told me Sasha had sold part of his art collection to buy the band's instruments. Now he went over to a battered leather case and lifted out a bass guitar with reverence. It struck me that for Lipnitsky the guitar in its velvet shroud was another icon. He slung it around his neck and began to talk about the troubled history of his band. "Nineteen eighty-four was our worst year," he said, and I could understand why. It was the year when the last of a succession of geriatric Soviet leaders, Konstantin Chernenko, came to power. A former propaganda chief under Brezhnev, he led hard-line campaigns that recalled the dark days of the Cold War. "When Chernenko became the Kremlin top guy," Sasha said, "they really started to crack down on anything connected with the West, and rock music was an obvious target."

This was the time when Art Troitsky had been exiled from the Moscow press, and Stas Namin had been forced out of music. It was a shock to realize that only four years before my meeting with Sasha Lipnitsky, the Kremlin had mounted a crackdown on rock 'n' roll that echoed the era of the Stalinist purges. "We did our first concert in eighty-four," Sasha said, "and that was just when the KGB were hounding rock bands. The concert was at my old school, and all the rock people showed up. There was a huge fuss, and the director of the school had a hard time with the authorities. I was arrested, but we still wanted to have more concerts. For some reason, I felt really brave."

Sasha Lipnitsky looked more like one of the ascetic saints hanging on his wall than a man who would choose to slug it out with the KGB, but he had a martyr's determination. He decided to invite a half-dozen top bands to play at his country dacha about twenty miles outside Moscow. "But then the KGB moved in. They went to Art Troitsky's house and threatened him, and then a half-dozen black Volgas arrived at my dacha. The KGB colonel was very aggressive. He shouted that this concert 'was obviously a Western-inspired provocation.' When the bands arrived at the dacha from Moscow, the KGB told them to leave and take their fans with them. They were really frightened."

Hearing the story, I felt I was tuning in again to a nightmare from the 1930s, slipping into a black hole from the years of Stalin's Terror. But a quiet-spoken musician made me understand that for his generation, the terror could be confronted. "I asked to see the KGB's orders. There was a ludicrous row about official stamps on our lyrics, and whether we could play without lyrics, and in the end, it seemed the KGB guys just lost interest." It was agreed Lipnitsky could have his birthday concert if it was on his own property. So he invited a hundred fans to hang out in his garden, and the concert began at last, with the KGB peering through the fence. "It was raining," he recalled, "and with all the electric cables lying around, I thought someone might get killed."

When the concert was over, Sasha had the hundred fans sleeping in his dacha for the night. His grandmother, who had spent years in Stalin's gulags, thought it was lots of fun. He dug out some photos he took that day. A girl in a bikini danced while a guy strummed a guitar and a crowd listened under umbrellas. I thought they looked like people left behind from a hippie commune in Haight-Ashbury. Kids ate salad and drank wine in a garden. A man sprawled asleep on a bearskin rug as if he'd fallen on the bear and flattened it. A fan slumbered on a mattress in the garden under a plastic bag. It was innocent and naïve and hopelessly defiant, and I found myself suddenly moved by the photos and by Sasha's story. Moved and angry. How could the vast engine of the Soviet state have stirred itself to lumber down a country lane just to bully a few kids with guitars? The whole episode gave me a new understanding of just how threatened authority must have felt, bewildered and flattened like that bearskin rug under the weight of music made by youngsters having fun in the rain.

Sasha put away the photos and for a moment he got lost in the memories of that day when the KGB had gate-crashed his birthday party. "There was a weird follow-up," he said. "I heard that Gorbachev made a speech to the Central Committee about how my rock 'n' roll birthday party had been organized by plotters against the state." This was startling. So only months before he became the top man and began to chip away at the Soviet iceberg, Gorby felt he still had to rehash the old paranoias about rock being a Western virus, sent to infect the U.S.S.R.

Chernenko was a sick man, and he died in 1985, only thirteen months after becoming the Soviet leader. The new top man, Mikhail Gorbachev, was a very different figure, nearly twenty years younger and full of fresh ideas. It was hardly surprising that musicians hoped for better times under Gorbachev—though some were still unconvinced.

As he was nestling his guitar back into its case, Lipnitsky said something that made me think Gorbachev might have been right after all about the seditious potential of rock 'n' roll. "I reckon," Sasha said, "Gorbachev is a result of the Beatles. I'm sure he was a fan." He snapped the case shut. "Gorby's naïve and romantic attempts to change Russia are a result of that Beatles romance."

9

"You should go and see Vladimir Pozner," said the British journalist Martin Walker. "He'll be able to give you the insider's take on why the old guys in the Kremlin were scared by rock 'n' roll and the Beatles." Walker had got to know Pozner since he came to report from Moscow, and he had a guarded respect for him as the Soviet Union's most talented and effective propagandist. "He's an interesting man," Walker said, "very bright and oddly enough I think he's pretty honest—for a Soviet journalist."

Like many Russia watchers in the West, I had become increasingly aware of Vladimir Pozner over the past few years. He was an intriguing and mysterious figure. Since Gorbachev had begun to shake things up in the Soviet Union, Pozner had become a kind of spokesman for perestroika. He turned up regularly on TV in America and the United Kingdom, beamed by satellite from Moscow like one of those puzzling aliens in *Star Trek*—the ones who look just like us, but not quite. Speaking in the unmistakable accents of New York City, handsome, urbane, and articulate, with his telegenic Slavic cheekbones, he was plainly an apologist for the New Russia.

Vladimir Pozner, Soviet-American journalist.

But we had never before heard propaganda fired back at us in our own voice, and with such eloquence and assurance. It was clear that for all the ambiguities of this American-seeming Soviet reporter, he might be able to give me some rare insights into how the Kremlin felt about the Beatles. Anyway, I was intrigued to meet the man who was becoming one of the West's favorite commies.

I trudged through the slushy snow, dredging up some of my half-forgotten Russian to find my way to his apartment. I finally tracked the place down in a quiet courtyard not far from the Kremlin. Pozner opened the door, instantly recognizable, and invited me in. It was like a film set for the perfect Soviet intellectual's flat. Books were arrayed round the walls and piled up on tables; on his desk my attention was caught by a glass model of the Empire State Building. As we began to talk, it was clear that Pozner was well supplied with the seductive charm that is often a key ingredient of the successful journalist. And he was disarmingly frank about the Kremlin's part in the propaganda wars with the West. "The picture supplied by our propaganda about America and the West was false. And when people here began to understand that, some time in the early sixties"—about the time, I thought, when news of the Beatles reached the Soviet Union—"what happened was that they did a one hundred eighty–degree turn. Everything about America and the West is great from that point on."

Pozner talked about that gathering divide between Soviet citizens and their rulers, and he had wonderful stories. "People would watch some report about the evils of Capitalism with pictures of poor blacks and drunks on skid row. But they would turn down the propaganda commentary, and focus instead on the miraculous displays of clothes and furniture and food in the shop windows."

He also began to talk about his own story. It was a drama as adhesive as any Cold War thriller. Over the years since then I have come to know Pozner well, and I count him as a friend. Along the way I have also understood something of the strains of his life as a man stranded between East and West, and of his fierce determination to survive.

On that first afternoon, I only got the headlines. Pozner's father was a Russian Jew who married his French mother in Paris and then fled the Nazis for New York early in the Second World War. Pozner senior worked in the movie business, and the young Pozner grew up in Greenwich Village, imbibing baseball and jazz and folk music. After the war as the Iron Curtain slammed down, the anti-Communist crusade of Senator Joe McCarthy pulled the plug on the Pozner family. The father, who remained a true believer in Stalin and the revolution, refused to renounce his Soviet citizenship. After a miserable interlude in Communist East Germany, the family arrived in Moscow in 1952, just before the death of Stalin. Vladimir Pozner struggled to settle amid the austerities of Soviet life, and his frustrations came to a head when he met up with young Americans who traveled to Moscow for the World Youth Festival in 1957. The festival reignited his longing for the music and the freedoms of his boyhood in New York. "Suddenly I realized how much I missed America," he said, "the way they acted, the way they joked, the way they sang. I got this terrible feeling of homesickness, and I decided I was going to leave the Soviet Union." He told his father he wanted to defect. The response was direct and brutal. "If you ever say that again, I'll report you to the KGB."

Pozner was stranded behind the Iron Curtain for the next thirty-eight years, building a life as a successful Soviet journalist, working for official magazines. His radio broadcasts from Moscow to the West in the depths of the Cold War, retailing good news about Socialism, were highly valued by the Kremlin. Pozner became a member of the Communist Party, and a believer in the ideals of Karl Marx. But he grew increasingly skeptical about the old men at the top. His outspoken comments cost him a chance to travel to the West, and that only increased his disaffection. The arrival of Gorbachev in 1985 had been his defining moment. From Leningrad, Pozner hosted the Soviet end of a pioneering Satellite Television "space bridge" between East and West with Phil Donahue as his cohost in the United States. Soon he got his long-awaited permission to travel. "At long last," he said, "I was able to visit America again. Coming over the Fifty-ninth Street Bridge, I saw New York and my heart stopped."

He took me for a drive along the vast boulevards of central Moscow, and filled in more of his story. "I was never fully trusted here," he said, and I felt again the restlessness of a man who was never at home in either of his worlds. It made him a wonderful interpreter between East and West, and as we drove along the Moscow River under the walls of the Kremlin, I asked him about the strange obsession of the Kremlin with the Beatles. "The Beatles were never invited here," he said, "and I think that really is an indication of the kind of built-in radar system of Communist officials. These were not stupid people, and they probably would have found it hard to explain what it was about the Beatles that made them jittery. But there was a kind of freedom, 'fuck-the-power-structure' thing—and they felt that. They had this detector sitting inside them."

It was fascinating to have this insider's perspective into how the Kremlin felt about the Beatles. I was particularly struck by Pozner's suggestion that their hard line was based not on ideology or political conviction, but on instinct and feeling. It confirmed my gathering sense that the Beatles' challenge to the Kremlin went to the heart of the Communist leadership's alarm about the ungovernable power of culture in Soviet society.

Pozner laughed as he turned on to a road that took us past one of the Stalinist towers overlooking the river. "High-ranking party officials do not really have a great sense of humor—apart from jokes about the toilet. The idea of anyone laughing at them, they couldn't deal with that. They saw it as undermining the status of the Communist Party."

"What do you think Brezhnev would have said about the Beatles if you had asked him?"

"I doubt he could have put his finger on it, but I guess he'd have said something like 'we don't need that.'"

I wondered if inviting the Beatles to play in Moscow wouldn't have been a better idea, to defuse the threat by embracing it. "No doubt," Pozner said, "but they couldn't see that. The more the Beatles were prohibited, the more the kids wanted them. 'This is somehow the apple we're not supposed to taste, so it must taste very, very good.'"

We stopped alongside a towering titanium statue of Yuri Gagarin. "He's supposed to spread wings and fly on his birthday every year," Pozner told me. Gagarin was still a hero for Soviet citizens a quarter-century after his pioneering space flight. As we gazed up at the statue, a "just-married" couple were piling out of a car. The bride's white dress swirled in the wind, and the impossibly young groom looked blue with cold. "They'll be coming to dedicate their marriage to the space hero," Pozner said. It was oddly affecting to hear that people were still paying their respects to the secular saint. "The Soviet Union has actually stood on a profound belief, shared by most people, that their system was the best in the world," he said. "Now that's beginning to fade, the whole edifice could fall apart." We drove away and I looked back at Gagarin, disappearing behind an anonymous block of apartments. "How has it all lasted so long?" I asked Pozner. "It's been held together by fear and by belief," he said. "The Beatles played a role first by helping to overcome the fear." He looked across at me. "And then they showed the belief was actually stupid."

I went out of Moscow for the weekend to Art and Svetlana's dacha. Even such a sophisticated and worldly couple shared the Russian obsession with having a place in the country, a painted wooden house with a prospect of their own stretch of pine trees. Svetlana cooked a chicken, and I updated Art on my Beatles explorations.

"Pozner was interesting," I told him. "He helped me to get a sense of why the comrades were so scared of the Fab Four." Troitsky nodded. "Yes, in the sixties we were coming to understand that we were living in a monster state, and we needed something else. Of course party hoods picked up on that, and so the Beatles were an obvious target for Soviet satire with the haircuts and hysterical girls. But I think the heavy-handed satire actually added fuel to the Soviet Beatles mania."

"Do you think that there was ever a chance they could have been allowed to play here?"

"No way. In the late sixties Madame Furtseva, who was our minister of culture, actually sent a guy to check out a Rolling Stones concert in Warsaw. Of course he was shocked and terrified, and the story he brought back absolutely closed the door to any hairy electric band—especially the Beatles."

We sipped the scotch I'd brought from England. "There was another thing that bothered the culture ghouls," Art said. "In the Soviet Union, we always like to follow a leader. And the Beatles were the leaders of rock 'n' roll. I was a little snob, so I knew the Kinks, the Pretty Things, and all those bands. But for most Soviet kids, there was one leading band, and that was the Beatles. They were on every tape machine, and they personalized the whole of rock music. So it was obvious that they shouldn't be allowed to come here."

Svetlana arrived with the chicken. Surveying the two middle-aged men trading memories, she said, "You guys remind me of a gang of Beatles fans in this country—mainly men. The girls were probably stuck at home cooking a chicken." It reminded me that Russia was still a remorselessly macho society, where drunken men staggered home on Women's Day to offer their wives a bedraggled flower.

Art seemed hardly to notice. He had more to say about the fantasy of a Beatles concert in the Soviet Union. "I think it would have been a bad idea anyway. The audience would have been stuffed with the children of Party creeps, and young activists with awful haircuts and terrible ties. That would have made us feel that the Beatles had betrayed us rather than coming to rescue us."

Troitsky leaned back in his chair. It was getting late, and I had to head back to Moscow. "You should come with me to Leningrad and meet a real Russian rock star. Boris Grebenshikov is due to play a big concert. I know he's a huge Beatles fan, and he'll tell you about that. But you'll also hear how we've found our own voice at last."

10

Standing at Moscow's Leningrad Station, the "Aurora" express was the longest train I had ever seen. Coaches stretched into the distance, and every door had a guardian—unsmiling, intimidating women with military caps, boots, and ticket machines. The conductors' style made me wonder if they had been recruited from the redundant guards at the recently dismantled gulags.

The Aurora had been the Soviet Union's fastest express train since the 1960s, but my compartment was like a set from a period movie; a little table with a white cloth, artificial flowers in a vase. A plastic-covered sheet announced: "Menu of complex dinners. Comfortable conditions for every passenger." A sinister item on the menu caught my eye: "Tongue, vow of silence." I flipped a switch, but the lights didn't work.

Thirty minutes out of Moscow, the train had traveled a hundred years back in time. Muddy tracks meandered through decaying wooden villages. I saw two men with bottles hugging on a dirt road. I thought this must be the kind of place where Art Troitsky's "peasants and redneck villagers" made their lives. What on earth could they have felt here about the music of four kids from another world?

Ambling through weary-looking stations where faded slogans flaked off crumbling walls, the Aurora rattled north toward Leningrad. At one stop, I took a few photos through the window: a babushka plods by with a painted bucket brimming with apples; a chubby girl in a dirty pink tracksuit wanders along the platform, smoking ravenously. Time seemed to have slowed to a crawl out here beyond the pull of Moscow.

I drowsed, and then jolted awake as a scratchy voice announced that we were approaching Leningrad. On the platform, speakers were playing heroic music and I had the feeling that I was an extra in a Soviet epic of the 1930s.

Out on Nevsky Prospekt, the film abruptly changed. It was getting dark now, and the city's main boulevard was a parade of illuminated arcades, almost operatic in its prettiness. There was little of Moscow's big-shouldered bossiness on display; the place felt like a gorgeous Paul McCartney ballad after the capital's Lennon-inflected snarl. Art Troitsky had told me he didn't really feel at ease in Leningrad. He had a distrust, shared by many Muscovites, of the second city's theme-park spectacle. "The city of bad memories," Art called it.

I went in search of Troitsky at the vast sports center where Boris Grebenshikov was due to play a concert the next night with his band, Aquarium. It was a special occasion: Russia's rock hero would perform alongside a top Western band headed by Dave Stewart of the Eurythmics in a striking display of musical glasnost. A banner declared AQUARIUM AND FRIENDS '88. The Hollywood director Michael Apted, a friend of mine from television, had arrived in Leningrad with six film crews to make a big-budget documentary about the concert and about Grebenshikov. The recent opening up of the Soviet Union after the decades of isolation had made the West hungry for stories about the former Cold War enemy. Soviet rock was especially fascinating, as it became the soundtrack for Gorby's amazing adventure.

Troitsky had told me something about the Grebenshikov mythol-

ogy and about the adoring fans who revered him as a combination
of poet, guru, anarchic prophet, and spiritual guide. Discovering
the Beatles in the early sixties—he kept a Beatles shrine in his
apartment—had changed Grebenshikov's life. He was transformed
from maths student to underground rock hero, the Soviet love child
of Dylan and Lennon. Aquarium's unique lineup of cello, bassoon,
violin, and guitars performed Grebenshikov's hypnotic anthems of
alienation and rebellion. Throughout the stagnant Brezhnev years
he had gathered a vast following through illegal gigs recorded on
reel-to-reel tapes and passed from hand to hand across the country.
His transcendent moment had come in 1980 at a rock competition in
the Georgian city of Tbilisi. Grebenshikov had outraged the judges
by lying down to caress his Fender Telecaster in a flagrant display of
sexual bravura worthy of Jimi Hendrix. All the judges got up and
left, and back in Leningrad Grebenshikov lost his job as a computer
programmer. He was expelled from the Komsomol and banned from
playing in Leningrad. But he gained a nationwide following as a sha-
man perfectly attuned to his generation, fearless, sexy, unstoppable.
Art Troitsky, who had invited Grebenshikov to Tbilisi, was in no
doubt about the significance of Aquarium's scandalizing performance. "It meant you are free to do what you want. It taught people
how to oppose the rules."

Seven years after Tbilisi, Grebenshikov was embarking on a dangerous flirtation with commercial Western rock, and his fans were
uneasy. Was he selling out? Would they lose him? It reminded me of
how faithful Beatles fans in Liverpool, the people who had turned
out for every gig at the Cavern Club on a wet Tuesday night, had felt
when the boys left them behind and vanished into superstar lives in
London.

The Leningrad concert was unknown territory for the Western
visitors as well. As Aquarium's cellist sawed away on the empty stage
and the film crews roamed around lining up shots, the big question
for the bloated Western rock caravan with its mountains of gear

seemed to be, "Where can we find some black paint?" Designers and roadies fluttered around, incredulous that in the whole of Leningrad they couldn't find anything to tart up the bleak stage. Observing the mutual bewilderments in the freezing cavern of the sports center, I felt I was witnessing the latest chapter in the centuries-old struggle by the city's founder, Peter the Great, to transform his city from a reclaimed swamp to a gilded outpost of European civilization. But Peter didn't have any shortage of gold paint to carry out his transformation.

Just a year before, Grebenshikov had risked his renegade status when the state record label Melodiya had released an album of Aquarium's underground tapes. It sold a quarter-million copies in a few hours, startling evidence of how Gorbachev's glasnost and perestroika were declaring a cease-fire in the endless battle between the Soviet state and popular music. Now Grebenshikov had challenged his legend even more by signing a contract with CBS records in America. The hookup with Dave Stewart in Leningrad would be an important test of his fans' loyalty.

As the film crews continued their self-important fussings, groups of nervous policemen patrolled the auditorium. They seemed to be mostly pale-faced boys, unsure of how to deal with this unruly invasion of foreigners with their intrusive cameras and endless demands. In a state where policemen had never had to wrestle with the ambiguities of civil liberties, the unpredictable mix of rock 'n' roll and Western film crews was an unfamiliar challenge. To compound the cultural tangle of Western rock extravagance with Grebenshikov's band of underground poets, a group of tiny girl gymnasts were rehearsing on the edge of the sports arena. They twirled and skipped and floated, a timeless Russian counterpoint to the tensions playing out around them.

The cello player was heading off the stage. I caught up with him and introduced myself. He said his name was Seva Gakkel, and he

seemed to have absorbed the personality of his instrument: dignified, quietly spoken, with an open aristocratic face. When I mentioned the Beatles, he lit up. "I heard 'Help!' in 1965, and it was a
revelation. I realized something had happened to me, and from then
on I couldn't avoid it. I just felt a kind of happiness." I was becoming familiar now with the feeling among the Soviet Beatles generation I met—that electric moment of the first encounter with the
music. Gakkel said he was struck by that opening jangled chord of
"Help!" with the force of a religious conversion. "I realized that it was
very personal for me, and very important. I realized that something
was happening out there in the world, a world of young people I
couldn't visit. It was a world I couldn't avoid, a world I wanted to belong to." He struggled for a moment to find the words. "It was something that allowed me to feel complete." Then Gakkel said something
that suggested a wider, more seditious impact of the Beatles and their
music: "It was probably the most important thing happening to us. I
belonged to their world, and somehow they generated my world. We
just didn't care about the system we were living in." That sense of being exiled from the world was a repeated theme of my conversations
with the Soviet Beatles generation, and the insistence on breaking
free of a life defined and constrained by the system seemed to have
combusted with the energies they found in Beatles music. For people
like Seva Gakkel, the certainties of their parents had dissolved into
irrelevance.

I followed Gakkel and his cello into the dressing room, where the
air was heavy with pot and Aquarium seemed to be taken up with
assorted rituals and mantras. Troitsky introduced me to Boris Grebenshikov. Slender and pale, with lips borrowed from Mick Jagger
and hair swept into a careless ponytail, he switched on a smile and
the charisma of an instinctive rock star. He was happy to talk about
how the Beatles had changed his life.

"Before the Beatles came," Boris said in impeccable English, "life didn't have any apparent meaning. After I heard them, it was clinched. That was it—now I know." It was the most evangelical expression of faith in the Fab Four I had encountered, and there was more to come. "I would remind you of the ancient Chinese sage who said that the mode of the music changes society." Ancient Chinese sage" gave me the authentic flavor of the Leningrad rock community, that curious mix of hippie and dissident I hadn't come across since London in the late sixties. "Here, we heard their music and the Soviet kingdom was ruined." Grebenshikov continued his meditation on the meaning of the Fab Four. "The Beatles came, and you couldn't copy them. And so the whole country listened to the original—and that started changing the way people think, the way people feel. And now people are feeling they can't live any more according to the old laws."

It was the kind of mystical musing that usually made me run for the door, but Grebenshikov talked with the quiet authority and hint of a smile that made me want to keep listening. I asked him how he had started his own band. "I began listening to the Beatles in sixty-four, I found my first instrument on a garbage heap, and my father made it into a sort of guitar. I figured out how to play the guitar around sixty-eight, I formed the band in seventy-two. We were so underground we never really had time to learn how to play."

The rest of the band were beginning to drift away for a long-delayed sound check, but Grebenshikov was in no hurry. "I started learning English, really learning English when I realized that the language they taught me at school and the language the Beatles were singing were the same"—he laughed—"like Tarzan books." He picked up his guitar and played a fragment of "Strawberry Fields." "You know," he said, "for us America and England were 'the West'— sort of a mythical country, like Shangri-la, the place where they make Coca-Cola, rock 'n' roll, and chewing gum."

He stood up, and his charisma filled the room. Grebenshikov was a star in any country. He turned and said, "You know, the kids who heard the Beatles back in the sixties, they grew up. And so hanging on to the Soviet regime has become rather difficult. Because we have millions of people who are actually on the other side."

Twelve thousand kids mobbed the sports center the following night. I stood in the midst of an ecstatic crowd, surging around the stage. Alongside me a boy flaunted a yellow satin jacket with the slogan GLASNOST 88 like the logo of a rock tour. A young girl held up a picture of Saint Boris, an icon in a plastic sleeve. Thousands wept and waved sparklers, moving their hands in a collective euphoria, dancing, punching the air. Looking out over the kids from the best seats set above the crowd, officials and party bosses sat stiff and uneasy, spectators at a revolution they could no longer control.

I was in the midst of a crowd lit up by Grebenshikov's belief that change was inevitable. But there was trouble at the heart of Aquarium. Troitsky told me it had been a terrible night. "There are rumors that Boris is having an affair with his bass player's wife. Boris's wife, Lyuda, tried to throw herself out of a window. Now he's arrived with his wrists cut by broken glass."

But Grebenshikov was a star, and his audience was at his feet. He roared into a thrilling set, singing in Russian. He played his new song "Radio Silence," the title track of his first American album.

"I feel like I belong here," he sang, "I feel like I've been waiting a long time, and now I can tell you some stories."

He radiated a magnetism I hadn't felt since filming a Rolling Stones concert almost twenty years earlier. Dressed all in black, commanding the stage, smiling his famous smile, he was the real thing—a very Russian rock star.

Grebenshikov introduced Dave Stewart, and they ripped through some songs together, singing in English. In love with Boris, the crowd were happy to forgive the English for now. Stewart told the crowd, "I'm from Sunderland, Boris is from Leningrad. We meet. It's

Boris Grebenshikov sings during his momentous 1988 Leningrad performance with Dave Stewart of the Eurythmics.

just a tiny thing. But it's better than killing each other." The crowd cheered. Surrounded by the children of the Cold War enemy that had once threatened to nuke me, it was a moment to savor.

And then, inevitably, the band struck up with "All You Need Is Love." I looked across the swaying crowd and saw a young Russian soldier hauling himself onto his girlfriend's shoulders. He spotted me taking his picture and waved a V sign in my direction. Then another soldier heaved himself over the crowd and joined in the celebration. Even the pale young policemen looked happy. Soon, though, as the vast Soviet empire began to unravel, that Beatles love-in with Boris and Dave would feel like an ironic soundtrack for the final act of the Soviet Union.

11

Alexander Dubček looked tired as he heaved himself out of a car. He offered his sad clown's smile and raised his hat. The leader of Czechoslovakia when the Soviet tanks rolled into Prague in August 1968 to crush his "Socialism with a human face" was back after twenty years in exile. Now it was January 1990, the Berlin Wall had fallen, and revolutions across Eastern Europe were sweeping away the fraying Soviet empire. Following the Velvet Revolution in Czechoslovakia, I was in Prague to interview Dubček, at his invitation. During his exile he had seen a film I had made, a dramatized documentary about the Soviet invasion of his country, and he wanted to meet the filmmakers, and particularly the actor who had impersonated him, Julian Glover. It was a memorable moment for me, coming face to face with the man who made the first dent in the Iron Curtain and showed the way for Gorbachev's perestroika.

We watched my invasion film with Dubček, and he relived the terrible days when he was hauled off to Moscow to be bullied by Brezhnev and forced to abandon his liberal reforms. As our actors marched into the Kremlin confrontation—reconstructed in Liverpool Town Hall, only yards from the Cavern Club—Dubček glared at our Brezhnev lookalike and murmured, "Demagogue."

When the screening was over, he dipped his head. Then he looked up and smiled his sad smile. "The only thing that really matters," he said, "is that people live happy and contented lives." It was, I thought, an unlikely, hippie-ish thought to have come from an old Communist leader, but then Dubček was never a regulation apparatchik. I remembered how he had joined the audience when the Beach Boys came to Prague in 1969, just as he was about to be sent into exile. They played "Breaking Away" for him, and it enraged the authorities.

After meeting with Dubček, I set out to find more about the rock revolution across the Soviet satellite countries of Eastern Europe in the 1970s that took its inspiration from his resistance—and from the Beatles. Czechoslovakia's rock opposition after the Soviet invasion was led by a band called the Plastic People of the Universe. The Plastics admired the political edge of John Lennon, and refashioned Lennon's radical notions to confront the Soviet-backed government in Prague. Their assault was uncompromising.

> *Throw off the horrible dictatorship!*
> *Quick! Live! Drink! Puke! The bottle, the Beat!*

The Plastic People were the vanguard for an army of rock groups across the Soviet empire in the 1970s who saw their music as a weapon to challenge the state. Many of them claimed their frustrations and their music were fueled by the Beatles, but their challenge to authority was all their own.

In East Germany, the band Renft sang about compulsory military service and the Berlin Wall. They were crushed by the state. A standoff between rock fans and police erupted on the twenty-eighth anniversary of East Germany's foundation. Four policemen were killed and sixty-eight wounded, while unknown numbers of kids were killed, injured, and arrested. The anger of a generation raised under Communism collided with the bewildered repressions of the state—and rock music had become the battleground.

In Czechoslovakia, Dubček's hard-line replacement, Gustáv Husák, mounted a fierce campaign against rock in the early seventies. Dozens of clubs were closed down, Western-style lyrics were banned, long hair and unconventional clothes were proscribed, decibel levels were regulated. Rock retreated to secret concerts in provincial towns and villages, but the police tracked them down. Violent battles between police and fans left dozens injured. Increasingly, the focus of official rage was the Plastic People of the Universe.

By the mid-seventies, the Plastics had turned their backs on official culture. They found a role as underground heroes, making their own sound equipment and sponsoring Festivals of the Second Culture in rural villages away from the authorities in the capital. But in March 1976, the Czech regime had had enough. The government declared that the Plastics would be put on trial. The indictment fulminated against lyrics that contained "extreme vulgarity with an anti-Socialist impact, extolling nihilism, decadence, and clericalism." The Plastics readily accepted the charge of vulgarity, and in their defense provocatively claimed the authority of Lenin himself—who, they pointed out, had used vulgarisms in his writings.

The result was hardly in doubt. On September 24, 1976, four of the musicians received sentences from eight to eighteen months. The judge called their lyrics "filthy, obscene." There was a torrent of protest from the West. Czech television responded by calling the Plastics "drug addicts, perverts, and devil worshippers."

The harassment of the band members who had avoided prison, and of their fans, intensified. A concert venue was confiscated and used for target practice by the military. Another venue was boarded up and declared an epidemic site. By 1980, the assault on rock music by the Czech state had been as deadening as any of Stalin's purges.

*   *   *

The rock 'n' roll carnage of the 1970s in the Soviet satellites of Eastern Europe reached the U.S.S.R. only as the sound of distant battle somewhere over the horizon. For the masses in the Soviet heartlands, the cultural commissars delivered the safe sounds of the "vocal-instrumental" ensembles. The VIA (Vocalno-Instrumentalny Ansambl) groups with their carefully sanitized rock appeared on television and were recorded on the state record label Melodiya, their lyrics and decibel levels as meticulously regulated as the length of hair. Their song lists had to conform to quotas that dictated percentages of Soviet, East European, and Western material. The VIA songbook featured songs about grain harvests and steel output, but some of the groups became genuinely popular.

The Happy Guys were a textbook VIA group, impeccably groomed, safely rock-lite. They were allowed to tour, given a TV show, and even released robotic versions of the Beatles' "Drive My Car" and "Ob-La-Di, Ob-La-Da." From the mid-sixties, another VIA group, the Singing Guitars, won fans across the country, featuring the safer hits of the Beatles and Cliff Richard. Their 1975 rock opera *Orpheus and Eurydice* gained lavish official approval. The story, of a rock star "crucified on the cross of mass culture," was very much in line with Soviet rejection of Capitalist rock. The inevitable echo of the Who's rock opera with its "deaf, dumb, and blind" antihero Tommy underlined the careful limits of official Soviet rock in the 1970s.

The VIAs drained much of the energy from underground Soviet rock, as exhausted musicians defected to the safety, security, and generous fees of state-approved pop. Pesniary, a VIA group from Minsk, began as another Beatles tribute band, but in the mid-seventies, they formally rejected the influence of the Beatles and soon prospered with official tours of Eastern Europe. In 1976, they were permitted to tour the United States, playing their polite and professional mix of Jethro Tull–style stadium rock and Russian folk music to polite and puzzled audiences from Virginia to Louisiana. Their manager told

American reporters that "the group wholeheartedly supports the program of the Soviet Communist Party."

One of the weirdest and most revealing episodes of this time was the story of "Mr. Tra-la-la." Eduard Khil was a popular singer with impeccable credentials, officially named a Distinguished Artist. His style seemed guaranteed to satisfy the most suspicious censor—clean cut, smiling, a neat little triangle of perfectly folded handkerchief peeping from the pocket of his impeccable brown suit. In the early 1970s, Khil planned to record a sentimental song called "I'm Very Happy to Be Coming Home at Last" with lyrics about a lonely cowboy galloping across the prairie to his girlfriend, who is knitting socks as she waits for him. But the hints of an American setting were enough to ensure that the song was judged unacceptable by the music censors. After several revised lyrics were also banned, Khil came up with an ingenious solution. He abandoned lyrics and tra-la-la-la'ed his way wordlessly through the song in a cheerful burble. It became a huge hit and he went on performing it for twenty years, becoming famous across the Soviet Union as Mr. Tra-la-la.

Art Troitsky told me about another curious mutation of Soviet pop in the 1970s. "Most interesting and daring pop songs grew out of movies in those days," he said. "And the biggest hit of all was a film called *Diamond Hand*. It was a crazy fantasy action movie, parodying the idiocies of Soviet life with several great songs."

The seditious messages were smuggled in songs delivered by unthreatening losers, including a spiv and a drunk. "The Island of Bad Luck," a song about a paradise where nothing works, was understood by everyone in the audience to be a wicked commentary on daily life in the Soviet Union.

"Only the censor didn't get it," Troitsky said. "Even better was a song about idle rabbits who didn't care about anything. It was sung by a hopeless drunk in the film, so again the censors failed to spot the allusions to the cynical existence of millions in nineteen seventies Russia."

The watchful pop commissars managed to domesticate some of Soviet youth's hunger for rock during the 1970s. But on the sidewalks outside the state record stores in Moscow and Leningrad a black market in cassettes of Western albums continued to flourish. On Saturday mornings, scores of fans gathered to swap tapes and buy bootleg Beatles or Deep Purple albums. The rarest items could command a couple of weeks' wages. In a spasm of repression reminiscent of the 1960s, vigilantes from the Komsomol youth organization mounted regular raids on the black-market gatherings, levying fines and handing out prison sentences to speculators and buyers. But the Soviet Union's increasing openness to foreign visitors and students ensured a continuing supply of those seditious albums from the other side of the Iron Curtain.

Meanwhile a multitude of amateur bands, as many as one hundred thousand by the mid-seventies according to an official estimate, entertained crowds at state institutions playing cover versions of Western hits. Many of them delivered efficient copies of Beatles songs, but the jazz-rock group Arsenal had a huge success with a stage performance of *Jesus Christ, Superstar.* The state's Melodiya label was now cashing in on the market for acceptable rock, registering nationwide hits with David Tukhmanov's "How Beautiful Is This World" and "In the Waves of My Memory," concept albums that blended poetry, Pink Floyd, jazz, and classical music. Melodiya also made a star of a dramatic young singer, Alla Pugacheva, who belted out her hits in a style that echoed Janis Joplin and Bette Midler. Over the next decade, the flame-haired diva would sell one hundred fifty million tapes and records, establishing a fan base on the scale of Bing Crosby or Elvis Presley.

One Western import did find favor with the nervous guardians of Soviet popular culture. Following the global success of *Saturday Night Fever*, disco was deemed acceptable. With its disciplined rhythms and anodyne lyrics, the dance floor was embraced as a safe place to corral youthful energies. In the mid-seventies, at a time when Melodiya had not released any Beatles album, the state label began distributing disco hits by ABBA and Soviet-bloc disco groups. Sound systems imported from the West were licensed for four hundred discos across the Soviet Union.

A visit from the German disco group Boney M in 1978 marked the climax of Soviet disco fever. The host bureaucrats of Gosconcert, the state agency arranging international cultural exchanges, had one major concern. Boney M's biggest hit, "Rasputin," with its refrain celebrating the czar's evil mystic as "Russia's greatest love machine," was deemed unacceptable, even sixty-two years after his death. Boney M accepted the official ban on the song, but "Rasputin" continued to roar through discos across the country.

But the ultimate popular musician for Soviet-bloc audiences for twenty years from the mid-sixties was Comrade Rockstar Dean Reed. I became obsessed with Reed, and his bizarre story wove through my life as I began making documentaries in the Soviet Union in the late 1980s and into the 1990s.

Trying to set up a documentary about Dean Reed became a long-running project for me. On a series of visits, I followed the story of the handsome all-American true believer from Colorado, who was recruited by bewildered Soviet culture bosses to come to Moscow as an official answer to the Beatles. Reed became a huge star across the Soviet bloc in the 1970s as the Kremlin's official answer to the hunger for rock 'n' roll. He looked like the answer to their dilemmas, a rocker from the West who mixed performances of "Blue Suede Shoes" and "Heartbreak Hotel" with songs about peace and solidarity. Reed saw his life as a Soviet epic, singing his song "We Are Revolutionaries" and starring in pop videos where he performed on the roof of a train blazing a new route into Siberia. He fed off the adulation of rock-starved kids, who loved him because he seemed to be the embodiment of every teenage fantasy about America. Fans mobbed him from East Berlin and Prague to Moscow and Leningrad, throwing carnations as he swiveled his hips and preached peace and love, wrapped up in sex, politics, and rock. With thick hair and a promiscuous smile, Reed was their American. I talked to a man who had been to one of Reed's Moscow concerts in the seventies and still remembered the excitement. "He was moving, always moving, nothing like our singers. This was rock 'n' roll. The girls were crying 'Dean Reed, Dean Reed.'" A Soviet official told me, "With Dean, for us it was like the Beatles in England."

Art Troitsky hated Dean Reed. "Anyone who would deep kiss with Brezhnev"—Art mimed a sloppy kiss—"was betraying everything about rock 'n' roll." He was plainly enraged by the memory. "Dean Reed became a huge star here. His mug was everywhere. It was even on plastic bags. He came from the land of the free and the home of the brave. And Chuck Berry," Troitsky added. "But it was only in a place as isolated and provincial as the Soviet Union that he could have become a star."

I had seen a preposterous video of Dean Reed, riding a unicycle as he sang "Can't Buy Me Love." It perfectly summed up everything Art hated, but it also radiated the charm that had made Reed a household name across the Soviet empire. It helped me to understand how this naïve and unremarkable pop hustler had managed to become a Socialist poster boy, crooning "Ghost Riders in the Sky" for Yasser Arafat, serenading the Marxist Chilean leader Salvador Allende, and delivering his starry smile for crowds of autograph hunters in Red Square. He was showered with baubles from admirers across the Eastern Bloc: the Communist Youth Gold Medal in East Germany; medallions in Czechoslovakia and Bulgaria; the Komsomol Lenin Prize in the Soviet Union. He adored the celebrity and the stardom he would never have known in the West. In the mid-seventies, he was for the Soviet masses the most famous American apart from Henry Kissinger. I could feel the overwhelming hunger among the children of Socialism for Western popular music during the cultural blockades of the 1960s and '70s. Even the pallid version offered by Dean Reed was irresistible.

Dean Reed, all-American Comrade Rockstar.

I knew that Reed had died in mysterious circumstances in 1986, drowned in a lake behind his house in East Berlin. It made him more interesting for me, but Troitsky was unforgiving. "He was finished here anyway. We had our own rock stars by then and we didn't need outsiders—not even Bruce Springsteen, still less Dean Reed."

After more than twenty years of circling the Soviet Union, Dean Reed's magic faded. The more I looked into Reed's story, the more I understood the hopeless failure of cultural bureaucrats to provide any Soviet alternative to Western-style popular culture. Trapped inside an inflexible ideology, officials never caught up with shifting public taste. When they attempted to claim a diluted version of Western culture—as they did with Dean Reed—it was soon out of touch. I watched a grisly video of Reed trying to teach *Ghostbusters* dance moves to an uncomfortable group of Soviet teenagers in the final year of his life, and it stood as a monument to the bafflements of official culture. Soviet officials were always much slower than their comrades in other Eastern Bloc countries to recognize shifts in what people wanted. Long after jazz had been overtaken by rock 'n' roll, campaigns were still being mounted against saxophones.

From the mid-seventies, there was a cautious twitching of the Iron Curtain. The Helsinki Accords of 1975 signaled improved relations between East and West. The Apollo-Soyuz joint space mission that summer provided a public relations spectacle of the new togetherness. In 1993 I met the Soviet commander of the joint mission, Alexei Leonov, who became something of a symbol for détente when he shook hands with an American astronaut in orbit. I thought Leonov, who was the first man to walk in space, was a perfect ambassador, jolly as Santa Claus. He showed me a painting he was working on to celebrate the spirit of superpower friendship. It showed Christopher Columbus's ship on its pioneering voyage to America, and Leonov pointed to where he had inserted a badge of the Soviet space program onto the sail of the Santa Maria. Art Troitsky recalled that Apollo-Soyuz cigarettes were everywhere at the time. "It was quite a pleasant thing," Art said, "because it seemed to be about a part-time ending of the Cold War." Cultural exchanges were also back on the agenda for the first time in twenty years, and rock 'n' roll was recruited to serve on the front line of détente.

Melodiya quickly made an agreement with the Beatles label in the U.K., and in 1977, *Band on the Run* by Paul McCartney and his group Wings arrived in state record stores. The release of a complete Beatles album was still years away, but a seven-inch disk with a few songs was permitted to trickle without publicity into stores inside a plain white cover. After the years of bootlegged X-rays and audio tapes, Beatles fans could at last buy a few real Paul McCartney tracks.

In the new spirit of careful musical diplomacy, Cliff Richard was invited to perform his safe and cheerful hits on a tour of twenty Soviet cities. A few other Western bands followed in Richard's wake. But Elton John's arrival in the spring of 1979 was a sensation. The culture commissars were largely untroubled by Elton's songbook. Just one item was ruled out.

The Beatles' "Back in the U.S.S.R." was judged too sensitive, and for nine concerts, the hand-picked audience of Communist Party faithful applauded politely Elton John's greatest hits—minus the forbidden song. At the very end of the final gig in Moscow, Elton exploded into the Beatles anthem. The kids stuck at the back of the hall poured past the uneasy officials to the front of the stage, cheering and screaming. Elton said it was one of the most unforgettable performances of his life—exactly the uncontrolled display of youthful enthusiasm the authorities had feared.

In fact, yet another conservative backlash against the unpredictable excesses of rock 'n' roll was already gathering. Rumors of a Beatles reunion in Moscow had released unwelcome indications of youthful hysteria; and when a planned concert in Leningrad by Santana, the Beach Boys, and Joan Baez was canceled by authorities, the police were called in to disperse thousands of angry fans massing in front of the Winter Palace. The ensuing confrontation, including water canons and smoke grenades, became known as the Leningrad Rock Riot, and it seriously rattled the authorities. It was becoming clear that the instinctive unease inside the Kremlin about the challenge of the Beatles and rock music, which had been fermenting for more than a decade, was reaching the boiling point.

Another clash between rock fans and police in August 1979, when Aquarium played an unauthorized concert in Leningrad, resulted in police dogs, truncheons, and 150 arrests. The police accused fans of committing acts of vandalism. For authorities alarmed by the mounting disorder, it was the end of the road.

At a congress of the Soviet Composers' Union in November 1979, in a tirade that recalled the fury of the Stalinist era, the head of the union, Tikhon Khrennikov, fulminated against rock musicians and their music. He denounced the "all-embracing permissiveness" and "vulgarity" of rock 'n' roll. As Soviet tanks rolled into Afghanistan, a tide of repression swamped the rock scene across the Soviet Union, snuffing out the temporary truce of détente. Art Troitsky had been right about that "part-time ending of the Cold War."

12

On the morning of December 9, 1980, I turned on the television in my New York hotel. For a moment, I thought I must be still asleep, lost in a dream. On the screen was a black-and-white film my film—of the Beatles in the Liverpool Cavern Club, playing "Some Other Guy." Then the announcer was saying that John Lennon had been shot dead, just up the street from my hotel. "This is the first film of the Beatles back in 1962," the announcer said, "and we're showing it now to remember John." Fumbling to grasp the news, I headed off to the Dakota apartment building where Lennon lived with Yoko Ono, just across from Central Park.

It was still dark, but crowds of fans stood in silence on the sidewalk next to the entrance, hemmed in by police barriers. An impromptu shrine was already piled with flowers and messages:

> *John was a flower, plucked in his prime,*
> *No one will replace you, all throughout time.*

A youth held up the cover of Lennon's latest album with a photo of John and Yoko kissing. A tearful girl was telling her friend, "He made his home in New York, and now we've killed him."

The shock waves were rippling out around the world. At his John Lennon Temple in Leningrad, Kolya Vasin sank to his knees in prayer. Across the U.S.S.R., there was disbelief and dismay. Almost immediately, Soviet propaganda began to refashion Lennon—for decades derided as a corrupter of youth—as a martyr for peace. Now the focus was on his heroic opposition to the war in Vietnam.

I joined the thousands in Central Park, gathering for a wake. Kids climbed into the bare trees with peace placards, and a guy displayed a hand-lettered banner saying WE LET YOU DOWN. "Imagine" echoed through the park, and there were tears. Soon, crowds were also coming together near Moscow University, playing Lennon's music. Police arrived to disperse the mourners; but grieving fans continued to gather in Moscow and across the Soviet bloc on every anniversary of Lennon's death, and the police were usually careful to avoid confrontations. Silver birches were sent from Russia to be planted at the Lennon memorial in Central Park.

Across the Soviet Union, Lennon's death provided an opportunity for propaganda highlighting the murder rates in America and the decadence of Western societies. And in the early eighties, it seemed that the Soviet Union and the West were entering a new ice age. The litany of bad news was endless: the Soviet invasion of Afghanistan, martial law in Poland, the shooting down of an airliner over the Soviet Far East, American missiles in Europe—and to confirm the standoff, Ronald Reagan denounced the Soviet Union as "an evil empire." For the first time in twenty years, there was serious talk of nuclear war.

With the death of Leonid Brezhnev, the Soviet Union had a new hard-line leader. Yuri Andropov was a former boss of the KGB, and he quickly ordered a crackdown on Western influences. Rock music was a particular target, and following their notorious performance in Tbilisi, where Boris Grebenshikov had scandalized officials by mimicking sex with his guitar, both Boris and Aquarium were banned from playing in Leningrad. They retreated to improvised recording studios, making the unofficial cassettes that transformed them into underground superstars across the Soviet Union.

The new head of Soviet ideology was Konstantin Chernenko, a long-standing scourge of all things Western, and of rock music in particular. Now he attacked the West for trying "to poison the minds of the Soviet people." Chernenko feared that Western ideological attacks were "threatening to undermine the commitment of Soviet youth to the Soviet system." Even disco music, recently acceptable, was now under suspicion. *Saturday Night Fever* was criticized for promoting negative attitudes, and a film about ABBA was withdrawn from theaters. In this climate of paranoia, Time Machine were denounced in the newspaper *Komsomolskaya Pravda* as "un-Russian."

Fearing a return to Stalinist repressions, Soviet cultural leaders scrambled to implement the new hard line. Overseas tours were canceled by Gosconcert, clubs and discos shut down. Youthful attachment to Western fashions and styles was savaged in Party newspapers.

In February 1984, Andropov died. He was succeeded by yet another geriatric leader with repressive instincts, the ideologue Konstantin Chernenko. The new leader immediately launched a fierce attack on the Komsomol youth organization, accusing its leaders of "blind imitation of Western fashions." The Komsomol chief called for a renewed cycle of vigilante attacks on music clubs and the censoring of repertoires. The Ministry of Culture decreed that more than three quarters of a band's music must be written by members of the Composers' Union, and established commissions to review all professional groups. Many failed the new tests and were forced to disband.

Musicians like Stas Namin gave up completely on trying to play their music. In this toxic atmosphere Order 361 was issued, an edict directed at popular music. The title of the order—"For Organizing the Activities of Vocal Instrumental Ensembles, and Improving the

Ideological Level of Their Repertoires"—catches the dismal mood of that era. It seemed Stalin's DNA had been preserved like some nightmare from Jurassic Park, and was stalking the Soviet Union yet again.

The attack on rock music reached beyond the musicians and club owners to track down recording engineers, who were accused of profiteering. A list of more than a hundred acceptable groups was issued, itemizing both Western and Soviet bands. The Who and Pink Floyd were not approved; the Beatles were not even mentioned. In provincial cities, the cull of unacceptable albums revealed the scale of the Western contagion. Of seven hundred records seized in two raids, only twenty-six had been produced in the Soviet Union. A studio owner in Volgograd was sent to jail for two years.

Discos did not escape the purge. Many were closed down, others were fined, and all Western records were banned. The Ministry of Culture raged across the rock landscape, savaging every aspect of the music and the musicians. The forming of the commission to re-view professional groups felt like the final blow for many bands. The venerable Time Machine feared extinction. Art Troitsky reported how they were stranded, unable to tour and "awaiting their fate." They survived their official review; and like many other groups, they kept their heads down, waiting for the storm to pass.

On March 10, 1985, Chernenko died. The new man in the Kremlin, Mikhail Gorbachev, was to change the Soviet Union, and the world. In the process, he gained the improbable label "Russia's first rock 'n' roll president."

Rock music became the soundtrack for Gorbachev's perestroika reforms, and Soviet rock blossomed from the mid-eighties. The spec-tacular curtain raiser was a performance in 1985 by the Moscow band Avtograf ("Autograph") during the global Live Aid concert, beamed around the world to one and a half billion viewers. Due to a technical hitch, the opening of Avtograf"s performance was scrambled with shots of peasants picking cherries, and Soviet viewers were only able to see fragments of their act. But soon the world heard Soviet rock loud and clear. State television remained cautious, and selections from Live Aid were not broadcast until a month later— when a Moscow paper claimed the event had been organized in part by Soviet television. A concert dedicated to raising money for starving millions in Africa was described as "a global event in defense of peace and against nuclear war."

In August 1985, in an echo of the World Youth Festival of 1957, which had first breached the dike holding back Western rock music, the Gorbachev regime sponsored the twelfth World Youth Festival. It was intended as a sop to domestic audiences wearied by years of stagnation, and the festival was presented as a "showcase of anti-imperialist solidarity." But as in 1957, rock 'n' roll flooded through the door opened by the festival. A hundred rock bands arrived in Moscow in an uproarious cacophony of heavy metal, reggae, folk, and punk. Bob Dylan came from America; Soviet performers included Stas Namin and Andrei Makarevich's recently rehabilitated Time Machine. But many more edgy local groups, beloved of Art Troitsky, were banished from the festival. For the cultural authorities, rock 'n' roll was still an unpredictable animal that needed careful supervision. Only safe, established bands were acceptable, and more challenging, political, and experimental groups were kept out of the mainstream.

"Changes," a song by charismatic underground star Viktor Tsoy and his band Kino, became an anthem that caught the mood of the time.

> *Time for Change, our hearts demand*
> *Time for change, we are waiting for change.*

I saw a video of Tsoy performing the song to thousands of ecstatic fans, and it seemed to express the frustrations of an entire generation.

In those early Gorbachev months, there were cautious signs of change. Soon after the Youth Festival, in the fall of 1985, an official "Rock Laboratory" was launched in Moscow. It offered recording equipment and rehearsal space to new bands. Then in March 1986, the state label Melodiya released the first ever complete Beatles album. Fans queued in disbelief to buy *A Hard Day's Night*. But only a limited number of copies of the twenty-year-old album were made available, and Moscow's rock community suspected that the official Rock Laboratory would suck the life out of the local scene. Art Troitsky was not welcomed at the Rock Lab.

Troitsky's benefit concert in May 1986 for families suffering after the Chernobyl nuclear catastrophe challenged the still-uneasy Kremlin monolith toward making real change. The British band UB40 pushed the limits still farther on their tour in the fall of 1986. Soviet minders tried to control the heady mix of rock and politics, mistranslating the band's outspoken remarks about censorship and police brutality and damping down invitations to their audiences to dance. The band found themselves bogged down before every concert in hours of negotiations with security officials, but to the distress of their minders they continued to speak out whenever possible.

The most striking evidence of a new climate for rock 'n' roll in Gorbachev's Soviet Union was the revival of the once-unacceptable Boris Grebenshikov. He was allowed to play sold-out concerts in Leningrad and he was soon established on the trajectory that would take him to the international concert with Dave Stewart I witnessed, and on to stardom in a Hollywood documentary.

By 1987 the trickle of change in Soviet rock was becoming a tidal wave. Michael Jackson, once reviled as decadent, moonwalked on state TV. Melodiya released an album by Aquarium. The underground hero Boris Grebenshikov was now the darling of glasnost. Driven by Gorbachev's new and dynamic minister of culture, Vasily Zakharov, the state tapped into the energy and the networks the underground bands had been creating for years. Albums of Soviet rock with titles like *Red Wave* were distributed in America and Europe.

The rock détente was confirmed in 1987 when Art Troitsky persuaded his new friend Paul McCartney to record an album of classic R & B hits—including "Kansas City," a song I had filmed the Beatles playing in the Cavern twenty-five years earlier. Recorded in just two days, specifically for release in the Soviet Union, the album was decorated with a huge red star and entitled *Snovo v CCCP—Back in the U.S.S.R.* McCartney joined in the euphoria of those heady days. "The new spirit of friendship opening up in Russia," he wrote, "has enabled me to make this gesture to my Russian fans, and let them hear one of my records first for a change." Years later I would discover how valuable that gesture would be for some of Paul's fans.

By now, playing the U.S.S.R. was an irresistible gig for Western rock stars. James Taylor, Carlos Santana, and Bonnie Raitt all made the trip. Billy Joel sang "The Times They are a-Changin" in Moscow's Olympic Sports Complex. But not everyone was happy about the explosion of rock glasnost. Battles on Moscow's streets between punks, hippies, heavy-metal addicts, and working-class toughs alarmed conservatives in the Kremlin. Sergei Mikhalkov, who wrote the Soviet national anthem in 1944, denounced rock music as "the moral equivalent of AIDS," leading the chorus of anti-rock statements from senior figures. Some of Gorbachev's conservative comrades were becoming uneasy with the relaxations of central control. The Kremlin's leading ideologue Yegor Ligachev, gathered support for a crackdown on rock music.

The concerns of the conservatives were not hard to understand. In the late eighties, there was, as they alleged, growing evidence of civil unrest and violent protest, sometimes spilling out of rock concerts. But by now the revolution of the Beatles generation seemed unstoppable. There were those who thought otherwise.

13

Returning from his morning run, my Soviet journalist friend Vladimir Pozner switched on the television. Instead of the news, he found an old recording of *Swan Lake*. "I realized that was the end," he recalled. "Whenever anything major happened in the Soviet Union, we were treated to *Swan Lake*. You weren't told what was going on." It was August 19, 1991, and what was going on was a power grab by Kremlin hard-liners, determined to abandon Gorbachev's reforms and turn back the clock. "So you had this terrible military takeover, tanks on the streets of Moscow," Pozner recalled, "and *Swan Lake*."

Suddenly, it seemed the rock 'n' roll years of perestroika and glasnost might be snuffed out. The dour gray men who had always hated rock music—the men who Pozner had told me couldn't handle being laughed at—were back in control. "I thought immediately I'd be in jail and the experiment was all over," Pozner said. "I was afraid. That terrible feeling of nausea came back and I realized the fear was still sitting there."

The attempt to seize power was mounted by a few Kremlin hard-line conspirators while Gorbachev was on vacation in the Crimea. For two desperate days, the people of the Soviet Union held their breath. Pozner got calls from all over the world asking for his reaction to the coup. Speaking out would be dangerous—and he had a visa to escape to New York. He decided he must speak. Via satellite, he appeared on American television and said, "The fate of democracy in this country is being decided." Then he joined the democratic forces who were massed outside the Russian White House. In scenes like the final act of a heroic opera, Boris Yeltsin climbed on a tank outside the White House and defied the hard-line plotters. Fearing they were losing control, the desperate coup conspirators went to seek the support of Gorbachev at his vacation villa. He refused to meet them, and on the night of August 21, the tanks began to leave Moscow. The coup was over.

Many in the huge crowds defending the White House building were rock musicians. During the massive concert that followed the collapse of the coup, a telegram was read out from George Harrison. Pozner recalled, "Nobody wanted to leave. This had been what they call in Russian their 'starry moment.'" And it was in many ways the defining moment for the Beatles generation.

After the final collapse of Communism in 1991, I worked on several projects that led me through the chaos of the new Russia. The streets of Moscow were a dismaying spectacle in those days, lined with desperate people trying to sell an empty Coke bottle or a single shoe to supplement their ruined currency. As gangster "biznissmen" looted state assets, everything was for sale—including information from state archives. For reporters and filmmakers, it was a bonanza. I researched a film about the abortive coup that had tried to overthrow Gorbachev, meeting up with disgraced politicians and shady generals in the backs of cars. I also spent time inside the fearsome KGB building, which was suddenly open for business. I heard that the KGB's swing band was available for hire to play Glenn Miller arrangements at weddings.

I pursued a film about the theft and smuggling of Russia's chaotic nuclear stockpile, but the trail was impossible to follow through the

dangerous criminal underworld. Paranoia, rumor, and macho pos-
turing blurred the borders between reality and fantasy.

Amid the wild freedoms unleashed during Boris Yeltsin's volatile
presidency, I was able to get inside two of Russia's most secret military outposts. In the chaos that had invaded every corner of the
country since the dismantling of the U.S.S.R. it was reassuring to
find that *Sgt. Pepper* and *Abbey Road* had penetrated some of scariest
places in the formerly Evil Empire.

I managed to film inside a top-secret nuclear missile base a thousand miles south of Moscow near the Volga River. I spent some time
with Russia's "roketchiki" as they stood ready to launch their giant
Topol missiles around the world. The affable colonel in charge of a
missile battalion told me he had never met a foreigner before; but I
discovered the Beatles had invaded the secret base. Colonel Petrovsky
invited me to a family party in the countryside alongside a lake
where his wife cooked lamb over a fire, while he fished with a fellow
officer. It was a scene from Chekhov, languorous but full of unreadable undercurrents. While the delicious smoke drifted over us and
we traded fraternal vodka toasts, a young roketchik lieutenant,
Yevgeny Pavlov, picked up a guitar and played "Yesterday." McCartney's melancholy ballad was a long way from home, but it felt haunt-
ingly Russian on that winter afternoon on the Volga. Back on the
base, I was treated to more from the Beatles songbook. A raucous rock
band of junior missileers thrashed out "Back in the U.S.S.R.," and I
wondered how the cultural dictators who had fought for years to exile
the Fab Four would feel about finding their anthem had breached a
nuclear citadel of Mother Russia. Art Troitsky's bold declaration about
how the Beatles had been more effective than nuclear missiles was being played out for real.

Star City, Russia's cosmonaut training center just outside Moscow,
was a shock when I filmed there. The cluster of high-tech facilities
that had been a showcase of Socialist achievement since Yuri Gaga-

rin led the world into space had become a dispiriting collection of grubby buildings where broken tiles littered the weed-infested campus. Only Gagarin's office remained as he had left it, Spartan and ready for action. The clock over the door was stopped at the moment of his death.

The Russian space program was broke, reduced to selling theme park visits to rich Americans who could pay five thousand dollars for a few days at Star City, where they were crammed into space suits and whirled around in the centrifuge until they were sick. I met up with Sergei Krikalev, a cosmonaut who had been stranded in the Russian space station for a year when Communism collapsed and the state ran out of money to bring him back to Earth. I also talked to veteran Russian cosmonaut Georgy Grechko. With a frizz of hair that shot up from his head as though it had got stuck in zero gravity, Grechko was unfailingly jolly despite the dismal state of the Russian space program. He told me he had taken Graham Greene's *Our Man in Havana* into space to help him cope in adversity. He also talked about the music he took into orbit. "Some of the younger cosmonauts had Beatles cassettes," he said, "but I had big bands, especially Glenn Miller." "Moonlight Serenade" was his soundtrack as he circled the Earth in the 1980s when there was still a U.S.S.R. to call home.

Art Troitsky provided an unlikely musical coda for the era of Soviet space heroics. In 1992, he helped to organize a "Gagarin party" at the Museum of Space Achievements in Moscow. With pensioned-off spacecraft hanging over them and strobe lights firing off like shooting stars, hundreds of kids gyrated in a thunderous techno-rave. After the collapse of the Soviet Union, Troitsky was becoming a little sentimental for the old days when it had been cool to be a Communist. "It was pleasant," Art recalled, "to be able to say 'here's Yuri Alekseyevich Gagarin, the man who managed in 1961 to destroy the whole American Dream overnight.'" By the time I got to the space museum a few months after the Gagarin party, it had become a used-car lot for imported Western castoffs. In the echoing hall where the retired spaceships had made their final landings, a gigantic portrait of Gagarin smiled down on a jumble of dusty Cadillacs and Chevys. As Art said, "In this new Russian reality, there is no space for space."

I checked in with Troitsky whenever I was in Moscow. His responses to the huge changes in his country were predictably unpredictable. He relished the messy liberations after the fall of Communism, becoming the first editor of Russian *Playboy* magazine while discovering a new taste for heroic Stalinist anthems. And of course we talked about the Beatles, and about their role in helping to wash away at the foundations of Soviet totalitarianism.

In the early nineties, I found Art fighting a heavy cold, shut away in his apartment with his vast collection of arcane CDs. I had made a bet with myself that the ultimate test of his hip awareness would be whether he had anything by the surreal Merseyside band Half Man Half Biscuit. Sure enough, as we talked, I spotted the Biscuit's 1985 debut *Back in the D.H.S.S.* on the shelf behind him. With its sideways allusion to the Beatles song, mixed up with the acronym of the U.K.'s unemployment agency, it seemed the ideal background to our talk about the continuing impact of the Fab Four in bankrupt post-Communist Russia.

"The fact is they alienated a whole generation of young well-educated Soviet kids from their Communist motherland," Troitsky said. "They wanted to live in an alternative world, consuming alternative culture, pursuing an alternative lifestyle." He was stopped by a sneeze. "Life in the Soviet Union as we saw it was like a boring, pale version of real life. And real life was elsewhere—it was in Britain, it was in America."

"OK, so now that it's all over and there's no more Soviet Union," I asked, "how significant do you reckon the Beatles really were in making it all fold up?"

Troitsky pondered for a moment and poured a scotch from the bottle I'd brought. "It's interesting," he said. "In the big bad West they've had whole huge institutions that spent tens of millions of dollars trying to undermine the Soviet system—you know, the C.I.A. and the F.B.I. and Radio Liberty and all that stuff." He took a swig of the scotch. "And I'm sure the impact of all those stupid Cold War institutions has been much, much smaller than the impact of the Beatles."

It was the most resounding statement I'd heard of how the Beatles changed the Soviet Union. And Troitsky had more to say. "The Beatles turned tens of millions of young people to another religion. And by the end of the eighties, the whole of Soviet ideology and Soviet power disappeared like fog in the morning." He looked saddened for a moment, and I felt how dismaying it must be, even for a man like Troitsky, who had spent his life opposing the Soviet system and had felt its unwavering hostility to the things he cared about, to find that it was gone and the decades of repression had been about nothing but the preserving of power. I recalled that the book Vladimir Pozner had written as he came to understand the betrayals of his Socialist convictions was called *Parting with Illusions*. Troitsky hadn't even had the illusions.

"It all vanished so quickly," he said, "because by then two or three generations of Soviet people, I mean anyone under forty, they were ready for a different life." I wondered how the Beatles fit into that hunger for change. It was a question Art had clearly thought about a good deal. "They prepared Soviet kids for a different lifestyle, different ideologies, different human values. They never articulated any of this, of course, but the music itself was very important. The message we took was that we're free, even though we live behind the Iron Curtain. You can pretend to be a young Communist, but at the same time you are someone totally different. You're a stranger in your own country."

14

In the vast space where the furious masses had gathered to storm the czar's Winter Palace and ignite the Russian Revolution in 1917, a clumsy boy in a baseball cap was fumbling with a skateboard. He fell off several times, tumbling onto the cobbles, and then gave up.

Leningrad had been rebranded under its prerevolutionary name as Saint Petersburg, but I thought it was looking decidedly down at heel. Bored girls with plastic shopping bags smoked in an antique coach, a prop for a street photographer. A pink stretch Hummer cruised by, shaking the Coca-Cola umbrellas outside a bar. Chunks of gilding had fallen from palaces, paintwork was flaking. A saxophonist was warbling a pretty version of Paul McCartney's "Here, There and Everywhere" in the bar of the Hotel Astoria—where legend held that Rasputin checked out without paying.

I walked through the exquisite arcades along Nevsky Prospekt on my way to see Kolya Vasin again. In chilly sunshine, the street looked perfectly operatic. I called in at a gallery where Art Troitsky was having an exhibition of his collection of paintings. They were entirely Art, I thought—quirky, sexy, indulgent, like the woman who owned the gallery.

I hunted through the labyrinth of passageways leading to Vasin's temple, getting lost in a blind alley. A woman with a broom made of twigs was sweeping a corridor. "Kolya?" I asked. She pointed with the broom and then led me to the familiar door with the plaque announcing the John Lennon Temple. "He's out!" she said, but banged on the door anyway with her broom. There was a scuffling, and Kolya threw open the door. "Beatles forever!" he yelled. Then he said, "I'm hungry!"

We headed out for something to eat. Kolya found the Patrick Pub, where the TV was raving away with a program called *The Comedy Club*. In a garish set, a screaming audience drove frenzied contestants to ever-greater idiocies. The Soviet Union of Vasin's youth had been a bad dream, but now Russia had different nightmares.

He was still bound up in his stories of survival long ago. "I used to take one of the Soviet badges with a picture of Lenin and stick a picture of the Beatles on it. I was walking down the street wearing my badge, and suddenly an old guy came up to me and started shouting about how I was a bad man with bad hair and a bad life. He ripped off my badge and threw it on the ground." Afterward, Kolya's friends told him to be careful because the man was a famous sculptor who had made a statue of Stalin in the middle of Leningrad. "A statue of that cockroach with the moustache!" Kolya spluttered. "He'd hardly be a Beatles fan."

He munched a leathery-looking steak and remembered another story. "I went to the Finland Station to get my train to work, and a policeman spotted my long hair." Vasin's face registered the incident as though it had happened the previous day. "The policeman said, 'You are not a Soviet man! You are living like a Western man.' And he grabbed my hair." The memory of how the cop dragged him along the platform by his hair while dozens of people stared and laughed was branded into him. "I was almost crying from the pain, but I had to keep silent. I was afraid the man would drag me off to prison."

Kolya devoured more steak. "All my life I've been hurt, insulted, kicked, and pushed around. I was taught all sorts of rubbish I never needed." He paused and looked at me. "That's why I'm not a complete human being—I'm crooked and scared." I was coming to understand that this sense of martyrdom, of suffering for his faith in the Beatles, was an essential part of his devotion. Coming from soggy old Britain, where the rain so often rubbed away the edges of our passions, I was finding the intensity of Vasin's Beatlemania strange and unsettling.

He finished his steak. The TV had moved on to some reality show populated by girls with startling legs and micro skirts. "Let's go," he said. "I want you to see something."

Back at the temple, Kolya found the video he had been looking for. As he slammed it into his antiquated player, he said, "I think they were just afraid of the Beatles' popularity. So they decided to deal with them straight away. You have to understand this was a spiritual struggle." An old black-and-white news item flickered on to the screen. "This was what state TV showed us in 1966."

It was a bulletin from the front lines of that "spiritual struggle," a piece of propaganda Stalin might have admired. Over a series of still photos of the Fab Four, carefully selected to be as unflattering as possible, a sneering voice delivered its message:

"Pop quartet the Beatles. Look how elegant they are! But when they started their career they were performing on stage just wearing swimming trunks with toilet seats on their necks. Then they met a kind fairy—London dealer Brian Epstein. This London fairy understood that these gifted guys could be real cash earners. Struck down with psychosis, the fans don't hear anything anymore. Hysterics, screams, people fainting! Demolished concert halls and fights are the usual finale of a concert. It's a world consisting of four walls covered with the photos of four singers with long hair."

Then there were pictures of kids dancing wildly, intercut with hooded Ku Klux Klansmen and blazing crosses, together with im-

took these pictures in October 1964, when the Beatles came into the Manchester studios of Granada Television to perform their new record, "I Should Have Known Better." I had come to know the Beatles a couple of years earlier in August 1962, when, as a very raw young TV director, I made the first-ever film of the Fab Four at the Cavern Club in Liverpool—shortly before they made their first record. By the time they came to our studios for "I Should Have Known Better"— and I took these pictures—there were ten thousand kids outside trying to break down the doors.

lost the negatives of these pictures for almost fifty years and only rediscovered them recently, so the photos have never been seen before.

ages of poverty in the Deep South. This was closer to Goebbels than Stalin. The narrator switched from sneering to snarling.

"Keep on dancing lads, don't look around. You don't really want to know what's happening. Keep on going, louder and faster! You don't care about anyone else!"

When it was over, Vasin looked drained. "This went on too long," he said, "much too long. For us it was the dark side of our lives." He shook his head and spat.

There was a bang on the door. Kolya greeted a tall shaven-headed guy, enveloping him in a hug. "Nick Brabanov," the man announced, "from Vladivostok." I thought Brabanov had something of the monk about him. He said he had a band called Good Night and they always played at Vasin's birthday celebrations for the four Beatles. Inevitably, Brabanov was another Beatles devotee. "It was my father's fault," he said. "He wanted me to learn English so he brought me some seven-inch Beatles disks from Moscow. I fell in love when I was a little boy." Like Kolya, he had a mystical take on the Beatles. "Their music inspired us because it was a great source of freedom—a piece of God's soul come to earth." He stroked Kolya's cat and sang a few bars of "Hey Jude." The cat purred. "Russian people were overwhelmed by the Beatles," he said looking up to the ceiling where a yellow submarine floated. "Nobody was neutral here—people loved or hated them for destroying some Communist fantasy they believed in. And of course the Beatles really did destroy those stupid things."

"But we survived," Vasin called out from across the room. "Our generation survived. We have lived through it all—Stalin and Brezhnev and all the other crazy old guys who warped our lives. Now we can celebrate our freedom on the bones of dead Russians and dead Russia." He was close to tears, but he gathered himself for a final flourish. "We want to water the soil they're in, to revive the free spirits who died, so that Russia can be a great country again." The outburst reminded me of why Solzhenitsyn was such a hero for Vasin, and why the great writer became such a troubling figure when he came to live in America. His messianic cadences and ultra-nationalist declarations had been hard to reconcile with the genius who had suffered in the gulags and had given the world a new understanding of that terrible time. It made me wonder again about the overlap between the devotion of a superfan like Kolya Vasin and the religious intensity of a fundamentalist believer.

Kolya was pouring tea for us from a Beatles teapot he had made. He pointed out the beetle on the lid as he filled our heart-shaped mugs, and then stirred our tea with spoons decorated with heads of the Fab Four. I was glutted with Beatles stuff; but Kolya had more.

"You must come to my John Lennon birthday party in October," he said, his eyes shining with anticipation. "I wouldn't miss it," I said.

15

I found Andrei Tropillo hunched over a mixing desk like something from the Starship *Enterprise*, nodding his head while a thunderous heavy-metal track bounced off the walls of his studio. Art Troitsky had told me that though Tropillo "suffered from mild delusions of grandeur," there was some truth in his declaration that he had "changed the course of Soviet rock."

Troitsky said that Tropillo had distributed millions of Beatles albums to the Soviet masses. Of course, I was keen to hear more about that.

Tropillo was a man of volcanic energies. A barely restrained pigtail streamed behind him like a vapor trail as he raced around his empire, an old factory in the muddy outskirts of Saint Petersburg, spilling out his wildly improvised version of English. An inventive sound engineer, he had dodged the Soviet system to set up recording studios and became a pioneering producer of bands like Aquarium and Time Machine. "He was a true believer in Soviet rock," Troitsky said, "never accepting money from musicians, while he endured all the hassles. Without Tropillo, we'd still be listening to the patriotic anthems sung by geriatrics with bad wigs."

Tropillo took a break from mixing his latest discovery, and in the lull after the heavy-metal attack, I asked how he had found his way through the stifling web of state controls to set up a recording studio. "I suppose it all goes back to my father," Tropillo said. "He was in jail for four years for insulting Stalin, but he invented a form of radar, which helped us to win World War Two. So my childhood was littered with galvanic cells and electronic marvels. I made my first radio receiver when I was a kid at school." In the late sixties as the Beatles generation began to make their own music, like countless other young Russians, Tropillo learned to play guitar. "But my dream was to build my own recording studio." He organized underground concerts for unofficial new groups, supporting musicians such as Andrei Makarevich and Boris Grebenshikov. "I was lucky," he said. "For some reason I never got caught by the militia." Tropillo remembered that his father, after spending those years in prison, was always fearful that Andrei would be arrested for organizing illegal concerts. "I took my father to a Time Machine concert, and he was sure that as soon as it ended the doors would open and there would be a line of black police cars ready to take everyone to prison. But it didn't happen, and I made enough money to buy some recording equipment. At that time in the early nineteen seventies a lot of Jewish musicians were leaving Russia and they wanted to sell the stuff they had used for jazz recordings, so I bought enough to start my first studio."

Tropillo hunted around for a place where he could set up his studio without being arrested. He tried a series of spaces in official buildings that might give him protection, such as the House of Pioneers and the Institute of Psychology. It was a constant battle to find a way through the crazed labyrinth of regulations, but he discovered a loophole. While you were not allowed to make more than six typewritten copies of a document, there was no limit on copying recorded tapes. "So I began to record Soviet rock bands and I never asked them for money"; that avoided the risk of being arrested for profiteering. "Instead I just took some rights in their recordings to make my disks."

Tropillo also funded his commitment to Soviet rock through the national obsession with the Beatles. "At that time, the state record company Melodiya released a special record a couple of times a year called 'Musical Kaleidoscope.' It was a collection of various songs. In 1967 they quietly included a Beatles track 'Girl.'" He sang a snatch of the song: "Is there anybody going to listen to my story all about the girl who came to stay . . ." "It was the key that opened the door for rock 'n' roll in Russia." The track was listed on the sleeve as "an English folk song"—with no mention of the Beatles. I guessed the state had released the Beatles' sweet, sad little item because they thought it was safe. But for Tropillo the release had an unintended meaning. It also signaled that a Beatles song could be official, no longer prohibited. "That meant that millions of copies of 'Musical Kaleidoscope' were distributed, which introduced 'Girl' and the Beatles to the masses."

Inevitably, the Melodiya record reached far beyond the privileged kids of Moscow and Leningrad to Art Troitsky's "rednecks and peasant villagers." It was a crucial moment in spreading the Beatles and their music across the Soviet Union. "People listened to the records, and it changed their minds," Tropillo said. "This wasn't the evil music the state had warned them about. This was beautiful." Other people had told me how actually hearing the Beatles after being bombarded by hostile state propaganda had made them begin to doubt the previously infallible state.

Andrei Tropillo became a fearless bootlegger, pumping out countless copies of Beatles records in the years before the Soviet Union finally signed up to international copyright agreements in 1995. "I believe in 'copyleft,' not copyright." His shoulders shook as he relished his joke. "I was sure that in Russia we should support musical piracy." His breezy declaration of rock banditry was, I suggested, an early version of the downloading revolution. Tropillo insisted it was

a weapon in the battle with Soviet cultural repression. "Musical piracy was a guarantee of freedom, an absolutely legal way to have free
information in Russia." I suggested that I wasn't sure how happy
Paul McCartney would be with Tropillo's Robin Hood campaign.
"Paul McCartney didn't live in Russia," he said with a smile.

In 1990, the pirate went legitimate. Tropillo became a director of
the State's Melodiya label. He had one crucial ambition: to use the
vast resources of the U.S.S.R. and the lack of international regulation to copy and distribute millions of Beatles records. "I knew how
Soviet people felt about the Beatles," he said. He had a wonderful
simile to describe the Soviet addiction. "It's like dogs and cats: they
don't understand what you say, but they feel your feeling. Russians
were the same with John Lennon and Paul McCartney."

So at last in 1990, twenty-five years after the Beatles had reached
the Soviet Union via crackling radios, bootleg X-ray films, and reel-
to-reel tapes, people could buy their albums in state stores. "The
government got the money of course, not me," Tropillo said. "But I
gave these records to people who had the right to hear them."

Tropillo said he wanted to show me something. I followed him,
trying to keep up as he scuttled down flights of stairs, chattering
nonstop. He opened a door into a high-tech factory where robot
machines were churning out endless shoals of silver CDs and DVDs.
"This is very clever," he repeated, skipping between the humming
machines and cascades of disks. He had, I thought, the gleeful and
faintly sinister assurance of Charlie lording it over his chocolate factory. Then he was already away and heading for another door.

It was quiet away from the machinery. We were in an office lined
with CDs, many of them by familiar Western bands. Tropillo led me
to the iconic Beatles' *Sgt. Pepper*. At first sight it looked just like the
album in a million homes, with a gallery of eighty-eight celebrated
faces—Einstein, Brando, Sonny Liston, Karl Marx, Mae West, and
all the rest. Then I spotted that an interloper had sneaked into the

back row. Peering out between Edgar Allan Poe and Fred Astaire was the face of Andrei Tropillo. But he wasn't the only gate-crasher. Between Laurel and Hardy wasn't that Kolya Vasin?

Tropillo had a couple of final surprises. He scampered ahead of me and stopped at a strange oil painting. It seemed to be a portrait of him in eighteenth-century costume, holding some kind of furry demon with staring eyes. "This is me as 'the Navigator,'" he said, "wearing the costume of the explorer Captain James Cook. I'm holding a creature that represents my work." Then I noticed a Masonic symbol. "Yes, I'm a very high Mason," he said, looking almost shy. "My role is to join God with people." Then he told me his ancestors were founders of the Knights Templar. Feeling faintly dizzy I asked, "You mean like the folks in *The Da Vinci Code*?" "Yes," Tropillo answered. "I have a drop of Jesus's blood in me."

I was relieved to get back to the Beatles. Tropillo found a little gray disk and handed it to me. "This is an X-ray flexi from the sixties with 'Can't Buy Me Love.' Please have it." It felt a bit like being given a handful of moondust, and I was touched. "This is what the Beatles did," Tropillo said. "They were the key that opened the door to Western culture. Western culture produced a cultural revolution here—and that cultural revolution destroyed the Soviet Union." Then his mood changed. "We destroyed the system, but other people have used the results—bullshit business people, and the old KGB creeps."

As I was heading away down the stairs, Tropillo had a final message. "Don't forget to come tonight and hear the new punk band I'm managing, the Oz. They'll be doing their punk opera, 'Che Lennon.'" I said I'd be there.

Down a backstreet near the main railway station, I found a small crowd, huddling against the rain. This was where Tropillo had said I'd find his new band, and its leader Igor Salnikov. It wasn't hard to spot Salnikov. Tall, skinny, dragging on a damp cigarette, he exuded the easy confidence of a would-be rockstar. He was also displaying a bright red T-shirt decorated with an image of John Lennon in a Guevara beret and the words CHE LENNON.

I introduced myself, and he offered me a starry smile. "I think I got almost everything from Lennon," he said. "There was a Beatles album a long time ago, and I really loved it." He spoke almost perfect English with a slight American accent, and he was cute. "Later I got some of John Lennon's albums, and I started to read a lot about him and his thoughts—and it changed my life."

So here was this kid, probably twenty-five years younger than Boris Grebenshikov, and the Beatles were still working their magic for him. "All John's songs are so simple," he said, "but they're so true. And I suddenly realized I can do the same thing, I can feel what he's saying. This thing is so huge for me." It was pouring rain now, and we took cover under an old archway. "It's my plan to change my name officially to John Lennon," Igor said. He made the declaration with a shy giggle, but he was plainly serious. "I have my second Russian name from my father, so it's gonna be John Vladimirovich Lennon. They say it can be done."

The doors of the club were open at last, and we went inside. A handful of youngsters stood around, dragging on cigarettes, skewered by a lurid green laser. Three nearly naked men began to thrash out angry punk. An elderly punkster sidled up to tell me all his friends hated John Lennon. "We liked George Harrison." I couldn't imagine what gentle old George would have felt about being the darling of the Saint Petersburg punks. Things didn't sound promising for the Oz band and their Che Lennon opera.

Looking as though he'd had a long day at the mixing panel, Andrei Tropillo introduced his new band to the sullen crowd. The Oz drifted onto the little stage, a teenage rhythm guitarist with the Che Lennon T-shirt, a wizened lead guitarist who looked like a truck driver, a lean drummer—and a boy wielding a trombone! You had to give the boys points for originality. Igor/John looked nervous,

The Oz belt out their punk versions of Lennon with their leader,
"John Vladimirovich Lennon."

fussing endlessly with a mike. And then, suddenly, they exploded into noise.

Igor screamed, the trombonist made elephant bellows, the others thrashed away. Somewhere in the midst of the din was Lennon's "Power to the People." The crowd looked as though they were elsewhere. As abruptly as it began, the song stopped. There was no reaction at all from the audience. And so it went on, Igor's cacophonous reworkings of "Working Class Hero," "Crippled Inside," "Jealous Guy" all received in glum silence by the crowd. Tropillo looked desperate. "Wait till you hear 'God,'" he said. "That's the show stopper." Igor/John gave it his all, kneeling on the floor, pouring out his anguish. "God" ended. Silence again.

The old punk slunk up to me again. "They're shit," he said.

16

I didn't make it to Paul McCartney's historic 2003 concert in Red Square. I was in Berlin, revisiting the source of my Russian obsession for a film about my time as a junior spy. Listening in on those Soviet pilots at the height of the Cold War before the Berlin Wall was built had sparked a fascination with their lives. How was it for them, peering back at us through the Iron Curtain? Was it really as grim in the Soviet Union as we had been told? In those days before television could take us to Moscow or Vladivostok in an instant, the lives of people in Russia were almost as mysterious as the dark side of the moon. But in Berlin almost fifty years ago, I sometimes felt I could reach out and touch those other lives.

It was haunting now to wander around the old Gatow air base, on the outskirts of the city, where I had been stationed. This place, deserted now except for a hare bouncing ahead of me across the airfield, had played a vital part in the story of those fearful years after the Second World War. The Cold War threatened to boil over into World War Three, and Berlin was always in the front line. Still devastated after the war, the city stood on the fault line between the superpowers. The partition of Germany after the war had left Berlin an island, stranded in the middle of Communist East Germany. The city was split into nervous zones controlled by America, Britain, France, and the Soviet Union. In 1948 Stalin resolved to tidy up his map and seize complete control of Berlin. He closed down all rail and road routes into the city in an attempt to starve the population into surrender. The Western allies began a huge operation to break Stalin's blockade of Berlin. More than two hundred thousand planes flew into the city bringing food and supplies. Many of those flights had landed here at Gatow.

The peaceful airstrip I was revisiting had handled hundreds of aircraft every day in a ceaseless thunder of landing and departing planes. American airmen, who became known as "candy bombers," dropped twenty-three tons of chocolate and chewing gum for the hard-pressed children of the city. Defying Moscow, the relief flights saved the city and its people. After a year of the Berlin Airlift, Stalin conceded and was forced to end his blockade in 1949.

The airlift was a memory by the time I arrived in 1957. Coming back now, I found other memories. A collection of ancient jet fighters from the U.S.S.R. had made a final landing in an air museum here at Gatow to recall the time when this place was a flashpoint of the standoff between East and West. I walked along the lines of decaying aircraft arranged on the airstrip and wondered if any of these fighter planes, pensioned off MiGs and Sukhois, had been flown by the people I listened to day after day. Might this battered hulk have been the owner of that call sign I scribbled down in my listening post? Could this have been Rain Two Six or Birch One Eight?

Did the pilot survive to become part of the Beatles generation? Or did he go down with his plane, like the man I monitored as he yelled that he was on fire? "Good-bye, comrades!"

I looked across the airfield at the fence that had formed the border with the Soviet Union—the fence through which those bedraggled

Russian soldiers had escaped in search of Elvis. And wasn't that the watchtower over there where I used to defect from my espionage duties to listen in to American Forces radio and the *Jazz Hour*?

While I was trawling my Cold War memories, a Beatle was in Moscow, wowing the Beatles generation with "Back in the U.S.S.R." It was their moment anyway, not mine. I recalled how Kolya Vasin had told me that he and his friends "breathed" through the holes in the Iron Curtain punched by the music. And now Kolya was in Red Square hearing Paul McCartney, along with a hundred thousand weeping fans who had been waiting for the Beatles for forty years.

When I did catch up with some of the people who were there on that unforgettable evening, they all remembered it as a key moment in their lives. "It was a beautiful event," Art Troitsky told me. "There was a spectacular sunset over Red Square, and the whole thing was like a huge religious ceremony." Inevitably, Troitsky had been involved in organizing the concert. I was accustomed to hearing his skeptical take on most things, but the Red Square concert seemed to have genuinely touched him. "A lot of people my age were standing there, silently crying. It was like one of those huge gatherings on the banks of the Ganges River, a mass baptism."

Troitsky's friend Sasha Lipnitsky, the bass guitarist with the band Zvuki Mu and a casualty of the Kremlin's hatred of the Beatles, was in Red Square. He turned down a chance to meet McCartney. "I just wanted to see the concert," he said. "I understood that it was something special, even for Paul McCartney. The result of this long love affair of Russians for the Beatles was the extraordinary feeling at that concert. It was the last nail in the coffin of Communist power." Seva Gakkel, the cellist with Aquarium, traveled from Saint Petersburg to be at the concert. "I felt, like thousands of other people, that it was a very important moment in our lives. It was like a beautiful idea that happens, and then it's gone. I felt sad that it didn't happen twenty years ago."

Andrei Makarevich, who dreamed of the Beatles when he was a schoolboy and was inspired to form the Soviet Union's most iconic rock band, Time Machine, was in Red Square to see Paul McCartney. "I felt I had to make a present for him," Andrei said, "because he did so much for me, and he changed my life in such a magical way." As a rock star himself, Andrei was only too aware that he could look like an idiot giving a picture he had made to a Beatle. "I went backstage, and it was funny because senior government ministers were standing in line like schoolboys to say hello to Paul. Then a bodyguard came to say he wouldn't have time, but somebody told Paul I was a musician, and he came to have a chat." At this magic moment, Makarevich found himself riveted by McCartney's small hands, as flustered as a starstruck child, "I stumbled out something like 'thank you very much for coming, we've been waiting for half our lives.' I managed to hand over the picture, and he said 'Really, for me—that's great' and the picture was taken away somewhere."

Andrei's story of Red Square had a conclusion that suggested that for the Kremlin the concert was more than a Beatles love-in. "I was in my seat when two guys in black suits came up and asked me very politely to move closer to the stage." He found himself placed next to an empty chair as McCartney ripped into "Can't Buy Me Love." "Then I saw a little group of officials striding toward me, and suddenly President Putin sat down in the empty chair. He said 'don't look at me, look at the stage.' Then a pile of photographers crowded around us." So while the Kremlin got its pictures of the youth-friendly president chatting to a rock star, Putin told Makarevich how McCartney had performed "Let It Be" for him when they met before the concert. Everybody won.

Sasha Lipnitsky also saw something of the concert's subplots. "The organizers and sponsors of the event were people from Alfa-Bank, and they were waiting for Putin during Paul's first few songs. They were looking at the Kremlin, desperate to see Putin, and I could see how thrilled and relieved they were when the president came and sat next to Makarevich."

Andrei summed up the ambiguities of the day: "Red Square is a strange place. Lots of people have been killed there over the years. But Paul's concert was like a real holy day." There were of course other ironies. The music that had been banned and derided by the Kremlin for decades was now being embraced and exploited to win hearts and minds. And it was Paul McCartney who was here, not Dean Reed. But I wondered about those anxious people from Alfa-Bank. If they were pulling the strings now, sponsoring a Beatle to sing in Red Square, wasn't that a perfect twenty-first-century deal between rock, money, and politics?

I wanted to meet one particular fan who had been at the concert. Sergei Ivanov was Russia's defense minister, and I'd heard that he liked to relax after another hard day overseeing the brutal Chechen War by listening to his favorite Beatles tracks. By the time I got to him, he had become Putin's first deputy prime minister, and I imagined he might be too busy to chat about the Fab Four. I was wrong. "Anything for the Beatles," he said.

I went to the Russian White House, where the government is based, to meet Ivanov. It's a grandiose building overlooking the Moscow River, and I'd spent some time there ten years earlier, exploring the endless carpeted corridors in pursuit of a film about the coup that had tried to overthrow Gorbachev in 1991. As I tramped the corridors again behind a wordless official in a black shirt and white tie, the place was so quiet it felt abandoned. I was shown into a reception room filled by a vast oval table. The flower bowl contained a microphone. A grandfather clocked ticked away the minutes, and as a couple of murmuring assistants checked me out, I took in the room. It was an immaculate post-Soviet nowhere: gold velvet curtains, glass candelabra, nondescript landscape paintings. The clock ticked and I studied the floor: inlaid stars and squares, the only bit of the room that didn't look like a reproduction. Then I heard hurrying footsteps, and the assistants came to attention.

Sergei Ivanov breezed into the room. "So sorry to be delayed," he said in perfect English, "I was with the president." How on earth did he make his excuses to Putin? "I'm sorry Vladimir Vladimirovich, I have to go and talk to Leslie about the Beatles." He sat down, and I had a moment to take in this cheerful-seeming man, with a politician's charm and car salesman's smile. I made myself remember that he was also a colonel general in the FSB, the latest version of the KGB. But he was already gushing on about McCartney's Red Square concert.

"That was great," he said. "I was sitting next to my wife, who was also a Beatles fan of course. We understood that Paul McCartney was playing in Red Square, but we asked each other 'can this be real?' We were happy that we lived in a time when it became possible." He giggled like a child on Christmas morning. I had heard that Ivanov was one of the officials who waited in line to meet McCartney before the concert, and it was apparent that even now the memory of that day was lighting him up.

We talked about how the boy who would become Russia's defense minister and potential president first found the Beatles. "I remember it well," he said. "It was 1963, and I was ten. I turned on the radio, and I heard 'Love Me Do.' Radio Luxembourg played it ten times in a row." So the young Sergei was already flirting with a foreign radio station. "I got interested, and I asked my mum about them. Surprisingly, she knew and she told me they were the Beatles." Soon all his friends were talking about the new group. "I remember that time in Leningrad when we had Beatlemania. If you walked down the street, you could hear Beatles music through the windows of every house you passed." This was at a time when the Kremlin's cultural commissars were working to stamp out the decadent English group. Ivanov's memories suggested how hopeless the campaigns had

Russian defense minister and Beatles fan Sergei Ivanov.

been from the beginning. "Of course," he went on, "there was Communist Party ideology, and there was real life. The Party said the Beatles were a negative influence. But propaganda was one thing. Real life was totally different."

I was intrigued to hear from an insider how Kremlin control was already beginning to fray in the sixties, and how Ivanov felt the Beatles were a part of the process. That separation of "real life" from the tightly controlled version of reality dictated by the state would open up an unbridgeable gap between the rulers and the ruled over the next twenty years. And in time, a government minister from the Beatles generation would be in the Kremlin, and a Beatle would sing to the president in Red Square.

I began to swap favorite Beatles songs with Ivanov. I imagined Putin waiting fretfully for his deputy while we traded titles like two old Fabfans in a bar. Ivanov offered "Love Me Do" and I gave him "Penny Lane." He suggested "Hey Jude," and I responded with "Lady Madonna." "You know," he reminisced, "I really began to learn English through Beatles lyrics. I remember "A Day in the Life" from the *Sgt. Pepper* album: 'Woke up, made my bed, dragged a comb across my head.'" He mimed the combing as he quoted the song. "That was the first time I learned what the word *comb* means." He beamed. "There's no end of this," he said.

The minders were looking restless, glancing at their watches. Ivanov got up and shook my hand. "I did this out of love," he said.

17

Moscow bound one more time, in 2008 I slumped in the departure lounge at Heathrow Airport, surveying the Glorious Britain Shop. Apart from Teddy bears with Union Jack waistcoats squatting on the bonnets of Mini Cooper toys, and plaques illuminated with quotations from Shakespeare, every other aspect of glorious Britain seemed to be wrapped up with the Beatles. There was a Beatles magnet set, a wash bag with Fab Four signatures, an alarm clock with Beatles faces, and a John Lennon stamp from Tajikistan framed with an old British shilling coin. So it appeared John was big in Tajikistan. At last my flight was being called.

On the plane, three excited Americans stood in the aisle chattering about financial armageddon. I heard "billions" and "Goldman Sachs." A burly black man in horn-rimmed glasses said "Lehman Brothers gone, Morgan Stanley gone!" He seemed thrilled by the disaster movie of Global Financial Meltdown. "You watch oil!" Another man, handsome as the Pixar prince in *Shrek*, flaunting a gold watch the size of a fist, offered "They asked Jesse James why he robbed banks. He said 'Cos that's where the money is.'"

I remembered something Lennon had said as the Beatles imploded along with the hippie dream of "money can't buy me love": "Nothing happened, except we all grew our hair, and the Beatles made seventeen million pounds." But even in this cold new world of grotesque money where Russian oligarchs competed to claim the biggest luxury yacht with the biggest helicopter pad, there was no getting away from the Fab Four. Channel 17 on the in-flight radio was entirely given over to Beatles songs, and the morning paper had a couple of stories about the Beatles and money. Someone was selling the drum skin from the *Sgt. Pepper* album cover for a hundred and fifty thousand pounds. Another woman was selling the hand-written lyrics for "Give Peace a Chance," which had been given to her by John when she sneaked into his bed-in with Yoko. The sales room thought they should make three hundred thousand pounds. It seemed that every Beatles castoff had become a commodity, on sale in the global market place.

Art Troitsky had said I would find him at a Moscow club called Ikra, where he would be singing with Zvuki Mu. It was after midnight when I arrived, and the girl on the door was hostile. She seemed to have studied hospitality under the harridans who had chased me out of restaurants in the eighties, furious that I was interrupting their lunch break. After a while, the door girl grudgingly slouched off to check if I really was a friend of the famous Art. While I was stranded at the door I studied the unusual fish tank in the lobby. No fish, just a pink Kalashnikov nestling amid seaweed. It was, I thought, a perfect image of Moscow in the twenty-first century: Damien Hirst meets gangster chic.

The sullen girl returned and wordlessly pointed into the gloom. I fumbled my way through blacked-out rooms, occasionally glimpsing Troitsky on TV screens, mouthing silently. At last, the thumping din of Zvuki Mu guided me to another stygian room where Art was twitching on the stage, without detectable singing. A pack of women stood around on precarious heels, smoking furiously, displaying their handbags, and staring at their cell phones. They looked to be less than half the age of the guys in the band. Troitsky took time out from twitching on stage to tell me he had just been playing a corrupt plastic surgeon in a movie. "I had a red Ferrari," he said happily. He told me I should go and meet a man called Maxim Kapitanovsky who had been making films about the Beatles in Russia. I escaped past the pink Kalashnikov, spotting a poster on the way out for a Sean Lennon gig.

It was snowing next morning, big soft flakes like artificial snow in the movie *Doctor Zhivago*. Instead of sleigh riding with Omar Sharif and Julie Christie, I was trudging through the streets with thousands of Moscow commuters, muffled up in identical anoraks. A torrent of cars swished through the dirty slush, and the only dash of color was an illuminated sign outside a music shop, a shining Gibson guitar. I thought of all the years when that would have been a mirage.

I waited for Maxim Kapitanovsky under the statue of a worker with a clenched fist. A plaque said this was Ernst Thälmann, a hero of East German labor. Now Ernst was guarding the door to a gigantic mall, a palace of consumerism. A stocky man in a leather jacket and a leather cap spotted me and I imagined he could be an East German Stasi cop watching over his hero's statue. He made his way through the stream of shoppers, smiling. "Maxim," he said. We went into the mall, past the array of cell phones and iPods, and found a coffee bar. Maxim laid a couple of DVDs on the table. I was longing to see his Beatles films, and they glowed at my elbow like smuggled nuclear isotopes. First, he wanted to tell me his story.

"We had no religion in the Soviet Union," he began, "so we had a gap in our souls. The Beatles filled that gap." Why did so many of the people I met want to link the Beatles to religion? It was as though the two faiths suppressed by the state, rock and Christianity, had become intertwined in a generation's determination to free itself from the control of the state. Kapitanovsky was in a band in the seventies, playing Beatles songs and joining the rush of kids with homemade guitars. He had great stories about improvising guitar strings from the control cables for model aircraft.

Then he began to tell me about his films. "My dream was a cycle of five documentaries about the meaning of the Beatles for my generation and about rock 'n' roll in the Soviet era. I had it all mapped out." Five films? It sounded like a fantasy project, but Maxim said he had interested a Russian bank in backing the idea. That was of course the ultimate deal in the new Russia: Beatles, rock, and money. "Here's how I planned it," he went on. "Film one would be about Beatlemania in the U.S.S.R., film two—Paul McCartney's concerts in Russia. Film three—blue jeans, the supreme objects of desire for the Beatles generation; film four, Russian rock." He had rattled through the list with the unstoppable conviction of a producer pitching a project in Hollywood. His final episode would hardly have won over a money man doing breakfast in Beverly Hills. "My fifth film would be about restaurant musicians. All the best people played there, because they had some choice over the music." I recalled those Soviet jazzmen of the 1930s who had flourished briefly in stylish Moscow restaurants before Stalin packed them off to his gulags. Anyway, the bank had loved it all, and Kapitanovsky had made grand plans.

"I would arrange for the Russian ambassador in London to welcome look-alikes of Paul, Ringo, Yoko, and Olivia Harrison as an introduction to the film. Then I'd interview Paul to link the cycle of films." He said the bank adored the whole idea and wanted to take it to Putin for his support. "But then they got sidetracked in personal rivalries and the whole thing fell apart." From what I'd heard of the murderous vendettas among Russia's new movers and shakers, I reckoned he was probably lucky not to have finished up at the bottom of the Moscow River.

He got more coffees for us. "Anyway," he said, "I managed to make two of the films—Soviet Beatlemania and McCartney's visit.

The McCartney film 'Seventy-three Hours in Russia' was a night-mare." Maxim had my sympathy. The prospect of finding a way through the combined obstructions of Russian security goons and Paul's superstar minders would, I imagined, have taxed the ingenu-ity of a Mossad hit squad. Kapitanovsky's own ingenuity in pursuit of McCartney was impressive. "When Paul was in Saint Petersburg, it was almost impossible to get anywhere near him. Then I found some guys who were just dismantling a huge crane near his hotel, and I persuaded them to rebuild it so we could get high shots of Paul's comings and goings." In Moscow, Kapitanovsky snooped foot-age of rehearsals for the Red Square concert during guerrilla warfare with McCartney's seventy-strong security force. "One of his body-guards smashed our camera, but it made a good moment for our film." He said his Beatlemania film, titled *The Beatles Are to Blame*, got shown repeatedly on Russian television, but *73 Hours with Paul McCartney* "just won bits of paper at Russian documentary festivals."

Kapitanovsky walked me through a blizzard to the Metro station, and I trundled back to the city center. It was still snowing on Tver-skaya Street near the Kremlin, and the old beggar woman was still kneeling in the snow under posters for concerts by Boris Grebenshi-kov, the Animals, and Charles Aznavour. I gave her some rubles and plodded to my hotel. Up in my room, a maid vacuumed around me as I viewed Kapitanovsky's DVDs. The "Beatlemania" film was fun, stuffed with crazy archive footage of bald apparatchiks trying out Beatles wigs and rock fans being rounded up by vigilantes. *73 Hours with Paul McCartney* looked as grueling as Maxim had suggested. It seemed mainly to be made up of Paul and Heather—Mrs., soon to be ex, McCartney—getting in and out of stretch limousines sur-rounded by human shields of security. There was affecting footage of fans, including the inevitable Kolya Vasin—waiting for a Beatle. "It is real Beatle?" asked an ecstatic grandmother. A banner pro-claimed, ONE SWEET DREAM CAME TRUE TODAY. There was a memo-rable shot of McCartney's limo racing past, Paul sticking his ever-perky thumb out of a window to make a perfect snapshot of superstar detachment. There was lots of footage of people shining floors, arranging flowers, and painting drainpipes in preparation for the arrival of Sir Paul. They would have made less fuss, I reckon, for Queen Elizabeth. Kapitanovsky's high shots from the reconstructed crane looked nice, and I enjoyed the tussle with McCartney's security squad in Red Square. Best of all was a delicious fantasy filmed during the sound check: Lenin and Marx look-alikes bopping together.

The room maid completed her cleaning marathon and headed for the door. Before she left, she turned and said shyly, "I love Bitles."

It had stopped snowing at last, and I walked across to Red Square. On the way, I stopped at one of the stands where hustlers try to push Communist kitsch—KGB badges, Red Army hats, Stalin T-shirts. I surveyed the armies of *matrioshki*, the nests of dolls that have become favored weapons in the arsenal of junk aimed at tourists. The Great Dictators (Genghis Khan inside Hitler, inside Stalin, inside Mao, inside Saddam Hussein) were lined up next to Harry Potter (containing the usual suspects). Then I spotted a Beatles set. John—clutching a guitar, circa 1966—was the container for the rest of the Fab Four. It was not his best look, regrettable slug mustache, dreary gray jacket with velvet collar; inside him was Paul, same bad mustache, same gray jacket, not even provided with a guitar; inside Paul, George, ditto mustache and jacket; inside George, Ringo—unrecognizable; and inside Ringo, a tiny guitar—presumably misplaced by Paul or George. I bought the Beatles and walked into the square.

Near Lenin's tomb, an old woman was selling postcards. She crouched on a stool, while a familiar voice spilled out of her battered tape recorder. After a moment I recognized the singer; it had to be Joseph Kobzon. The inevitable Kobzon has followed me over the years, wherever I've gone in this part of the world. I always thought that if Brezhnev could sing, he'd sound like this. Kobzon the rousing tenor who became the most-awarded artist in Soviet history; Kobzon

Beatles matrioshki dolls, on sale near Red Square.

belting out patriotic ballads and heroic anthems, a favorite of the
Kremlin and the inescapable performer at every state occasion for
thirty years. I remembered Kobzon for a couple of reasons: first there
was his disastrous wig; more surprising, his story sometimes seemed
to parallel and mirror the Beatles.

Kobzon's first album was released in 1962, like his Liverpool dop-
pelgängers. His breakthrough came in 1964, as the Fab Four were
sweeping the Soviet Union. And although Kobzon was awarded
"People's Artist of the U.S.S.R.," he was something of a rebel. While
Lennon handed back his medal presented by the queen of England
to protest the Vietnam War, Kobzon—who is Jewish—had outraged the Kremlin by performing Jewish songs in support of Israel.
He had been expelled from the Communist Party for that gesture,
though he was later rehabilitated. Kobzon then became the first celebrity to perform in Chernobyl and risked his life as the key nego-
tiator in rescuing hostages during a terrorist siege. After the collapse
of Communism, Kobzon was sometimes called "Russia's Frank
Sinatra" because of his contacts with the Moscow mafia. He insisted

that as a popular entertainer, the contacts were unavoidable, but the allegations cost him an American visa. His concert tours of South America, Africa, and Europe continued, and he has become a deputy in the Russian parliament. Recently, I had heard that Kobzon and the Beatles had finally converged. The ultimate official singer had made a pilgrimage to Liverpool, and then starred in a Russian celebration of Beatles music that climaxed with Kobzon's rousing performance of "Hey Jude."

The old woman packed up her postcards and tape recorder, and I spotted a group of American tourists on their way to visit Lenin's tomb. Their guide, a sharp-featured little woman with the people skills of a gulag wardress, was clearly finding her flock unsatisfactory. "Please pay attention, dear visitors," she shrilled. She told the group she was the same height as Lenin, and they should know his hair and fingernails were still growing. Someone tried to ask her a question, but she brushed it aside. "At the appropriate point," she barked. She had important facts to deliver. "Lenin is not a wax figure, like Mao Tse Tung." The war of the embalmed leaders was not getting through to the tourists. They shivered, clearly looking forward to taking refuge for a while with Lenin and his fingernails in the tomb. Then the guide spotted me. "Go away! Do not listen! This is private party!"

I headed across the square to look for the restaurant where I was due to meet Art Troitsky. It was getting dark now, and the golden domes of the Kremlin were illuminated, magical in the dusk. The red star on the top of a Kremlin tower that had somehow been spared the mass execution of most statues and symbols of the Soviet era was glowing like a beacon. A black limo sped out of the Kremlin gate and headed for home. In the space in front of Saint Basil's cathedral where Paul McCartney had played "Back in the U.S.S.R." and thrilled thousands to tears, a handful of kids were laughing and circling around on their mountain bikes, crunching over the frozen snow. A boy in a bright yellow anorak came to a halt when he spotted the Beatles matrioshki I was carrying. "Beatles forever!" he shouted.

I found Troitsky in a restaurant called Chlam, a stylish construct of distressed brick with Chet Baker whispering from concealed speakers. I thought how these restaurants had become showcases of the new Russia, dizzyingly expensive, with the life expectancy of a journalist investigating a gangster businessman. "Chlam" meant "trash," and the place was virtually deserted. "I love Chet Baker," Art said, giving me a hug. He spotted my Beatles matrioshki, and we agreed that the doll-makers could have chosen to celebrate the lads at a time when they'd abandoned the slug mustaches. We munched steaks as costly as gold bars, and Chet drifted into another smoldering ballad. I asked Troitsky if the Beatles were effective as aids to seduction. "Oh, I think everyone of my age in the Soviet Union would agree their music had huge sentimental value. Every Russian teenager met his first date and had his first kisses to a Beatles soundtrack. And now when they hear 'Yesterday' I'm sure they have beautiful memories of things that will never happen again." The thought stirred some memories of his own. His marriage to Svetlana had ended years earlier, and I knew he had four children with four different women. "I'm a spoiled boy," he said cheerfully.

I told him I had watched Maxim Kapitanovsky's film about Beatlemania and had been struck by the old archive film of kids being rounded up by vigilantes for buying rock records. "As I told you once, we were living in a monster state. If you really want to get a glimpse of those crazy times, I hear the KGB has opened a museum. Everybody is a businessman these days." I said I'd check it out, and as Chet sang "Let's Get Lost," we toasted the KGB.

"I love the Beatles," said Vera, my tour guide as we walked past the old KGB headquarters, which had been the focus of nightmares for generations of Soviet citizens. "I still listen to 'Girl' and 'Yesterday' and all those pretty songs," she recalled, and she sang a snatch of her favorite: "I believe in yesterday . . ." The vast yellow KGB citadel, known as the Lubyanka, looked almost benign in morning sunshine, but for a woman of Vera's generation it was still a fearsome place. A statue of Feliks Dzerzhinsky, the murderous head of the Bolshevik secret police, used to stand in front of the building, but it had been hanged from a crane and hauled away by demonstrators in 1991. The plinth was still there, like a ghoulish warning that Stalin's "devout knight of the proletariat" hadn't really gone. It reminded me of the photographs that had been doctored during the Great Terror. In some, Trotsky had been painted out but his boots had been left in, to remind any supporters about the dangers of opposing the dictator.

Vera found the door to the KGB museum, tucked away on a side street. She said the place had been set up in 1984 to train young agents in the best traditions of the security services, and had opened to the public more recently. We were greeted by a cheery little KGB colonel in a suit, who promptly sold me a badge for the FSB, the KGB's successors—"same studio, different head," Art Troitsky had said.

The museum was chilling. Like the Stasi secret police museum I had visited in East Berlin, it was a frozen record of a hellish state ruled by madness and paranoia. Here was a letter written in blood by a KGB prisoner, there a wreath for Dzerzhinsky's funeral made entirely from bullets. I peered at crazed spy techniques, microdots buried in newspapers and bibles, and at lunatic killing devices: walking-stick swords, poisoned spectacles. I couldn't find anything to match the Stasi's more fiendish relics: jars to preserve the scents of dissidents so the dogs could hunt them down (dogs that had had their voice boxes amputated). But that was perhaps because the KGB museum was mainly a monument to the evils of the Cold War enemy in America, and skipped over decades of home-grown horror. There was a conspicuous absence of more recent KGB heroes, from Andropov to Putin. No wonder, I thought, Kolya Vasin exiled himself in his apartment and defected with his beloved Beatles music.

On the street again, Vera told me she was a passionate democrat: "Just two percent of people think like me." And she had a sobering story. "Just the other day a honeymoon couple asked me to take them on a tour of Stalin's Moscow. They especially wanted to see the House on the Embankment where top officials lived and from where they were regularly seized and executed."

In a kiosk on the street, I found a Russian magazine called "A Hundred Men Who Changed the Course of History." The issue was devoted to the Beatles. On page eight, there was a still from my film in the Cavern Club. A feature told how the lads had fought for peace, and against the Vietnam War. In the back of the magazine was a section about celebrities who featured in the Beatles story: the Stones, Andy Warhol, Mia Farrow, and . . . the British queen, Elizabeth the Second. She made it on the basis of having awarded those Member of the British Empire medals to each of the Fab Four in 1965. Inevitably, the magazine recorded how John handed back his medal as an antiwar protest. It was some sort of confirmation that Lennon, who had once been a target for extermination as one of "the Bugs," was now revered as a heroic fighter for peace—and a man who "changed the course of history."

18

"Today is the birthday of John Lennon, like the first day of our world!" On a golden Saint Petersburg morning in 2009, Kolya Vasin was euphoric. "It's like the day when people first came out of their caves wearing animal skins, found a piece of string, plucked it, and started singing." He threw back his huge shaggy head and sang, "All you need Is love." Kolya did a little dance, and the Beatles button pinned to his battered Stetson flashed in the sun. He was unstoppable. "Today is super day; today will be great concert. Russian people will sing John Lennon's music. John is daddy of all—number one!"

I watched as Vasin and a few of his friends began to unload a truck. With the reverence of curators receiving Picassos for a major retrospective, they gathered up his Lennon hoard and carried it through a doorway into an old redbrick building. A plaque announced that this was THE TRIADA CLUB. Before he followed his treasures, Vasin had more to tell me. "John Lennon is a Russian man for us. He is like Gulliver, and me and my friends are like Lilliputians dancing around his feet." I couldn't help thinking Kolya was a pretty chunky Lilliputian, but then he became serious. "John is about pain," he said, screwing up his face. "Russia is full of pain, so for us his

songs are like folk music." Pain—it was a version of the Beatles I
hadn't heard from anyone else, but I could feel that it went to the
heart of Vasin's Lennon obsession. His years of battling with a state
that had no place for him, and fighting for the music the state de-
spised, must have been hard. He had told me something of those
battles—the policeman who dragged him by his hair, the famous
sculptor who tore off his badge. I guessed there must have been a
whole lot more struggle—and pain—than I knew. But Kolya had
survived, and now it was Lennon's birthday.

I followed him into the club. It was a single room, bare brick
walls with a bandstand at the far end. As I got used to the gloom, I
became aware of a figure on the stage, stirring under a blanket. A
man was sweeping up broken glass and the harsh scraping merged
incongruously with the Beatles' "Ob-La-Di, Ob-La-Da" playing
somewhere. Vasin wandered through the glass, oblivious. He found
what he was looking for: life-size cutouts of John, Paul, George, and
Ringo, standing near the stage. They looked oddly unsettling, as
though they were about to stir into life. I noticed that Paul's left hand
had fallen off. Vasin picked it up, seemingly puzzled. He found some
duct tape and handed it to a friend in a herringbone overcoat that
looked several sizes too big. It was cold in the club, and a mirror ball
turning on the ceiling, scattering Kolya and the cutout Beatles with
occasional flashes, felt more like a police warning light at an accident.
Vasin was still euphoric. He looked across to me and laughed. "This
is my favorite day," he said, "the birthday of my guru and hero, John
Lennon. We started these parties back in 1971, and we make one for
each of the Beatles on their birthdays. But this one is special for me."

Arranging those parties more than thirty years earlier when Leonid Brezhnev's culture vigilantes were on the lookout for rock 'n' roll
troublemakers must have been risky and exciting. Even this morning, I could see how it energized Kolya, gave him a purpose and a
meaning. Now the battles were over, but the parties had become an
essential part of his life. Four times every year, in February and

June, July and October, he would gather his friends and the Beatles faithful of Saint Petersburg, and he would be the master of ceremonies, the moving spirit of the celebrations, welcoming a dozen tribute bands.

Vasin went over to the cutout of George and put his arm around its shoulder. "George put it very well," he said. "We gave people hope, and we gave people the chance to have fun. We gave people the chance to forget boredom and all the other crap—political, cultural, spiritual stupidity. The Beatles made us forget all that, and gave us a reason to celebrate." Kolya picked George up and moved him close to Paul, as though he were introducing them for the first time. The figures wobbled on their cardboard stands, and they seemed almost to have life for a moment. Then the man with the big overcoat broke the spell. He walked up to Paul with the duct tape and tried to reattach his broken hand. He stepped back and Paul's hand fell on the floor.

A giant pair of spectacles began to unroll from the ceiling, followed by John Lennon's nose and then his chin. The painting filled an entire wall of the club, blue and red and yellow. It stirred odd memories for me of those colossal portraits of Lenin or Stalin that used to loom down from the walls of factories and offices, the ultimate Big Brothers. Soon, John was everywhere in the Triada Club, in several more big paintings—a yellow psychedelic portrait, and a somber gray head. There was the famous photograph taken in New York. Then a poster scrolled from ceiling to floor with the lyrics of Lennon's song "Love": "Love is truth, truth is love."

"Back in the U.S.S.R." was playing somewhere in the background, and Kolya had stripped off his coat and hat now, revealing a T-shirt with a Lennon portrait. He wandered around happily, telling me about his visit to Britain and America. "It was in 1989. Suddenly there was a phone call and I was invited to visit rock 'n' roll places connected with the Beatles and Elvis. For me it was a rebirth." The biggest surprise for him was the statues. "I saw how people in the West celebrate their musical heroes. I saw statues of the Beatles and Elvis. We have statues of baldies with mustaches all over Russia. They have heroes of rock 'n' roll. And they put plaques on the houses where the Beatles lived. That made a huge impression on me."

When Vasin returned from that trip he had a revelation. "Something in my soul turned. After a huge concert in Saint Petersburg where ten thousand people listened to local bands playing Beatles music, I had a dream about building a temple." I had seen a little ceramic model of the dream temple in Kolya's apartment, which he also called a "temple of love." The model, smeary like a melted candle, suggested a strange tower with two shimmering spheres. I knew he was obsessed with building the thing, three hundred feet high, somewhere in Saint Petersburg. It sounded crazy, and Art Troitsky had told me Kolya had lost a lot of friends because they didn't support his campaign for the temple. I thought the whole idea sounded like a fantasy, but as he paced round the Triada Club there was no mistaking his belief in the project. "I realized I couldn't just go through life as a fan. I must do some real work. As John Lennon said, 'The Beatles were my school.' After they fell apart, I really started working. And he sang 'I Am Reborn.' I had the same kind of personal perestroika inside me."

Vasin's temple project had taken over his life. I found it hard to respond to his heady cocktail of spirituality, religion, and Beatle worship, or even to make sense of it. The campaign to turn the dream into an actual structure had consumed him for the past eighteen years. He lobbied city authorities, wrote letters to the Queen of England and the American president. The temple idea had blossomed and expanded like a science-fiction monster. "For me, it was the beginning of a new battle, a spiritual battle with the world around me. Although the Soviet Union collapsed, the new Russia didn't grasp the meaning of freedom, the spirit of the Beatles. I used to struggle against the cops, and now I had to struggle with these fools who did business and worshipped the dollar. My temple will stir the new Russian generation. I hope it will affect everything."

Kolya's vision seemed to have exhausted him for a moment. As he'd been pouring out his dreams to me, the preparations for the birthday party had been going on. The man in the coat was still trying to reattach Paul's hand, another man was lighting candles. More portraits of Lennon were crowding the walls as Vasin surveyed the gigantic painting. I wondered how I might process the meaning of his temple obsession. Beneath the craziness, it struck me his utopian project had odd echoes of the ideas that had driven the Russian Revolution, notions about creating the perfect Soviet man and engineering the human soul. But I didn't really see Kolya Vasin as a new Lenin.

He wandered across to me. "I've found a place for my temple at the mouth of the Smolenka River, which flows into the Gulf of Finland. There's a pretty little island at the mouth of the river, and it's a perfect size for the temple." I was surprised that the fantasy had found such a realistic base in his head. "I'll take you to see the place," he said. He was subdued now, and I could tell he was aware I was not going to be recruited into his small band of temple believers. "You know," he said quietly, "the world outside my apartment is a sort of hell for me. Maybe if I hadn't had to survive all that anger and violence in Soviet times, maybe I wouldn't have had the idea of this temple."

We went back to Vasin's apartment, leaving his friends to carry on the birthday preparations at the club. I hoped Paul would have been reunited with his hand by the time we got back. Kolya wanted me to see a book he had just published after years of work. We walked through the labyrinth of passageways leading away from the traffic-clogged street near the station. In the courtyard where Kolya's yellow submarine sculpture sailed along a wall under winged angel

Beatles, he led me to a little bookshop. Among a pile of sober Russian novels and travel guides, we found "Rok na Ruskich Kostyach"—"Rock on Russian Bones." The cover was a riot of Kolya's enthusiasms. Spiraling around an X-ray disk of a skeletal hand were guitars, vinyls, shouting text—FREE TERRITORY OF RUSSIA, PLAY LOUD, LOVE, WE NEED THE TEMPLE—and a disk-shaped version of the *Abbey Road* album cover with the Fab Four walking across the zebra crossing yet again. I turned the book over and was greeted with a smiling Kolya, holding a gold record of *Imagine.* The caption read, "This is my best moment." I bought the book, and the man behind the counter asked me, "Did you actually meet John Lennon?"

Back in Vasin's apartment, I cleared a space in his Beatles hoard to look through the book. I moved a plastic Paul McCartney, and Kolya said, "that's John Lennon's friend." On the book cover was a quote: "Sometimes I wrote in a lucky trance, as if I had written 'A Day in the Life.'" As I turned the pages, "Rock on Russian Bones" certainly had a trancelike feel. It put me in mind of those hippie effusions, psychedelic album covers dreamed up during acid trips in San Francisco. A photo of Jude the cat with flowers sat alongside a painting of a scarecrow in Strawberry Fields; a rooster played a guitar; Beatles lyrics in English wove through pages spattered with Russian text in a hundred styles; a collage of guitars was wedged between photos of Kolya at Lennon's old house in Liverpool and kneeling at Elvis's grave in Memphis. Little Richard's timeless slogan "A wop bob a lu bop, a wop bam boom!" shared a spread with an old monk playing a guitar. There was a raffish painting of a Stilyaga youth in 1958 with bouffant black hair, a garish bathing-belle tie, and red socks, smoking Camel cigarettes. There were urgings to "Go Johnny, go!" "Have some fun tonight!" There was a walrus and a painting of Lennon on a tightrope carrying a red guitar case. The 474 pages were numbered backward.

Tucked away in the midst of it all, I found a painting that made me stop turning the pages. On a hot-pink background, imprisoned inside a tilted black cage, a shadowy face with yellow eyes stared out. It seemed to have horns. Across the bottom of the picture, scrawled in English, was the single word SCARED. I remembered Kolya's quiet words in the club about having to survive the anger and violence of Soviet times. Then, under a photo in the book of a pair of sheep, I found another quote: KOLYA, DON'T BE AFRAID! It was signed MAMA.

Back in the Triada Club, things were moving slowly. A scatter of musicians slumped on the floor, hugging guitars. Paul McCartney's hand had been reattached at last, secured by a duct tape bandage, but not much else seemed to be happening. Forty minutes late, the first band tried to begin a sound check, competing with music playing at a thunderous level on the club's sound system.

After more unexplained delays, Vasin jumped onto the stage to launch Lennon's birthday party. He was certainly dressed for the occasion, in a shining white suit festooned with Beatles badges, and a white Stetson studded with more badges. By now, a crowd had gathered, an oddly assorted group of fresh-faced young kids, jolly matrons, and gnarled veterans. They stood around in the near darkness, waiting for something to happen.

It started very quietly. Kolya stuck his beard into the mike and began to growl, so softly I could hardly hear him. A tall man in a long yellow coat that put me in mind of a Chinese magician joined Vasin on the stage, and added his own quiet growling. The audience shifted uneasily. Abruptly, Kolya let out a yell that turned into words. "Yes, I'm lonely!" he yelled, and the Chinese magician yelled that he was lonely as well. I guessed they were channeling John Lennon's pain, but it was hardly the stuff of a fun birthday party. Happily, they soon subsided, and Kolya launched into a speech. "At last," he said, "we are ready for our celebration of music beyond space, beyond time, beyond the universe." There was quite a bit more of this, but finally he rambled to a conclusion. "We are celebrating the birthday

of a great man, the kindest of men, the man who sang to us all the
songs we will hear tonight." The audience stirred in anticipation.
"Let's listen to our anthem!"

The speakers crackled into life and the opening notes of the
"Marseillaise" fired across the room. "All you need is love!" Kolya
shouted, and he threw a cascade of paper into the air. As the sheets
fluttered down on the crowd, Lennon's hymn of togetherness was
picked up in the audience. Swaying lines of people slung their arms
around the person next to them and roared out the old song—word
perfect in English: "There's nothing you can do that can't be done . . .
It's easy!" I remembered that night in the summer of sixty-seven,
watching the Beatles singing the song for the first time on my black-
and-white TV at home in Manchester. The band wore garlands of
flowers and we called it "the summer of love"—when that was still
possible—and four hundred million people around the world tuned
in for the first global satellite linkup. More than forty years later,
Kolya's party was tuning in one more time—and Kolya at least was
still a true believer.

It was the trigger that started the celebrations. The tribute bands
followed one another onto the stage, awkward kids with bow ties,
haunted old geezers with guitars, fumbling through "Revolution"
and "I Feel Fine" and "Do You Want to Know a Secret?," and "With
a Little Help from My Friends." The crowd waved cigarette lighters
for "Imagine." The bands had names like Bluebird and Number
Nine and Yellow Pillow, and they were having a ball. Vasin gave
each of the acts a little goody bag as they left the stage, presumably
his Beatles spoons or a heart-shaped mug. Most of them were pretty
hopeless, but it didn't matter. The audience sang along with everything, pretty girls danced with each other, wrinkled couples rediscovered their old moves. Kolya moved through it all, arms waving,
eyes closed, ecstatic. He looked across at me and gave me a huge
wink.

Standing in the crowd, I found myself touched by the tide of feeling. Alongside me, a boy of twelve or so sang along with every word, his face lit up with happiness. Nearby an old man mouthed the lyrics without missing a word. I was realizing more than ever that the Beatles had mattered here—really mattered—and still mattered far more than they had for us in the West. I also had an overwhelming sense of slipping in time. Standing with this crowd, singing the old songs that had been so fresh and vital when I was young, was a kind of hallucination. I was back on that morning in 1967 when a friend unwrapped his brand-new vinyl of *Sgt. Pepper*, and I was transported to join the millions who believed the world might be remade. It seemed that Soviet Beatles generation was still living on that morning when the music was new—and they had infected their children and grandchildren with the virus.

Kolya had asked me to say something to the crowd about filming the unknown Beatles in 1962, and now he invited his "new friend Leslie" to the stage. I reckoned they'd much rather keep on dancing, but he was insistent. He gave me a huge hug, and I stumbled through my story one more time, ending with a rousing "Beatles forever!"

The bands and the music rolled on, Vasin did lots of bearish dancing, and a man with a beard clasped my hand and told me, "You are doing God's work." The fresh-faced boy I had spotted singing along with every song found me to ask how old I was when I made that first film. I told him "About twice as old as you are now," and he looked puzzled. A woman in an ABBEY ROAD T-shirt told me her nine-year-old son had asked her recently why "Yellow Submarine" was in English since he knew the Beatles were Russian.

A grizzled guitarist called Leonid delivered a rousing set of Beatles classics ending with "Yellow Submarine," which he managed to transform into a defiant protest song—as though reluctant to abandon his decades as a rock dissident. I was by now glutted and weary and ready to call it a day. But of course Kolya still had to deliver his final message. As Lennon's record of "Imagine" rolled over the swaying, waving crowd he bombarded them with flowers from a huge bunch in his arms. John sang, "And the world will live as one" and like this big gentle man in his white suit it was impossibly sentimental—and affecting. "All you need is love!" Vasin yelled.

I was heading for the door, but Kolya wouldn't hear of it. "You must stay for our feast," he said. With a crowd of veteran devotees, I drank sweet Russian champagne from bottles labeled TEMPLE DRINK—ONLY FOR BEATLES FANS and munched cheese and tomato sandwiches. Many noisy toasts were exchanged, and I was told that Vasin's John Lennon party was "a matter of love." A couple of old guys claimed me to insist that "Saint Petersburg and Liverpool are two brothers." Kolya was at the heart of it all, still glowing. "A beautiful, beautiful, beautiful day," he said.

At last, I made my farewells. A young man, blond and nervous, followed me to the door. "What was John Lennon like?" he asked. I fumbled for something fond. Then the man looked at me intensely and said, "Are you happy?"

19

I had been wanting to meet up with Mikhail Safonov for some time. He was a senior researcher at the Institute of Russian History in Saint Petersburg, and he had written an eye-opening article about the impact of the Beatles in the former Soviet Union. It was surprising to find a Russian academic straying into this territory, but Safonov had not pulled any punches. "Beatlemania washed away the foundations of Soviet society," he declared. "One could argue they did more for the destruction of totalitarianism in the U.S.S.R. than the Nobel Prize winners Solzhenitsyn and Sakharov."

Safonov was standing in the lobby of my hotel, an unassuming academic in a raincoat, muffler, and flat cap. He seemed nervous, and I wondered if he was going to recant and shuffle back to the safety of his institute. When we got to my room, I quickly discovered recanting and shuffling weren't Safonov's style. He took off his raincoat, and it was as though Superman had stepped out of his phone booth. The mild-mannered researcher shimmered. His suit was iridescent silver, strobing and dancing, transforming him into a glam rock star. As we began to talk, it became clear that the hidden raver within the conventional exterior was the core of Mikhail Safonov's secret.

"I first heard of the Beatles in 1965," he began, in an accent as thick as borscht. "It was a strange story about how someone called Ringo Starr had had his tonsils removed, but his fans had thought it was his toenails. And then the Liverpool post office was swamped with letters requesting Ringo's nails." For a geeky teenager on the other side of the Iron Curtain, this must have been an unfathomably exotic fable. But Safonov was intrigued. He heard "A Hard Day's Night" on the radio, scorned by the announcer as a song about the pursuit of money. He didn't care for it at first, but he got swept up in the Beatlemania of his school friends.

"The music came to us from an unknown, incomprehensible world and it bewitched us," Safonov said. "I began to listen to Beatles tapes on our big wooden radio–tape recorder at home, repairing the broken tapes with homemade glue. Soon I became a friend of the Beatles." Safonov recalled how he came upon that first Beatles track to be released in the Soviet Union. "I will never forget how I first found 'Girl' on the Melodiya 'Musical Kaleidoscope' collection. I could scarcely believe a Beatles song could be released in our country. But of course it was not credited to them."

For millions of kids, the overlap of the immortal name "Lenin" with the Beatle "Lennon" was irresistible but dangerous. To make jokes about that could wreck your education and your career. "If you changed Lenin for Lennon, it was really serious." Safonov thought that for many kids who were up to that time more curious than seditious, the absurd overkill was the beginning of doubt in the system they were supposed to revere. Like nearly everyone of the Beatles generation, he began to compile a book of their lyrics. And like the others, pondering those lyrics fired up his grasp of English.

Again like many others, young Mikhail grew his hair. He reached into a pocket, sending a psychedelic ripple through the silver suit. He pulled out a photo. "My friends called me 'Ringo,'" he said. And there he was forty years earlier, a long-faced serious boy, in sober pullover, shirt, and tie—with hair as Beatley as a Beatle wig. He smiled proudly as he held up the photo: "Ringo" Safonov looked back at the bald academic he had become. "This picture is very dear for me," he said.

He won a silver medal at school, but to collect it, he had to glue his hair down with sugar and water to try and achieve a "state haircut." As he was leaving the Palace of Culture after receiving his certificate, he was grabbed by police who branded him a long-haired deviant. They only let him go after he showed them his new certificate. Forty years later, the incident still angered him, and I got the sense that it had somehow shifted his life. Now he said, "The history of the Beatles' persecution in the Soviet Union exposes the idiocy of Soviet rule."

He told me a fantastic story about how a Leningrad school had staged a show trial against the Beatles. Mimicking the Stalinist trials of the 1930s, they had a prosecutor who railed against the Fab Four, and the whole charade was broadcast. "I heard the thing," Safonov said, "and how the schoolkids had to denounce 'the Bugs' as the Beatles were called. They were found guilty of antisocial behavior." Safonov shook his head. "The more the state persecuted the Beatles, the more they exposed the falsehood and hypocrisy of Soviet ideology. And in attacking something the whole world had fallen in love with, they isolated themselves even more. It made us more doubtful that our beloved country was right after all."

I thought of this decent man, laboring for decades in his institute to try and reconcile the orthodoxies of the infallible state with these unsettling ideas from the Cold War enemy. "Everybody who had absorbed the culture of the Beatles began to live another life," he said, "because they understood that Russian totalitarianism was criminal and it's no longer possible to live like that." Art Troitsky, Andrei Makarevich, Boris Grebenshikov, and Kolya Vasin had all told the same story, about the widening gulf between private and public moralities.

For me, that brought back something I had been told by the man who wrote the program for Alexander Dubček's Prague Spring in Czechoslovakia, the audacious document that set the stage for the explosive reforms of 1968. Zdeněk Mlynář was an idealistic young Communist who had studied in Moscow along with another reform-minded young man—Mikhail Gorbachev. Mlynář said that the crucial thing about Dubček's "Communism with a human face" was that his reforms—free press, freedom of speech—"banished fear." For the first time since the Communist takeover in Czechoslovakia twenty years earlier, private and public morality, what you felt free to say at home and at work, were the same. It was that liberation which the Kremlin was determined to crush with its invasion of 1968. Now I was understanding how the Beatles' music had helped a Soviet generation to "banish fear" and insist on living another life.

Safonov wanted me to understand how, like Vladimir Pozner, he had found himself "parting with illusions." It led him back to the theme that had wound through his life. "I think John Lennon was the killer of the Soviet Union. The Beatles hardly sang about politics, and they didn't think about the collapse of the Soviet empire, but the fall [wouldn't have been] possible if people hadn't been freed inside. They helped to make that possible. It was very important to kill the slave inside us, and they helped to take our fear away.

"We had always been taught to love the collective and the masses. Now we began to realize that the individual is hugely valuable, and that changed us. In the seventies and eighties the Beatles generation began to take jobs that had always been locked up by Party hacks. It became a non-Soviet generation." Millions of people like Mikhail Safonov, "Ringo Safonov" with a silver suit under his raincoat.

He stood up, and pulled on the raincoat. "I don't think the Beatles thought about all this," he said, "but they did it. So I say thank you very much."

At the Catherine Palace outside Saint Petersburg, trumpeters dressed like defectors from Sergeant Pepper's band welcomed guests arriving for the Pushkin Ball, also known as the Golden Autumn Ball. The gilded fantasy of the palace, which used to be the summer residence of the czars, was reflected in a thousand puddles, but the rain couldn't dampen the highlight of the social season. Flunkies with umbrellas shielded the hundreds of guests arriving in their ball gowns and tuxedos and escorted them past a receiving line of statuesque women in golden shrouds.

Kenneth Pushkin, a remote descendant of the great Russian poet, was here to welcome his guests. Handsome and charming, his diamond-studded cufflinks sparkling in the spotlights, he told me: "If anyone in Western culture could compare to Alexander Pushkin, it would be John Lennon." Kenneth Pushkin is an anthropologist who used to study Eskimos and now runs an art gallery in Santa Fe. He also has a blues band and writes songs—"and I'm a huge Beatles fan," he said. Kenneth had a strange story of how he discovered his family connection to the nineteenth-century Romantic poet. "I was in the Russian Far East working with Eskimos when a woman I hardly knew asked me to deliver a package to an Admiral Pushkin in Moscow. When he opened the door he looked at me and said, 'You are the real Pushkin.'" After that, Kenneth met many other relatives, and made regular pilgrimages to visit Pushkin shrines in Russia. He set up the International Pushkin Charity Fund, a charity to help Russian children, and the Pushkin Ball became an annual event.

Gold-embossed nymphs and cherubs gazed down on the elite of Saint Petersburg who included descendants of the Romanovs and other grand prerevolutionary families. It was a gathering to make Lenin weep, I thought. Lennon would, no doubt, have invited the guests to shake their jewels to applaud the orchestra, as he had at a Royal Command Performance in London. I knew the Catherine Palace was in fact accustomed to rock royalty and had recently hosted a party for Tina Turner, Whitney Houston, and Sting. Bill Clinton had also dropped by.

In the Grand Hall, the mirrored walls reflected an overload of

opulence. The hundreds of pounds of gilding on the walls, the towering ice sculptures, the dwarf in eighteenth-century costume—it
was a dizzying display of the new Russia on a posh night out. A procession of thirty flunkies in gold jackets filed past to serve a banquet, as the orchestra pumped out a selection of Strauss waltzes and
Kenneth Pushkin led the dancers in a swirl of silk and perfume.

There was a pause. Out of the chatter, a familiar intro emerged—
and the orchestra launched into a rather gawky version of "Yesterday." The dancers twirled again, and Paul McCartney's endlessly
replayed lament for a lost love, played now on a tinkly piano and a
sour trumpet, felt hard and brittle, like those ice sculptures.

After forty years, Beatles' music had dissolved into the fabric of
Russia so that it could take on any form. Not long ago I had seen
how Lennon's music was being reshaped as Russian punk, and now
McCartney was providing dance music for Russia's high society.

Kenneth Pushkin was laughing with a friend, another sleek, perfectly groomed man called Nico. "Nico's a musician," Pushkin said,
"and I write songs." "He just does it for seducing young women,"
Nico said. "That's true—the beautiful young women of Russia, most
beautiful in the world." Pushkin blew a kiss to a passing girl. Tiring
of their testosterone joshing, they moved on to the Beatles. "They
invented the culture of having a band and being a band," Nico said.
"Kenneth's band plays blues with a Russian soul." I wondered how
that would sound. Pushkin shrugged. "It's like talking about what
Pushkin means to Russian poetry," he said. "The meaning of the
Beatles to the popular music of the world is like saying what is Pushkin to Russian literature." Then he said in Russian, "Dlya nas, Beatles vsyo." For us the Beatles were everything.

20

In the fall of 2008, I met Kolya Vasin again on a cheerless street at the edge of Saint Petersburg. It was hard to reconcile this drab place of apartment blocks and graffiti-spattered warehouses with Kolya's vision of a "pretty little" location for his temple. This was a world away from the czar's city of gilded palaces and handsome boulevards. Vasin came up from the Metro station, unmistakable in a white New York baseball cap and a big black overcoat, muffled up against the slicing wind. His shoulder bag had borrowed the Beatles logo from Ringo's drum. We hugged and in his black-and-white outfit, it was like being hugged by a panda. "Let me show you," he said.

As we headed for the river, the wind grabbed us and pushed us together. In this faintly sinister backwater, I had a memory of other meetings, when the Soviet empire was still a dangerous place and I would get together with dissidents in out-of-the-way parks for whispered conversations. Kolya was no whisperer, and he shouted his story at me as we walked through a wasteland of cracked concrete and weeds. Plastic bags, tangled up in the undergrowth, flapped in the wind. A seagull screamed and whirled away toward the river.

We battled with the gale, and Vasin poured out the story of his eighteen-year struggle to build his temple. "I'm not Saint Francis who built a temple all by himself. I'm a scared boy from the outskirts of a big Russian city." Somewhere under the wild fantasizing, there was a core of self-knowledge and a fierce determination. "I went to the authorities first of all. I had to officially register the temple construction committee with the mayor's office. I found ten people who could actually work on it: designers, architects, project engineers, accountants who were also fans of the Beatles." I was surprised to hear that Vasin's dream seemed to be anchored in some reality. "The thing started to move, there was a buzz. But the authorities were very vague. They never said anything concrete. Putin never replied to me." I couldn't imagine how Kolya's vision for a three-hundred-foot-high temple to John Lennon would have been received in the Kremlin—even if Putin hadn't been an ABBA fan.

Remarkably, the authorities did suggest a place for the temple, alongside a lake outside the city. "But they never said a word about money. Is it really so hard to find sixty million dollars?" A plastic bag skittered across the wasteland and wrapped itself round my ankle. Sixty million dollars? I untangled myself, and the reality of Kolya's project blew away with the plastic bag. He was undaunted. "What is sixty million dollars to Saint Petersburg? It's nothing. It would give us a place to save our souls—like Hyde Park in London." But Kolya said it wasn't just the money. "Officials from the Orthodox Church were envious. They said they would do anything to stop the temple."

We arrived at a low wall along the edge of the water. The sky was a dirty rag, pressing down on the horizon. In the distance, I could see a few dockyard cranes. It recalled for me the desolate remains of Liverpool docks, abandoned and derelict along the River Mersey. Kolya looked at the slate-gray water and stuck his arms in the air to celebrate. "Beautiful place!" he roared.

"Many of my friends said 'we know a great place for your temple,'" he yelled at me. "It would have the best view over the sea." I

Kolya Vasin celebrates at the site of his proposed John Lennon Temple in Saint Petersburg.

asked exactly where he would put the temple. He stopped and pointed to a featureless patch of scrubby ground. "I'll put it here." I thought it would challenge even his supercharged imagination to see this joyless nowhere as the paradise of his dreams. He seemed determined that his unquenchable belief should make me see the spot through his eyes. "This place will be perfect for the spirit of the temple, because it will be like a lighthouse." He looked out to sea. "That way is Liverpool; from here there will be a long and winding road for John to come back."

Standing here at the place he had chosen to make his dream a reality, Vasin seemed to unhitch from his moorings. The wind snatched at his hair, giving him the look of a biblical prophet. He began to spiral into a vision that sounded more like something from the Book of Revelation than a prospectus for a building on the scruffy outskirts of Saint Petersburg. "I will be sitting at the top of the temple, looking for John Lennon's boat where he'll be rowing toward me with only a guitar on his back." Kolya mimed John's rowing, rotating his arms wildly. "He'll be rowing toward our temple, where a spiritual revolution in Russia will begin."

It was impossible to read how seriously he was taking all this. A teasing smile never left his face, and I half-wondered if he was having a joke at the expense of this man who had come all the way from England to hear about his fantasy. But the prophet had more to say. "The crowds of people will gather like they did when Christ came. And people will get switched on, and they'll realize they can't live like this any more." Kolya waved at the gloomy tower blocks. "They must have music, they must dance."

Like an astronomer observing the formation of a star from a cloud of interstellar gases, I sometimes had a sense that in the passion of the Soviet Beatles generation I was getting a snapshot of how religions are born. It reminded me of those syncretic religions that have blended Christianity with voodoo, or animal worship with Buddhism.

I made a film once about the iconography of Che Guevara. The inevitable photo of Che in his beret—taken by Cuban photographer Alberto Korda—had been adapted and reshaped in a thousand images. There was Green Che, Gay Che, Che on beer bottles and bicycle bells. I was especially intrigued to discover how a man who died in a squalid Bolivian village after a disastrous guerrilla campaign had been morphed into a saintly redeemer. I found images from across Latin America of Voodoo Che, Saint Che—and finally Chesus Christ. Here was Che in his beret, rifle slung across his shoulders in a pose echoing Christ on the cross with the inscription ECCE HOMO; and here was Che presiding at the Last Supper with Latin heroes from Zapata to Carlos Santana. Then I came across a picture from Mexico. On a green hillside, Che—naked except for his beret—hung on the cross, surrounded by kneeling peasants. The punk band I'd seen recently in Saint Petersburg with their album *Che Lennon* blurred the cult of the Beatles with the reverence for Guevara.

For Vasin, it seemed that John Lennon had taken on the saintly aura of Che Guevara. His tangling up of Lennon and God and the temple gave shape and meaning to his life. But now the dream was stalled. Kolya's friends had lost interest, some of them thought he had gone a bit crazy over the temple. The city authorities, the Kremlin, and the church had dismissed the idea with a shrug. But Kolya's belief in the temple sailed on, impregnable as the yellow submarine.

We watched a dirty cargo boat plowing across the bay. Then Vasin started to sing. "We all live in a yellow submarine, yellow submarine, yellow submarine . . ." A blast of wind snatched off his baseball cap and tossed it in a puddle. He scampered away to collect the cap, bubbling with laughter like a schoolboy. "Beautiful place," he roared.

21

Down a quiet street lined with trees showing off their fresh summer leaves, I found Pushkin Boulevard. It was June 2008, and I was near the center of Kiev, the unexpectedly handsome Ukrainian capital of parks and gold-domed churches, when I spotted what I was looking for. A curtain of old vinyl LPs dangled from a purple awning, and unmistakable music drifted from a doorway. This had to be the Kiev Kavern Club. I went down the steps and found myself in a Beatles wonderland.

An ABBEY ROAD NW6 street sign was propped on the bar under a clock made from an old LP inscribed LET IT BE; Beatles photos covered the walls, Lennon in his NYC T-shirt, Ringo in an army beret from *Help*. Beatles faces, Magical Mystery Tour vintage, were painted on the brickwork in psychedelic reds and yellows and greens. "Penny Lane" soared out of speakers. There was a *Hard Day's Night* album cover in Russian, "Vyecher Trudnovo Dnya." An ancient radio stood on a shelf, the Cyrillic stations on the dial like a roll call of the vanished Soviet empire: Vilnius, Minsk, Tbilisi, Kiev.

Polishing glasses behind the bar was a small man in a gray track-

The Kiev Kavern Club, keeping the faith.

suit. I introduced myself, and asked him about the place. Vova Katzman told me he was the owner. The Kiev Kavern was "really my way of sharing my crazy love for the music," he said.

I told him his club looked a bit like the original Cavern in Liverpool, and he had a surprise for me. "I saw that film from the Cavern in 1962, and when I found this place, it reminded me of that so I decided to make my club here." I tried to tell him that I had made the film, but he was already lost in his own story. "I first heard them in 1966 when I was just five, listening secretly to Voice of America. I started learning English through the Beatles songs, and they made my life better."

"Could you get hold of any records?" I asked him. He looked wistful. "It was illegal. There were no records. It was a different world." Now the world had changed again for Katzman and his generation. The Soviet Union was gone, and Ukraine was a new country, struggling to come to terms with the mess and confusion of democracy. The Kavern Club, transplanted from another time and another place, felt like a refuge from all that.

Hanging on a wall was an electric guitar, circled by a quotation: A GUITAR'S ALL RIGHT, JOHN, BUT YOU'LL NEVER EARN YOUR LIVING BY IT"—AUNT MIMI. "That's for my mother," Vova told me. "She said, 'Don't listen to that music—teach mathematics.' She grew up with Communism. Now my mother loves the Beatles." Vova looked over his shoulder at his bar, which was also a shrine. A smile lit up his tired face. "Beatles forever, love forever," he said.

I came to Kiev for a huge free concert Paul McCartney was due to play in the city's Independence Square. He had been invited by a Ukrainian oligarch, Victor Pinchuk, in support of an AIDS charity run by Pinchuk's wife. The event was a heady post-Communist brew of mega-money, conspicuous philanthropy, and big media— since Pinchuk owned a batch of Ukrainian television channels and planned to broadcast the concert across the country to an audience of millions. McCartney's company MPL would, as usual, own all the rights. We had all come a long way since I watched John Lennon squeezing his sweaty shirt into a bucket at the Cavern Club. And now I was here with another film crew, British and Ukrainian, to shoot at the concert, and to talk to local fans.

I had checked the McCartney fans' website Macca-central.com before I left home, and its comments on the upcoming Kiev concert seemed to catch perfectly the tone and spirit of charity rock in the twenty-first century. "This exciting event," it declared, "will allow people of different ethnicities and religions, political preferences and geopolitical orientations to come together around ideas of peace, love and unity—the very ideas that Paul McCartney with the Beatles helped to bring into the world." There was some uplifting stuff about how "the ideology and spirit of the Beatles helped build the demo-cratic aspirations for much of the Soviet society, and eventually led to the peaceful collapse of the U.S.S.R." Paul had added a "thumbs-up" personal message: "Pull together, groove, rock and roll."

The fans gathering at Katzman's Kavern Club were elated. "It seemed impossible," Vova told me, "that any of the Beatles would ever come here, except in my dreams." A crowd was gathering now, wrinkly survivors of Socialism and the long battle with Soviet authority to keep faith with the Beatles. I spotted an upright old guy clutching a *Sgt. Pepper* album, framed behind glass like a holy icon. It was evident that old Beatle schisms were still fresh here, most of all the long-matured grievances about how Yoko Ono had destroyed the band. A chubby veteran spilled out of a T-shirt with the slogan: STILL PISSED AT YOKO.

"People have been coming here from everywhere—Russia, Belarus, even Australia—looking for concert tickets," Vova said. Fans wearing Paul McCartney Independence Concert T-shirts flooded the bar as a band of teenagers took to the little stage. They wore natty white shirts and narrow ties, reminding me of the Beatles as I first saw them in 1962. "We're Brown Sugar," a youth brandishing a red guitar told me. They may have borrowed their name from a Rolling Stones song, but they launched into an old Beatles classic, "I Saw Her Standing There." And it was terrific. Even the incongruous presence of a pianist in the band failed to blunt the drive and energy of the performance—including authentic Beatles style, head-shaking howls: "So how could I dance with an other—wooooooo!" It felt as if the yell echoed from Liverpool to Kiev, like an animal cry flung across the rain-forest canopy. Absurdly, I found a lump in my throat. Maybe it had to do with that memory of my first contact with the young hopefuls who went on to fire their music around the world.

As the band got stuck into "Lady Madonna" I sat down for a snack with Katzman. The menus were his homage to the Fab Four, laid out like the labels on Beatles LPs: Magical Mystery Food and All You Need Is Eat and All You Need Is Sweet. I scanned the options: Please Please Me (canapé with black caviar), Yesterday (vegetable omelet), All My Loving (veal medallions). It had to be Back in the U.S.S.R.—pelmeni. Maybe I should have From Me to You for afters—that's chocolate mousse with liqueur. The Kavern food was a glorious melange of Ukrainian, Jewish, and scouse—a bit like Katzman himself.

He had a good story. Talking so quietly that I sometimes had trouble hearing him over the band and the chatter of the old fans, he told me how it had been with him and the Beatles back in the depths of the Cold War and Soviet paranoia. "There was a place in the botanical gardens where a man sold black-market Beatles records. We knew it was risky, and there were police raids sometimes. Anyway, I saved up some money—half a month's salary for an engineer—and I bought a Beatles album. The police saw me, and I was arrested. They grabbed hold of me and cut my hair, and then sent a threatening letter to my school." He smiled. "I didn't care. I loved the Beatles." Then he added, "All my friends supported me."

That must have been the real problem, I thought, for the bewildered rulers, the fumbling policemen, the nervous teachers, the geriatric Party bosses in the Kremlin. How should they deal with an incoherent mass movement, millions of kids like Vova and his friends, who simply grew their hair, listened to "Can't Buy Me Love," and laughed at them?

Then Katzman looked straight at me as though he had suddenly decided to throw off the diffidence he'd been deploying to shield him from some half-remembered fear. This mild, middle-aged man in the mouse-colored tracksuit needed me to understand something. "The Beatles changed the world," he said, "and they destroyed Communism—more than Gorbachev. If something's illegal, people want it more and more. If the Kremlin had allowed the Beatles, Communism would still be going on."

After all my journeying in search of the Beatles legacy in the old Soviet empire, and all the stories of the faithful, I was still impressed by the force of Katzman's conviction that four rockers from Liverpool could have shifted the world. Something real had plainly happened here.

We listened to the band for a little while, recycling a Wings song. A grizzled man, the one clutching the *Sgt. Pepper* album cover he had framed like an icon, sidled up to the table. "I am Sergei Gorashko and I have come from Donetsk," he said, thrusting his icon at me. "I want you give this to Sir Paul." I had an image of McCartney's basement stacked high with love tokens from fans, hopeless paintings, awkward poems, blurry photos, the detritus of adoration. I tried to explain to Gorashko, gently I hoped, that this was not going to be possible. He retreated with a sigh, trailing the weight of his disappointment.

A wispy woman told me her husband had been hoping to sing "Yesterday" for me, but he was too shy to come into the club and he was sitting outside. I told her to bring him in. She returned a few minutes later, looking upset. "What happened to your husband?" I asked her. "He became melancholy, and went home," she said. The sad icon man, and now the melancholy singer—it was as though Russia's attachment to wistful yearning, all that pining for birch trees and cornfields, had been distilled into a hopeless passion for the Beatles and their music.

Katzman's passion had been consummated in Red Square with Paul McCartney's concert. "It was like a fable," he said. The euphoria had faded now, a half-dozen years later, shouldered aside in Russia's new oil-fueled dash for national assertion. Big money and oligarch macho seemed to be the new rock 'n' roll. I remembered those nervous bank people, waiting for President Putin to arrive at McCartney's concert and guarantee their investment. But for people like Katzman, that moment in Red Square had lit up their lives. And now a Beatle was coming to his city.

The night before the concert I headed off to meet some of the oligarch's people. Crawling through clogged traffic in hot, thick rain, I spotted the concert stage, a vast construction site in the main square, lit up like the *Apollo* launch pad on the eve of liftoff for the moon. Hunched over his wheel, Evgeny my driver cursed: "Bloody Paul McCartney blocks up whole city." He slammed on the brakes again.

At last we reached "Horizon Office Towers—Where Business Wants to Be!" I survived the stares of the hulk with a gun checking my passport, and ran the gauntlet of the metal detector. In the lift, the Muzak played "A Man and a Woman."

Olga Serdyuk welcomed me in her office crammed with stuffed Teddy bears. The teddies had something to do with a campaign the oligarch's wife was mounting to help children in hospital. Olga was exquisite, illuminated with what my journalistic hero James Cameron once called "the intolerable bloom of youth." She said "frankly speaking" a lot, and she was very nice. Only her spectacles, as exquisite as Olga herself with perfectly crafted scarlet frames, hinted at an oligarch's high-powered assistant.

She was engagingly frank about the madness of organizing a massive concert for an ex-Beatle. "I've been getting furious calls all day," she said, "about how Paul is messing up the traffic. Even my father called to complain—and he lives two hundred miles away." She sighed prettily. "I'm also getting dozens of calls from people who—frankly speaking—I haven't heard from in years, all begging for tickets."

We moved on to a rooftop bar with a view of an operatic square decorated with a gold-domed cathedral. Olga had more stories about preparing the way for a rock legend. Her big problem recently had been confetti. At one point, McCartney's stage show calls for a cascade of confetti to pour down on him and the band. But not just any confetti. "Paul's people told me to collect six different grades of confetti—from coarse as gravel to fine as sand—and send them to London for Paul's personal scrutiny and approval." Now she was working on the opening of an exhibition of McCartney's paintings at the oligarch's gallery in Kiev. "Frankly speaking, I think they're childish," she said.

Olga's husband, Dima, bustled in, dark and a bit menacing, packed into a Hawaiian shirt. He was keen to let me know that Kiev was very old and very expensive. Then he was telling me that he got the exquisite Olga to make him soup at midnight. I couldn't tell if she was embarrassed or thrilled. Dima was determined to make enough money to buy a Brazilian island where he could swim with dolphins. Olga looked at her watch.

Dima was right about the prices in Kiev. The bill for our drinks was unfeasible. It had been a long day.

22

Concert day in Kiev started hot and sticky. By ten A.M. the platoons of security ghouls were already gathering, patrolling the orbit of the vast stage, murmuring into radios. During the night, the construction gangs had transformed the heart of Kiev, diminishing the scale of things, dwarfing gilded fountains with giant video screens, throwing up concrete barriers across old cobbled streets.

My film crew, cameraman Roger Chapman from London and assorted Ukrainian technicians, had the look of a refugee family fleeing a war zone. The concert checkpoints around the city center made moving around with our equipment a sweaty ordeal. We piled cameras and microphones and tripods into a wonky shopping trolley, bumping over the cobbles and trundling down alleyways, looking for ways to navigate the security net. Only Roger's booming laughter helped to sustain our farcical little convoy.

That laugh, a whooping, joyous outburst like the cry of some exotic primate, had turned heads wherever we had filmed together. I had worked with Roger in some odd places. At the Shaolin Temple in China where kung fu was born we had filmed the training ordeals of new recruits, drilled like Mao's armies as they dreamed of learning to fly and become movie heroes. We didn't see any flying monks, but we did record kung fu monks breaking baseball bat–size clubs over each other's heads. "I don't believe what I just filmed," Roger had said. The laughter had come later.

Rattling through the streets of Kiev with Roger and the trolley, we decided that those kung fu monks had been more hospitable than Kiev's guardians of rock 'n' roll. Now, police in shiny boots and dark glasses were sweeping the concert area, pushing people further and further to the margins. It was all very orderly and well organized. "Why are you doing this?" I asked a handsome young steward in a cream jacket. "Paul asks for it," the guy said, looking uneasy.

I dodged a couple of cops and found my way to the edge of the stage. A chubby, affable-looking man with Pinchuk Foundation credentials hanging around his neck was taking a breather, leaning on a barrier. "Nikita," he said, shaking hands. His card told me he was a "Ph.D. in Political Science." It became clear that he was a Beatles superfan, as well as an oligarch's enabler. Nikita insisted the Beatles had been his tutors. "My English teacher suggested I should listen to the Beatles, and it changed everything. They opened the whole world."

Nikita mopped his face and looked up as a helicopter clattered across the sun. A camera crane swooped over the stage, and spiraled up and away. Nikita was talking about the hazards of getting hold of illegal Beatle records when he was a teenager. "My treasures," he called them as he told me about how being caught with *Abbey Road* could cost your job or place at university. "The Beatles transformed me very quickly from being a good young Communist, and I understood that I lived in a very strange country."

As we talked, I was watching the invasion of Kiev's grand square with its heroic statues and triumphal memorials by the bloated juggernaut of Western rock. But Nikita wanted me to understand what the Beatles invasion had meant for one Ukrainian boy. "The main thing they brought me was the idea of freedom, personal freedom. It's like you meet friends after being alone for a long time. I understand there's nothing unreachable, nothing impossible. Everything is in my hands."

He pointed at a glass-sided building behind the stage. "You should have a look at our Beatles museum. At the opening ceremony, we cut an audio tape. Those secret tapes we made of Beatles songs hanged the Communist Party of the Soviet Union—because they couldn't control the tapes. It was the beginning of the end."

The museum was only yards away, but the security cordon demanded a sweltering detour with our shopping trolley. At least our little caravan provided some entertainment for the increasingly frustrated crowds.

At the entrance of the Beatles museum there was a giant blowup of the *Sgt. Pepper* album cover. The scale of it put me in mind of those epic Soviet propaganda posters where brave workers marched toward a Socialist utopia. The museum's version of utopia was to put yourself in the picture with the cast of *Sgt. Pepper* by sticking your head through a hole in the blowup alongside John Lennon in his acid-yellow coat. I resisted the temptation, and moved on to look at the other relics.

It was a strange assortment—a life-size cutout of the Fab Four on stage; a 1960s Soviet car—the model I recalled being driven by cosmonaut hero Yuri Gagarin; a photo of a Brezhnev-era Ukrainian footballer; a jolly history of the Beatles decked out in psychedelic swirls. My favorite items were tucked away in a corner. The curators had assembled a modest time capsule of a Cold War teenager's bedroom. It was an affecting tableau, and it transported me to an era of stifling drabness when the color and fun of the mop-tops must have felt like a heady escape. A spindly chair covered in faded ginger nylon squatted alongside a plastic television set. A gray cardigan hung on the wall. I remembered again Art Troitsky's lament: "There was nothing that reminded me of my dreams."

Oleg, who told me he was the secretary of the Ukrainian Beatles Fan Club, was cruising the museum. With his ponytail and Lennon

Paul McCartney plays Kiev: mega rock with mega security.

specs he could almost be an exhibit himself. I imagined the ghost of a teenage Oleg haunting that mock-up bedroom in the museum. Like many of the veteran Beatles fans I met, he seemed worn down by the years of struggling to keep the faith.

Oleg remembered discovering the Beatles in 1968, as the Soviet army invaded Czechoslovakia to snuff out the hopes of the Prague Spring. "There was the smell of war in the air," he said, "and we were scared. We listened to illegal radio stations like BBC and Voice of America to try and find out what was going on." I suggested that didn't seem a promising place to find the peace-and-love songs of the Fab Four, but his face was alive with the memory. "In between the reports they played music. And that's where I heard a few of their songs. I didn't find out the name 'Beatles' until a year later."

Oleg's memories of trying to improvise his own Beatles collection at a time when the records were as rare and dangerous as plutonium told me how quickly the virus had spread. Somehow, even here five hundred miles from Moscow in a provincial city, when a typewriter was seen as seditious, the idea of scratching "A Hard Day's Night" onto Grandma's X-ray photo had been passed on. "The best thing about those records on bones," he said, "was you could fold them up and hide them in your sleeve where the police couldn't find them." I had heard about those folding X-rays in Moscow and Saint Petersburg, and the idea seemed to have been handed on through a kind of homemade "Internet," giving a whole generation a way of bypassing the state's snoopers to listen to the music they loved. Tapes were even better, of course. Oleg pointed to a clunky reel-to-reel tape deck with big plastic spools in the museum. "I had one like that," he said.

We toured the museum together, and Oleg peered at an acoustic guitar with the word ROK printed on its belly. I recalled that the word means "bad fate" in Russian, so the guitar must have declared a special defiance. An electric bass guitar with a scuffed body was paired with a Tiger Guitar instruction book. Oleg was talking now about the dangerous times when the first real Beatles records were smuggled through the Iron Curtain. "I was arrested twice for having a foreign LP with me on the street where Beatles fans were hanging around and swapping records." We stopped to look at a flimsy little gramophone. It reminded me of the Dansette that had a lifesaving place in my own teenage bedroom.

Defying the monochrome austerities of Yorkshire in the 1950s, I had painted my Dansette purple, and my bedroom walls canary yellow. The garish reds and greens and blues of my jazz album covers topped off my mild Technicolor rebellion. Looking at the little museum with Oleg, I tried to imagine the desperation of feeling that even my record collection could get me into serious trouble. "Often my precious Beatles records were confiscated by the police," he said. "It felt like a tragedy. I reckon the police just wanted the records for themselves."

We came to a scatter of Beatles relics. A color photo of John and George was stuck on the screen of a television set. A battered photo frame had portraits of the four boys, copied from the cover of the *Let it Be* album. The force of the yearning was soaked into the tableau. Oleg looked at the dusty collection and it triggered a sharp little memory. "I was in trouble once at school. My desk was covered in the Beatles' names I'd scratched into it. I was accused of damaging state property."

And then the museum's spell was broken. A couple of girls with a digital camera climbed over the ropes that corralled the bedroom display. Leaning over the bass guitar, one girl struck a cutie pose borrowed from 1950s men's magazines, bottom thrust out, finger on chin. It was a version of sexy that used to be accompanied by a beach ball and a big swimsuit. The camera flashed and they swapped places. The other girl peeped out from behind the old TV, displaying a pout and miming a kittenish wave. It didn't appear to be a retro performance or a postmodern comment on the venerable Beatles. Finally the girls traded poses and photos in front of a sign spray painted KIEV WAIT FOR YOU! A teenager with Union Jack headscarf had been taking in the little charade. I felt I was drowning in the swirl of images and memories.

Camera on his shoulder, Roger followed a fat man with a straw boater and a tuba, marching behind a Dixieland band belting out "Yellow Submarine." The parade, with Roger in tow, squeezed through a door and into an auditorium at the Kiev Conservatory crowded with hundreds of kids wearing yellow shirts and yellow scarves. One section of the audience seemed to be military cadets with white shirts and epaulettes, upright and unsmiling. The Dixie-land band climbed up onto a stage bordered with blue balloons. They finished the song with a flourish and it cued the entry of a striking couple.

The host was a middle-aged man with fading hair and gray shoes. His partner was dressed in the style of a Christmas tree fairy. Her full-length ball gown in shiny cream nylon cascaded around her so that she seemed to be cruising the stage on wheels. Her hair was a torrent of golden curls. Brandishing their microphones like Kalashnikovs, the hosts yelled at the audience, informing them that this was the final of a nationwide talent contest to choose the best young musician per-forming Beatles songs. The audience looked underwhelmed by the prospect, but Roger looked happy and I couldn't wait.

We were not disappointed. First on stage was a big band, identi-cally fitted out in shimmering silver jackets that looked as though they had been supplied by Mikhail Safonov's tailor. They were con-ducted by an enthusiastic veteran with a silver mustache and a golden tuxedo. The band launched into an upbeat version of "Can't Buy Me Love," featuring enthusiastic but ragged solos by assorted teenage saxophonists. Then a young woman teetered onstage in heels high enough to qualify as stilts. She seemed alarmingly certain of her sexiness, belting out her vocal with a fine disregard for pitch. There was a scatter of bored applause and the band straggled off the stage.

We filmed as the roll call of Beatles wannabes wound on. A fresh-faced little boy with a set of pan pipes as big as his head trilled a ver-sion of "Yesterday." A tiny girl in a party frock pounded a piano in an oddly moving "Hey Jude." A couple of gawky youths with saxo-phones offered an off-key reading of "Ob-La-Di, Ob-La-Da." Yet another shot at "Can't Buy Me Love," this time reworked as a Balkan dirge waltz, came from a girl with dreadlocks and matador pants who climaxed her vocal in a growling rant.

My favorite by far was a slender youth with long blond hair whose solo version of "Let It Be" moved from a cooing murmur to an alarming falsetto howling that sounded like a wounded animal and seemed to go on forever. The audience looked stunned. With Roger, I wandered the backstage corridors where hopeful contestants were practicing their trumpets and guitars and saxophones. It was all endearingly earnest, and the unjaded determination of these kids to make the Beatles' music their own felt like a series of small triumphs.

They had even managed to bring some fun to the gloomy conservatory. "You have to see this," Roger said as he tracked into a side room. We shot a cameo that seemed to sum up the spirit of the competition, dotty and unexpected. A large woman watched over a monster cake, lovingly crafted in the shape of a yellow submarine. It floated on a sea of aquamarine-colored icing sugar. "Love it!" Roger murmured.

We walked back toward the auditorium, where I could hear a girl singer tearing into "Come Together," along the oppressive acres of turd-brown linoleum, past a succession of closed doors. The conservatory reminded me of that visit I had once made to the fearsome KGB headquarters in Moscow. The memory illuminated the reality of what was happening here. In a place where this music was once derided and banned, and even listening to it could derail your life, these youngsters were finding excitement and inspiration in the old songs that had changed the lives of the Beatles generation.

Back on the street, the joy evaporated instantly. We trundled our shopping trolley into Independence Square, where it was almost time for Sir Paul's sound check. By now, the security put me in mind of the protective fantasy surrounding a visit by an American president to a war zone. Solid ranks of police had pushed the crowds back into side streets where there was no chance they would catch a glimpse of the great man. When the sound check began, even the giant video screens stayed blank. "Hey Jude" echoed somewhere in the distance.

The music that had shifted my guts all those years ago in a Liverpool cellar had become this thing, vast and remote and untouchable, sealed behind barriers, summoned by oligarchs, pumped around the planet like gas or oil. But here, of course, Beatles also meant the timeless songs millions sang along with, the melodies claimed by those kids at the conservatory and hummed by the geezers in the Kavern Club.

We found a café where we could park the trolley and watch the crowds streaming by. They looked like crowds in any city now, differences of twenty years ago scrubbed away. Most of these kids, I guessed, had no memories of living with Communism. Just across the street, I could see teenage girls pouring into the new Kira Plastinina megastore, in pursuit of pink fripperies dreamed up by a fifteen-year-old Russian-American fashion phenomenon.

Abruptly, it began to rain, and soon Kiev was inundated by a torrential downpour. People crowded under awnings and cowered under huge Coca-Cola umbrellas. In minutes, the street was a river, inches deep. A gang of young braves seized the moment to rip off their shirts and dance dementedly in the deluge. I wondered if they had ever heard of the Woodstock Festival when thousands of hippies stood in the mud intoning "No Rain! No Rain!" In Woodstock and in Kiev, the rain poured on.

For a while it was fun. Four hours later we were huddling in the crew van with the deluge still pouring down on Kiev. Just an hour before the concert, it felt somewhere between farce and nightmare. In the darkness, Independence Square was an endless maze of barriers and checkpoints. We made a long detour through backstreets to get as close to the stage area as we could. The crowds packed into the "fanzones" were taking the full force of the storm. Even the trusty shopping trolley had to be abandoned as we sloshed our way to a gap in the fence where McCartney's chief gatekeeper, Stuart Bell, was fighting a losing battle with gangs of sodden pressmen. Peering out from a lilac-colored plastic rain hood, Bell struggled with a sheaf of release forms that were rapidly dissolving into pulp. As I reached him, he yelled through the hammering rain that I must sign one of his mushy releases, guaranteeing that I would not bootleg any of Sir Paul's performance, restricting my filming to ninety seconds of the opening song. It was hard to believe Bell could see anything through his rain-spattered glasses, and he seemed to be giggling at the absurdity of it all.

We trudged into the square, along corridors cordoned off by police tape. The place was unrecognizable now through the sheets of rain, slashed by searchlights. The arena in front of the stage felt like a scene from *Blade Runner*, packed with steaming people. Water flooded over my shoes, and when I looked down I saw that tangles of electric cabling were completely submerged. Didn't I remember a bunch of rock guitarists who were incinerated on rainy stages, victims of that killer cocktail of electricity and water? I didn't fancy being a footnote to Sir Paul's rain-spattered Kiev gig, remembered in Beatles legend as "the barbecued film guy."

I noticed that the VIP platform behind me stood well clear of the flood, and I tried to talk my way to privileged safety. My way was barred by Denis, the guardian of the VIP stairway. Denis was as cheery as his canary-yellow waterproofs, and while he was unyielding about access to privileged heaven, he was happy to talk about the Beatles. As the rain cascaded over us like a pressure hose, he told me his story. "I was born back in the U.S.S.R. Rock music was just forbidden. I was six years old, and we would sit at night in the kitchen, trying to catch Radio Liberty. For us, Beatles was a touch of freedom—of another life."

McCartney was due on stage in just a few minutes now, but Denis told me they were talking about canceling the concert. For him, that would only confirm the impossibility of his fantasy. "I could imagine being a cosmonaut in outer space, but I could never imagine that a Beatle would be playing right here in the heart of Ukraine."

Foiled in the quest for safety and dry feet, I hauled myself onto a little perch provided for photographers. Roger found a nearby perch for himself and the camera. For the first time, I had a view of the

stage. It was an unforgettable spectacle, tens of thousands of umbrellas heaving and glistening like a black ocean. Roger zoomed in
on a single rain-crazed fan, hoisted above the throng, gyrating naked in silhouette against the arc lights. On the giant screen alongside the stage, they were playing a video now, an express trip through
Beatles history. I caught a fragment of my little Cavern film, and
then the familiar parade of images: arriving in New York, singing
for the queen, filming *A Hard Day's Night*, sending "All You Need Is
Love" to four hundred million TV viewers round the world, playing
a sad gig on a London rooftop as the band fell apart. And now a
Beatle was in Kiev to sing for a billionaire.

Victor Pinchuk was the very model of a modern oligarch. Relaxed
in a leather jacket and white Paul McCartney T-shirt, he talked to
me about his concert as the rain hammered on his umbrella. "It was
my dream for many years. You know the influence of Beatles and
Paul McCartney during Soviet times was so huge, so great. Maybe it
was the only source of fresh air, of freedom for Soviet people."

It was obvious that this was not a man who was about to cancel a
concert his TV stations were due to broadcast to an audience of millions. He told me his first open-air concert was when he played his
precious record of "Can't Buy Me Love" through his bedroom window at the age of six. Now he had the impregnable assurance of a
man in command of a billion-dollar fortune, and the power to make
his dreams come true. "I thought I would invite Sir Paul. If he will
sing his songs about love, about friendship, about freedom, about
real human values it will help to unite our country." Pinchuk looked
up happily as if welcoming the storm to do its worst. "Now in this
incredible weather, people are speaking about freedom, and unity
and love, and this proves I was right."

With the concert only moments away, my mobile phone rang. An
anxious voice fought with the drumming rain. "You must stop shooting and return camera immediately! Rain will destroy my camera."

It was the man who hired us the only DigiBeta in Kiev, and he was desperate. So were we. I shouted "Yes!" and we carried on shooting.

"Are you ready?" boomed a voice. The crowd roared from beneath its umbrellas, counting down "Three—two—one!" And here was Paul McCartney, tiny in the distance, vast on a video screen. He gave us the inevitable thumbs up and, in Russian, a cheery "Privyot druzhi"—"Greetings, friends." The familiar cheeky boy's face still haunted the old features, powered up still with the adrenaline that has fired this man through thousands of concerts. How many gigs, how many countries? I remembered those crappy Manchester clubs, those cheerless TV studios. What drove this man, rich beyond imagination, one of the most famous faces on earth, to do it one more time on a wet night in Kiev? I guessed that the hunger I'd witnessed on that night in the Liverpool Cavern Club, the need that fed the spaniel charm, was still burning inside McCartney, the unstoppable Beatle. "It's going to be great here in Kiev," he declared through the deluge. "We're gonna have a great evening, OK?"

And then, thrillingly he roared into the opening riff from "Drive My Car," and I was back in the Cavern forty-six years earlier. Cutting through the lasers and the gargantuan staging, and the impossible weather, somehow the spark was still there, and the visceral contact with the crowd. And for this crowd in this place, there was something else. But, as Denis said, "to understand what really happened, you had to have been born back in the U.S.S.R."

23

RINGO IS A TIT! In the men's room of the Casa pub on Liverpool's Hope Street, I read the message, scrawled in felt tip on a toilet door: RINGO IS A TIT! The angry words curdled with the smell of piss and bile—bile for Ringo, who had enraged local fans by saying there was nothing he missed about the city. I thought it had been a dangerous remark in this city where the passionate loyalty of its citizens, their obsession with their place, is matched only by New Yorkers or maybe New Orleanians. They all bred people who were sure that no matter how impoverished their city is, there is no other place you could live, or ever want to live. Liverpool, New York, New Orleans: port cities where fabulous music was born.

I was in the city to meet up with Yoko Ono. For Beatles believers around the world, Yoko had penance to do. "Still pissed at Yoko" that fan's T-shirt in the Kiev Kavern Club had declared, and everywhere in Russia I met gnarled survivors of the Beatles generation who had held on to their grievance against Yoko Ono over decades. For them, John Lennon's widow was still the woman who broke up the Beatles. Oh, Yoko! No matter that John loved you; you brought it all to an end, you stopped the music.

Heading off to meet her now, I replayed the images: Yoko in the Abbey Road studio, always clinging to John as the Beatles imploded; Yoko in bed for peace with John; Yoko in a bag, doing Bagism with John; Yoko stunned and dignified on the day John was murdered. How would she be now? I had my own questions. I had been intrigued to discover she had some Russian history, and I wanted to know more.

It was also International Beatles Week in Liverpool, and I hoped to meet up with some old acquaintances who were making the pilgrimage from Saint Petersburg and Moscow. On a sunny August morning in 2009, all roads seemed to lead to the Beatles. There were signs for the Beatles Experience, the Beatles Story, Beatles Tours, Beatles Hotel, and the feisty old city was clearly flaunting its most famous sons—despite Ringo's brushoff. I found Yoko's hotel in a quiet street not far from the docks that had once made the city rich and had provided the gateway for the flood of music from America that had inspired the Beatles.

Zipped into a tiny black tracksuit and sporting her inevitable jaunty fedora, Yoko was a surprise. I had been preparing to negotiate her fierce reputation, but she was instantly friendly and approachable. Her familiar face was impish, and as we began to talk, the Japanese-flavored American accent sounded charming rather than scary. I brought out my ever-reliable calling card, telling her the story of my first film in the Cavern Club. She listened intently, saying "amazing" from time to time, laying her hand on my arm, almost flirtatious. When I told her I had seen that film again on American TV on the morning after John was murdered, and had gone to join the grieving crowd outside the Dakota building, she said "that wasn't a coincidence. You should have been in touch then!"

I didn't know how to respond to that, so I moved on to talk about my explorations in Russia. I told her about how the Beatles generation had inscribed "Love Me Do" onto X-ray film, about making guitar pickups from vandalized telephones, about kids who had risked their education and their jobs to keep faith with the Fab

Four. She lit up when I told her about Kolya Vasin, who had made his John Lennon Temple of Peace and Love in his tiny Saint Petersburg apartment and was planning a three-hundred-foot memorial to John. "Please send him my love," she said.

Then Yoko told me her own extraordinary story. "I had a Russian aunt who was a famous violinist and lived in great style outside Saint Petersburg. She married my father's brother Sunichi Ono after he graduated from the university in 1916." She said her aunt's Russian ancestors had known the great Russian poet Alexander Pushkin. "He was a frequent visitor to their country house," she said, and as she talked I tried to construct a picture of the Onos and the Pushkins hanging out together in the family mansion. But Yoko had already shifted to another century. "I have always felt a connection with Russia," she said, "though I didn't go there until I was invited by Mr Gorbachev to an international peace gathering in the late eighties." Yoko's recollection of her meeting with Gorbachev and his wife, Raisa, gave me an unexpected cameo to add to my search for the impact of the Beatles in Russia. "Gorbachev told me he admired John's peace campaigning, and said 'he should have been here now.' Then Raisa sang a line from John's song 'Woman' and said she and the president were fans of the Beatles." Yoko must have been familiar with famous fans around the world confessing their love for John and the Beatles, but even twenty years after that meeting with the Gorbachevs she glowed as she told me about it. I remembered all the stories I had heard about the repression of the Beatles generation in Russia, and wondered how those people I had come to know would have felt about this late conversion of the man in the Kremlin.

Yoko headed off for a packed schedule of appearances at International Beatles Week. "We'll keep in touch," she said. Ringo might have smudged his image in Liverpool, but Yoko was still John's widow, keeper of the legend, and a star. I had noted that during our talk, she invariably spoke of "John and Yoko."

* * *

I went down to the Adelphi Hotel, where the Beatles Convention was being held. The venerable old place in the city center where I'd first met Brian Epstein almost fifty years earlier was looking pretty down at heel, I thought, with the defeated atmosphere of a once-grand mansion living off memories of better times. The lobby was teeming with the Beatles faithful, tired men in anoraks, heavy women with shopping bags. Grizzled Germans with guitar cases said they were a tribute band and asked where they should go to play their gig. The place was buzzing with Beatles talk, veteran fans sharing stories of Fab festivals and swapping news of Paul's next concert and Ringo's recent betrayal. There were foreign voices, too, visitors from Italy and America, Japan and Russia, peering around as though they expected to catch a glimpse of Paul, or more probably of Paul's brother, Mike.

I bumped into Edward Shornik, an English teacher from Siberia who I remembered meeting in Liverpool a year earlier. He had brought a party of schoolkids, and said he had fallen in love with Liverpool. He told me how in 1969, he was at summer camp in Turkmenia "and we danced to 'Ob-La-Di, Ob-La-Da.'" He said he was still hoping to invite me to his arts academy in Novosibirsk to talk about the Beatles, and "to sample sturgeon soup and Siberian vodka." I thought that sounded like fun, though I hoped it wouldn't be in the depths of a Siberian winter.

I pushed through the crowds into the main hall. The vast ballroom had been taken over by a Beatles bazaar. Every available space was jammed with stands and stalls offering a dizzying array of stuff. Voracious fans checked out Beatles nylons and Beatles toothpaste, Beatles talcum powder, Beatles soap, and Beatles lipstick, the clutter from teenage bedrooms of a half-century ago. Now they were preserved like relics from Tutankhamen's tomb and on sale at prices that would bring a smile to the face of a London art dealer. I spotted a Beatles Wig Game and tried to imagine how even the most resourceful game maker had managed to devise a mop-top entertainment based on a nylon toupee. A brooding man called Richard sat at a table, displaying an unremarkable framed photo of himself with the Beatles. He said he was planning to auction the thing in London for ten thousand pounds. "I sell soap now," he told me. There were Beatles disks of infinite varieties, rare vinyls and strange Portuguese and Japanese compilations, the sleeves decorated with mysterious stains. There were aged copies of *Merseybeat* magazine, faded and tattered but displayed with a reverence more appropriate for the Dead Sea Scrolls. The hustlers of this hoard were a strange tribe, suspicious men in pullovers and bosomy women who sat knitting as they watched over their treasures.

An American man with red and green hair and a purple beard was loudly boasting of his acquaintance with the Beatles to a rapt crowd. In a side room, the elderly German band trudged through "We Can Work It Out," while next door a respectful crowd gazed at silent black-and-white film of the Beatles hanging around in a hotel room.

I felt a huge weariness with it all, and retreated to an alcove where the din of the Beatles traders was less overwhelming. What did it mean, this recycling of junk and faded memories? In the Soviet Union, I had seen how the music had changed lives and shifted a superpower. The curdled nostalgia being peddled here felt shabby and diminishing, the final whimper of that thrilling sound I had found in the Cavern Club. Then someone started to play an old seven-inch single of "Can't Buy Me Love" and it sounded fresh and vital all over again. I heard someone calling my name and I saw some familiar faces. Dimitry and Alexander from Saint Petersburg came over, carrying plastic bags full of things they had bought. "We met at Kolya Vasin's birthday party for John Lennon," Alexander said. I remembered him, glowing with good feeling, embracing the Saint Petersburg faithful at the party. I was happy to be reminded of that extraordinary evening when the Russian Beatles generation celebrated and joined in the old songs. It made the scavenging in the hall for leftover trinkets seem even more dispiriting.

"We traveled here from Saint P in a bus," Dimitri said. "We come every year." How would it be, I wondered, to be part of that magical mystery tour, rattling in an old bus for days on the pilgrimage to Liverpool. Did they sing the whole way, and swap stories about Paul's dog? Alexander told me he ran a Beatles website in Russia, and it seemed the Fab Four ruled his life. He said he had fallen out with Kolya Vasin over Yoko Ono. I didn't explore further. We looked out over the crowds, and Dimitri watched a couple of matrons haggling over a rusty tin of Beatles talcum powder. "I hate Beatles fanatics," he said.

24

The pianist was rippling through "Hey Jude" in the hotel lobby as I arrived in Minsk. In this ultimate bastion of Soviet-style repression I wondered for a paranoid moment if the music might be a provocation, targeted to flush out the subversive Beatles infiltrator from the West. I knew this was one of the worst places on earth to be a journalist. I had heard that Alexander Lukashenko, the president of Belarus, relished his reputation as "the last dictator in Europe," and was not a fan of rock 'n' roll. He saw it as dangerous stuff, a stage for confrontation, potential fuel for unrest and even revolution. Unofficial musicians were exiled from TV and radio, lyrics were scrutinized by the Committee for Ideology and Censorship. Official music—patriotic ballads or blameless Europop—were a regular tool of government. If you thought all this was a joke, making fun of the president could land you in jail.

On the way into town from the airport, I felt I was marooned in a Soviet time warp. It was the winter of 2009, twenty years after the fall of the Berlin Wall, but the Stalinist tower blocks stranded in dirty snow seemed determined to insist that the Cold War was still in business here. I had spotted a looming statue of Lenin, and the guidebook wanted me to know that Belarus was the only country in Europe that retains the death penalty. I had wanted to come here after following the Beatles generation in less extreme outposts of the old Soviet empire. Now I hoped that Belarus, like a dinosaur trapped in the ice, could give me a real sense of how it had been when the state was determined to rule rock 'n' roll.

Still, the florid hotel pianist was clearly free to decorate this "outpost of tyranny," as President George W. Bush had labeled it, with a Beatles soundtrack. Accompanied by a tormented toss of the head, she was giving "Hey Jude" the full conservatoire treatment. Unmoved, the black-suited bouncers lowering at the door of the in-house casino looked like any other guardians of bourgeois indulgence. My Amex card was welcomed with a smile by the chic young receptionist.

I came to Minsk to meet Yuri Pelyushonok. I had been wanting to catch up with Pelyushonok on his home territory since I came upon his irresistible little book *Strings for a Beatle Bass: The Beatles Generation in the U.S.S.R.* Packed with anecdotes and memories of growing up as a Beatles-starved teenager behind the Iron Curtain, it gave me a new understanding of the joys and heartaches of being a Fab fan in the Evil Empire. He described how it began for him and his friends: "We felt that somewhere abroad there had appeared something noisy, happy, hairy and awfully nice."

Pelyushonok led me into a parallel universe where guitars had to be secretly carved from kitchen tables, where wild myths blossomed about how the Beatles had played a secret concert near Minsk. And he confirmed that the news about how to make X-ray records had reached him on the western edge of the Soviet empire, spreading as fast as the Beatles virus. Pelyushonok also wrote about living with the constant fear from authorities who could crack down at any moment on the "antisocial elements" who listened to the Beatles. It was the story I had heard everywhere and it made me wonder if the rock 'n' roll epidemic hadn't become one of the strongest unifying forces in the fraying Soviet empire.

For decades Yuri Pelyushonok worked as a hospital doctor under the lunacies of totalitarian rule, learning to recognize the tiny mark on a patient's records which indicated this was an important Communist official who would expect special privileges and could bring down wrath from high places if he didn't get them. He became an expert at locating vodka to bribe the morgue orderlies and ensure the smooth transfer of dead Party bosses out of his hospital before their families made a fuss.

In the 1980s, Pelyushonok sailed the world as a ship's doctor watched over by floating commissars. In 1989, his love for the Beatles delivered a bonus. Arriving in Belgium, he discovered that the record Paul McCartney had made especially for the Soviet market in the high days of perestroika was a rare collector's item in Europe, worth real money. The vinyl earned him enough to import a twenty-year-old Ford Mustang to Belarus, and for the next two years McCartney's disk became the main source of foreign currency for Soviet sailors buying cars abroad. They called it the "golden disk." "I thought we should have replaced our statues of Marx and Engels," Yuri said, "with Paul McCartney."

After decades of fighting the assorted craziness of life in the U.S.S.R., Pelyushonok finally had enough. As the Soviet Union unraveled in 1991, he stowed away on a merchant ship and started a new life in Canada. But he took with him his passion for the Beatles.

I had finally met Yuri for the first time on a blazing August morning in suburban Ottawa. I found him hiding from the heat in his crowded living room with his tribe of Beatle pals. He looked just as he should—casually biblical, barefoot, with a grizzled beard and straggling gray hair circled by a hippie headband. His tribe looked equally in character: a Vietnam War escapee, a sweet man with a Beatles Convention 1996 T-shirt who told me he'd met George Harrison's sister, and an urbane Englishman in a blazer. I realized I was dipping my toe in an ocean of Beatles brotherhoods. All over the world there must be groups like this, sharing a sixties neverland, yearning for another time. Yuri's den was an encounter between Soviet intellectual retro and Fab icons. Fringed lamps and framed portraits of bearded ancestors jostled with yellow submarines, Blue Meanies, and Beatles matrioshki. Presiding over it all like the maharishi in his ashram was Yuri Pelyushonok himself, a guru with magical stories to tell.

"The Beatles were a religion . . . some bright light in a dreary life," he said. Speaking in an ecstatic whisper so I had to lean forward to catch the words, Yuri recalled how the seismic tremor of the early Beatles reached him through the Iron Curtain. "You can just feel it. You know it's in the air, I can't explain. But everybody knows it. It was so awfully good, you know, and so nice that you fall in love when you hear this music." Yuri seemed to unwind as he recalled that first passion. "Of course there was absolutely no official information about them, but we felt it."

In this Canadian anywhere it was hard to tune in to Yuri's boyhood memories of his Beatles epiphany amid the Krushchev-era apartment blocks and dusty courtyards of Minsk. But he had found a way to haul those memories halfway around the world and make them live again. His Proustian memory-jogger was a song he had written, "The Yeah Yeah Virus." And now he wanted me to hear it.

The setting could hardly have been farther away from a Soviet backyard. In the garden of his house, jammed in between the flower beds and trimmed hedges, Yuri had assembled a band of Canadian Beatle devotees to belt out his song for me. Presiding on a petrol-blue bass guitar, he counted down his own fab four: two guitarists—a Lennon with shiny black shoes, a Harrison with white slacks and sandals—and on drums, a smiling Ringo.

A gutsy, sliding riff rattled the plastic yellow submarine on a garden table. For a moment, the raw energy stirred echoes of my first encounter with the soon-to-be Fab Four in a Liverpool cellar. Then Yuri's lyrics yanked me into another place.

Yuri Pelyushonok and his band perform "The Yeah Yeah Virus"
in his garden, Ottawa, 2008.

> *While in the West the Beatles stepped on all the rules,*
> *The sixties beat was echoing through all the Soviet schools.*
> *Every Russian schoolboy wants to be a star,*
> *Playing Beatles music, making a guitar . . .*

The song summoned up those Soviet schoolrooms, well-ordered, disciplined, portraits of Lenin and Gagarin on the walls, the Communist Party's program to build young Socialists suddenly faced with a bewildering, unsettling new challenge.

> *Teachers looked upon all this as if it were a sin,*
> *We were building Communism,*
> *But the Beatles butted in.*
> *Each comrade's child was in a band,*
> *The yeah yeah virus swept the land.*
> *And things were getting out of hand.*

Pelyushonok was unreadable, an Easter Island statue with a bass guitar, as his song about the revolution that had changed his life wound to its conclusion.

> *What could they do? What could they say?*
> *A generation gone astray—they walked away.*

And now, eighteen months after that get-together in a Canadian garden, here was Yuri, sweeping through the lobby of my Minsk hotel, unmissable in his headband. He had agreed to make a trip home to help me track down that Beatles virus that had infected his boyhood forty years earlier.

We talked in the empty restaurant, murmuring like conspirators as the pianist trilled away in the background, mining rich seams of Slavic melancholy from "Yesterday." Yuri had my days mapped out. I'd meet a veteran Beatles nut in a shed somewhere, hook up with a fellow fan from Pelyushonok's schooldays, and join a reunion of his old band after a quarter of a century.

Yuri had a bizarre story. "This will help you to understand where we are," he said. Not long before I came to Minsk, he told me, the Free Theater of Minsk, a mildly radical bunch who played in a small private house, had been raided by the police during a performance. The entire cast and stage crew, plus the audience, had been arrested and held overnight. People who had been in the theater that night had soon lost their jobs. It sounded more like Absurdistan than a state on the edge of Europe. I was tempted to laugh, but Pelyushonok was deadly serious.

Glancing around the empty restaurant he said, "We must be quick and inconspicuous. We don't want to attract the attention of the police." Police? For meeting a man in a shed? I had thought my paranoia about being there was just a personal indulgence, a bit of spice to be recycled over a drink in a London bar. Yuri's warning was making this place alarmingly real. Now I was beginning to feel like Holly Martins in *The Third Man*, trapped in a noirish movie, directed by a man in a headband.

Yuri headed off into a sudden blizzard, adding to my sense of having arrived in a Cold War fiction. Upstairs in my room, I powered up my laptop and found President Lukashenko's MySpace site—or rather, a biting parody page sending up the Belorussian ruler.

The site informed me that the president's nickname was Daddy, and that his heroes were Lenin, Stalin, and Hitler. His "Mood" was "angry." Daddy's "Interests" included "dialectical materialism" and "military stuff." His "Top People" in "Friendspace" featured KGB tyrant Beria, Leonid Brezhnev, Mr. and Mrs. Milošević, and Kim Jong Il, the Dear Leader of North Korea. There was a photo captioned MY BEAUTIFUL RED GUARDS, two blondes in army uniforms with Kalashnikovs. The only crack in this nightmare edifice was listed under "Music." Along with Shostakovich, Stravinsky, and Wagner, Lukashenko registered an enthusiasm for "dance music." I had a sudden vision of the despot strutting his stuff to the Bee Gees doing "Staying Alive." Obviously Lukashenko's site had been hacked by a Belarussian Mel Brooks—but the hilarious parody gave me a snapshot of how his people felt about their president.

I also dug farther into the regime's control of music and culture. The official guidelines for television gave me the flavor: "Your master is the government, and you express the government's point of view." The state's leading ideologist was the former commissar of a fiberglass factory, a close chum of Lukashenko.

Popular music seemed to be a particular target of official nervousness. An open letter from blacklisted musicians said: "We have been stood on tiptoes and a noose has been placed around our necks. Apparently we haven't been hanged yet, but you can't call it a life." It was evident that Lukashenko and his gang had been petrified by the role of pop music in Ukraine's recent Orange Revolution and had decided to snuff out any local rock dissidents. The president had promised to "wring the neck like a duckling of any opposition protest." But this weird twenty-first-century version of repression often felt as though it had been scripted by George Orwell for Monty Python. Censorship is illegal in Belarus, but the refining of bureaucratic obstacles had become an art form of its own. Live shows, broadcasts, and music distribution all needed permits from the Belarussian KGB, the Ministry of Culture, or the Ministry of Religious Affairs. Refusals were regular, but reasons were seldom given; so appeals were impossible. Concerts were often canceled at the last moment, with improbable explanations: "because the kids will cut the seats" or "the hall is mined." There were no printed edicts, and official bannings were usually delivered by telephone, creating fear without a paper trail. Seventy-five percent of all broadcast music was ordered to be "of Belarussian origin"—though singing in the Belarussian language was strongly discouraged, since it might foment nationalist feeling. Russian was the approved language for lyrics, which were required to be checked by editors, and broadcast playlists had to be submitted a week ahead to station bosses.

Official pop stars, such as the band Siabry and its leader Anatoly Yarmolenko, delivered the kind of paeans that might have made Stalin blush. A recent offering, taking its title from the president's favorite nickname, was called "Listen to Daddy." The lyrics were an anthem of loyalty:

> *Daddy can do anything,*
> *Daddy's better then anyone,*
> *Listen to Daddy*
> *Morning, noon and night.*

Lukashenko sent a letter of congratulation, and Siabry were given a prestigious state award.

Belarus has competed in the Eurovision song contest since 2004, and in Daddy's wonderland the selection of the national entry has become the most important cultural event of the year. The Eurovision's cocktail of blameless celebration and national uplift has had an inevitable appeal for Lukashenko, and he has intervened personally in the vetting of the Belarus entry. Year after year, the jury in Minsk has awarded maximum points to the Russian song. The pinnacle of Daddy's efforts to blend politics and pop came in 2005, when ten-year-old Kseniya Sitnik, in pink tutu and white knee boots, won Junior Eurovision. Singing alongside pictures of handsome workers and girls in folk costume holding ears of wheat, Kseniya smiled out from the top of the presidential slogan "Za Belarus!"

Faced with this stifling embrace of popular music by the regime, thousands of musicians have emigrated. Those who have stayed behind have often been energized by a sense of being Soviet-era dissidents. Lukashenko's crackdown on "unofficial" music has given Belarussian rock music "something to play for," as one dissident musician put it. Unlicensed concerts are advertised via the Internet, often switching venues at the last moment to evade police harassment. Rock musician Vladislav Buben enthused, "It's like the days of the Soviet underground."

Unofficial musicians often quote the metaphor of Chernobyl. The disaster happened over the border in Ukraine, but seventy percent of the contamination fell on Belarus. For many, the baleful regime that infects their country feels like an alien import, bred in the Soviet Union decades ago and still polluting their lives.

Long after midnight, I closed my laptop. A blizzard was still swirling outside my window as I collapsed into fevered dreams of a warped spectacle where sinister children waving Kalashnikovs glowed and melted in a decaying theater.

Next morning, new snow had decorated the cheerless blocks in the city center. A taxi pulled up in front of the hotel and Yuri bounced onto the street. "Now we'll go and see my mother," he announced.

This was an intriguing prospect. He had told me something

about his mother, Liliana, and she had an unforgettable story. When she was a girl in the 1950s, as a star gymnast she was summoned to Moscow to be part of a May Day parade in Red Square. Hoisted to the top of a tower of heroic athletes, she found herself looking directly into the eyes of Comrade Stalin.

And now, more than fifty years later, I was meeting the woman who had eyeballed the Soviet despot and survived to tell the tale. She invited me into her tiny apartment crowded with trophies from her life as a physical training teacher, and souvenirs from Yuri's adventures as a ship's doctor. A little stuffed crocodile grinned from a shelf. Liliana had the face of an indomitable Soviet matriarch, strong-featured, silver-haired, ready to challenge the world from behind her no-nonsense spectacles. With her spotless crocheted shawl, she immediately put me in mind of one of those epic Socialist posters extolling the spirit of a heroic mother, eyes alight with the prospect of a better tomorrow.

But when Liliana began to tell me about her son's obsession with the Beatles, she sounded like every mother with an exasperating child. "I think his dedication to the Beatles was a bit too much. We always had a problem with that. What can I say?" She fluttered her hands with the memory of her frustration. "Can you understand me as a mother?"

Liliana raised her eyes to the ceiling. "Ever since he heard the first Beatles songs, it was like he was shaken. He only had the Beatles on his mind. They were like gods to him!" She laughed, and then sagged back on her chair. "Beatles, Beatles, Beatles!" she said, and it sounded like a lament.

As his mother talked, Yuri sorted through photos of himself as a teenager. In a couple of the pictures he flaunted an unconvincing beard, a tentative rebel. Liliana was speaking more quietly now, almost talking to herself as she remembered the dangers of her son's flirtation with the seditious young men from the Cold War enemy.

"Back then we were told that young people shouldn't get involved with Western music." Recalling the powerful taboos against unofficial music even now, I could imagine how alarming her son's musical heresies must have felt forty years earlier. "The Beatles were considered a really bad influence!" Liliana said. "If someone got hold of a record, Yuri and his friends were getting together and listening to the music. But the government didn't allow it, and if you were caught they could expel you from school or college."

Yuri had found some photographs of himself with a guitar. He looked impossibly young, hugging his instrument like an only friend. Liliana lit up as she saw the pictures. "He said to me that he wanted a guitar. First I enrolled him in the class to play the accordion. He did well but that wasn't for him. Then when he saw the Beatles with their guitars, he kept on saying, 'Mother, I want a guitar!' I didn't have much money and I couldn't just run into the shop. Then I looked at him, and I could see he just had to have this guitar." Yuri got his guitar, and his gang.

"This was my band when I was at school," he said, "the Blue Corals, we were for a while." He was looking at a picture of a group of youngsters slouched against a wall dragging on cigarettes and defying the camera with their guitars. "It was like a virus. You just hear it and you want to do it. You want to be like the Beatles; you've never seen them, but you want to be like them." Another picture, yellowed with age, showed a quartet of lads leaping off a wall brandishing guitars. Frozen in midair before they hit the ground, preserved in a permanent ecstasy of youth, the photo reminded me irresistibly of the Beatles' antics in *A Hard Day's Night* when everything was fresh and new. Looking at the photo, Yuri seemed to shed years. "You get together with your band, you play, and you're happy," he said.

For his mother, there were other memories. "It was all so loud! The whole house shook." She grew more animated as she acted out the drama of finding herself besieged in her little apartment with a rock 'n' roll band. "On the streets people would stop, young people

Yuri Pelyushonok's band, Minsk, 1960s.

would open the windows so they could hear. But neighbors from all the other flats would come and say, 'We can't get our baby to sleep with all this music! Can't you turn it off for ten minutes?'"

Yuri joined in with his own memories of those thunderous rehearsals in his mother's kitchen. "We used to play so loud that people who passed on buses—the windows of the bus closed, my apartment window closed—all the passengers were looking up at us." Liliana sighed. "What could I do? That's how he was growing up with Beatles music."

She bustled off into her kitchen to make yet more snacks for the visitor, and Yuri took a final look at the photographs with his band. He talked about the farcical attempts of the authorities to quarantine their kids from the Beatles virus: special scratching devices installed at the airports to wreck any smuggled records, clamping down on bands playing Beatles songs. "Official life was going on in its official way," he said. "But you have something in your heart, something secret—you don't let anyone touch it. There was a huge

gap between the kids and the rulers. It was a quiet revolution in our
brains."

On a raw morning with the ice cracking under our feet to make
mucky puddles, we plodded through a wilderness of rusting sheds.
On the outskirts of Minsk, the place looked more like a Latin American shantytown than an outpost of Daddy's utopia. It was weirdly
quiet out here, as though a population had been rounded up and
deported.

Pelyushonok looked uncertain. "He said shed number eight-o-
one," he murmured, "but I don't see any numbers." It was a perfect
spot, I thought, to reignite my paranoia. Would a police helicopter
come roaring down on us with loudspeakers blaring orders for the
Beatles dissidents to surrender their seditious posters? Would rusty
doors burst open to reveal a hit squad waiting to grab the Western
infiltrator?

Then Yuri spotted some numbers daubed in whitewash on a wall.
"I think it's down here," he whispered. In the next alleyway, we saw
an open door and heard the sound of someone tinkering with machinery. And I was sure I could detect a faint hint of "Norwegian
Wood" drifting from a tinny speaker. We came upon a young guy,
bending over a derelict-looking bit of car engine. He looked up and
Yuri said, "Are you Igor?" The man stuck out an oily hand. We had
found our Beatles fan.

Igor's shed was an Aladdin's cave of Beatles stuff. Strewn around
amid the broken bits of long-dead cars he had preserved his relics.
Tacked to walls, tucked in behind old license plates was a hoard of
posters, the sleeve of a Russian "Hard Day's Night" bootleg, a "Let
It Be" calendar for 1990, a program from the Liverpool Cavern
Club. Everywhere there were battered photos of the Fab Four. Igor
gave a hopeful tap at his dead engine, and looked around his kingdom. "I feel good when I look at my collection," he said. "My friends
come here, and we play our guitars." The image of Igor and his pals

jammed into this shed to play the old songs, shut away from suspicious neighbors or Daddy's culture cops, was affecting and sad. I wondered how this quiet young man, who seemed entirely innocent of dissident bravura, had joined the Beatles opposition. "When I was young," he said, "my father played his guitar—always Beatles, Beatles, Beatles."

He scrambled over a ruined car door and found an audio cassette that he had propped on a shelf. "My father gave me this Beatles cassette for my seventh birthday," he said. He put it back in its place with the reverence of a curator in the Hermitage Museum handling a Fabergé egg.

We met up with Yuri Pelyushonok's old schoolmate Yakov in front of an imposing building not far from the center of Minsk. "This used to be our school," Yuri said, "now it's some kind of smart institute." They stood chatting together, and I suddenly recognized that this was where that photograph had been taken thirty years earlier—lads slouching against the wall with their cigarettes and guitars. I guessed the one with the risky long hair in the photo must be Yakov, and now he had become this cozy-looking man with a neat beard and an anorak.

As these middle-aged men swapped stories about their struggles to play rock 'n' roll in the early 1970s, the memories of cheeky rebellion and ingenious mischief seemed as seductive for them as the music. The scheming to outwit teachers and authorities clearly spiced their recollections with a tang of sedition that had kept the details fresh for them over the years.

"You had to register yourself as a Russian folk music ensemble," Yuri recalled. "Then you would have a place to rehearse at school where you wouldn't be chased by the militia." Electric guitars were reviled by the authorities as "an enemy of the Soviet people," and Yakov remembered that every group had to list two trumpeters and a balalaika player as well as guitarists. "We found a couple of drunks, and then told our teachers they would join the group soon when they'd finished playing at a funeral." "You had to think like a rat," Yuri said, "insisting that 'Jailhouse Rock' was a protest against political prisoners." To complete the Alice in Wonderland checklist of playing rock in seventies Belarus, groups had to provide a fire extinguisher to accompany each amplifier.

The battle to conjure up the elements of a rock 'n' roll band—the guitars, pickups, amplifiers, and loudspeakers—filled the days of Soviet kids like Yuri and Yakov, driving them to fantastic improvisations. Desperate teenagers sawed up their grannies' kitchen tables to make a guitar body, copied slavishly from precious photos of the Beatles with their instruments. It was understood by everyone that of course the Beatles had invented the electric guitar. "I made a neck for my guitar in the school workshop," Yuri said, "telling the teacher it was a handle for a shovel." Like Andrei Makarevich in Moscow, Yuri struggled to find a guitar pickup. Then he saw an article in *Young Technician* magazine. "Dear friend," it said, "a pickup is assembled in much the same way as a telephone receiver." Like Makarevich, he joined teenagers across the Soviet Union, ravenous as locusts, to get hold of the coils in their handsets. The crisis made the front page of *Pravda*. Pelyushonok remembered how he and his pals rang up telephone repair men, and then rushed in to harvest the newly replaced coils. "But we were always too late, and another group had plundered the coils before us."

Loudspeakers sprouting from every building to broadcast uplifting propaganda and martial music were hijacked to belt out rock 'n' roll. But Yuri recalls that his biggest challenge was to find strings for his new passion: his bass guitar, modeled on Paul McCartney's famous Höfner. Balalaika strings, cello strings, nothing would make the authentic sound. "Finally, we 'liberated' four strings from the school piano," Yuri confessed. "During the singing of 'The Internationale' at an assembly to protest against nuclear war the piano sounded a bit odd. But nobody spotted our crime until the piano

strings snapped my guitar like a mousetrap during a school dance."
His teacher screamed that he was a "vandal." Yuri smiled, transported
to another time. "Those memories warm my heart," he said.

We trudged through the melting snow to another anonymous
building. "This is School number Thirty-three," Yuri announced.
"Kids were taught Spanish here, and they always envied us because we
English students were learning the language of the Beatles. We told
them we only get taught 'British capitalism is an enemy of progress.'"
Yakov recalled how they would sit around with the kids from School
Thirty-three. "Someone would bring a little reel-to-reel tape recorder
and we'd put it in a milk can to amplify the Beatles music. We listened to 'Oh! Darling' and swapped stories about the Fab Four."

The elaborate fantasies spun by those kids in the schoolyard were
just a fragment of the vast web of dreams and longings inspired by the
Beatles across the Soviet Union. Fed by the repression of real information, and by dreams of fabulous riches enjoyed by the Cold War enemy, the stories multiplied and blossomed. Yuri recalled, "One of us
would tell how the Queen of England had given John Lennon a
golden car. Someone else would insist it was silver, not gold. Pure gold
would make it too heavy for John to escape his fans."

Yuri and Yakov looked across the frozen schoolyard and told me a
story. It was their version of the "secret concert" myth, the fantasy
about how their heroes had once touched down near them, close but
tantalizingly just out of reach. It seemed to encapsulate every Soviet
kid's yearnings about the Beatles, and I had heard versions of the story
wherever I went. I remembered Andrei Makarevich's school friend
who waited in the snow for a glimpse of John Lennon; and there was
Vladimir Matietsky's chum who saw Lennon buying bread on Gorky
Street. Standing in the old schoolyard, Yuri and Yakov seemed transported to that time when the Beatles lit up their lives and sent them
on an adventure.

"We were sure they had landed here once on their way to

Japan—on some secret airfield not far from Minsk," Yuri said. "And as the story was passed around, we told each other that the Beatles had stepped onto the plane's wing to play an impromptu concert." Yakov took up the story. "This girl Tanka had lots of photos of the Beatles, terrible copies with stripy stains running down them. We decided that meant that the Beatles traveled in cages for their protection, so we reckoned they would be flying on a military plane." Yuri, Yakov, Tanka, and another girl, Marienka, decided they would try to find the place where the Beatles had landed. The crazy plan to smuggle their way into a military base to pursue a schoolyard fantasy seems like childish romp, but in paranoid Belarus it was—and still would be—very dangerous.

They trekked out to the air base, crawled under the fence, and found themselves confronted by a young soldier with a Kalashnikov. The dialogue between the frightened kids and the bewildered recruit is a poignant snapshot of how the Beatles had become a myth shared by an entire generation. "We put our hands in the air and pleaded with the soldier, 'Don't shoot us, we're your own people! We just wanted to see where the Beatles landed.'" The recruit looked at them with scorn. "The Beatles didn't land here," he said. "Everyone knows they landed in Leningrad. You should be ashamed of not knowing that!"

The tower block appeared unchanged since the Khrushchev era, dumped down on the bare earth fifty years earlier, gray and featureless as a filing cabinet. I trudged up five flights of stairs with Yuri, Yakov, and a couple of friends. The apartment belonged to Tolik, a quiet man built like a bull, who we found sitting on a sagging sofa, strumming a guitar. I could just recognize him as one of those kids in Yuri's photo, and I remembered that Tolik had once been a guitar hero, a boy who could play anything, the star of Yuri's band. He was nicknamed Jimi, after Hendrix.

Pelyushonok had brought me to Tolik's apartment for a reunion of their band, getting together for the first time in more than thirty years. He had managed to recruit his two friends from the original group—Tolik and Yakov—and they were immediately swapping stories about the old days.

Yuri had told me about the bizarre rituals of forming a "Vocal Instrumental Ensemble" in 1970s Belarus. It was the story of a forced marriage between rock 'n' roll and Soviet bureaucracy. "First of all," he said, "we had to have 'a roof'—an official institution to provide patronage and security." The roof could be a collective farm, a factory, a school, or a military unit. Without your roof, you would have nowhere to rehearse, you couldn't get hold of any decent equipment, and you couldn't even play at a wedding without risking a fine for making "unearned income." Yuri and Tolik were lucky. They were both members of the Belarus youth fencing team, and they found their roof with the Institute of Physical Education.

The next hurdle for their new "ensemble" was to choose safe songs. It was never easy to know which Western groups were banned, along with their songs. Chicago were taboo because their name suggested gangsters and sedition; the Rolling Stones were approved because Marx had said that cobblestones were weapons of the proletariat. The official "song police" could sometimes be pacified by claiming that a song's lyrics were protests against Western evils. "Can't Buy Me Love" was presented as a comment on prostitution in the decadent West, while "Taxman" was a protest against the exploitation of taxi drivers by the Cold War enemy.

But there were still dangerous trip wires for groups playing music "foreign to the ideology of the Soviet Union." Like every band, they were required to take part in official competitions, organized by the Komsomol Central Committee. Playing rock 'n' roll was strictly taboo at the Komsomol contests, and casting around for something safe, on one occasion they almost got into real trouble. Pelyushonok announced "an American anti-NATO song," and without realizing its significance, the band launched into "The Battle Hymn of the

Republic." Within a few seconds, the police ordered them off the stage. "We were lucky not to be charged with ideological sabotage," Yuri said.

As the group gained confidence, they got louder. They almost caused a riot playing "Dizzy, Miss Lizzy" at an army cultural center, and their notoriety got them an invitation in 1977 to play at a major festival in the Armenian capital, Yerevan. It was the first-ever rock gathering in the U.S.S.R., and it was the climactic moment in the story of Yuri's band. It was also the end of the road for Yuri, Yakov, and Tolik.

They got home to discover the dean of their institute, who had always secured their roof, had been replaced by an ex–prison guard. The new dean forbade the group from "dancing to the tune of the West" and confiscated all their gear. When he commissioned a thug with an axe to chop up their guitars, Tolik tried to hit him. The final act was a "comradely court," held in the largest auditorium at the physical education institute. The "Battle Hymn" incident was raised in evidence—"a disgraceful anti-Soviet episode"—together with the riotous army concert. The "orgy in Yerevan" did not escape the new dean. Before the inevitable verdict was announced, Yuri and Tolik ran to the music store to check out some new guitar strings. They were sent off to the army.

And now, more than three decades on, these middle-aged men were meeting up again to play together one last time. Yuri slumped contentedly over the end of the sofa with his guitar, watching Yakov tapping away on his improvised drum, an empty plastic bottle. "Nobody changed too much—except for me," Yuri said. "The last time we played was in 1978. Now Tolik grabbed a guitar, I grabbed guitar, Yakov grabbed this empty canister, and we created this song. And it was quite amazing . . . as if we went for a smoke in 1978, and then we came back, just fifteen minutes later."

Yuri's song, sweet and tuneful, recalled those days when Soviet kids were hungry to make rock 'n' roll.

In the yard between the flats, by the light of the windows,
With cheap guitars remade for Rock,
Infected by the Beatles, we tune up
Playing to the whole street.
If you play your guitar through an amp,
Or through a little radio,
You can play something like Rock
And make a drum from an old bottle.
Hey, man! Don't wake people in those Khrushchev-era flats.
They won't dig your guitar here.
I made myself a guitar of wood,
I made a pickup from a phone.
But it collapsed from the tension
When I played my favorite song.
Hey, man! Don't wake people in those Khrushchev-era flats
With your songs and your Oh yeah chorus.

In July 1991, after a year of voyages to Africa as a ship's doctor, Yuri Pelyushonok was looking forward to some leave at home in Minsk. Then he got a phone call from Zheka, an old flame who used to sing with his band, and was now working in television. The call triggered a rush of events that were to invade Yuri's life and bring his obsession with the Beatles to a crisis. It was also the start of a drama that became a perfect tragicomic demonstration of the Soviet state's paranoia about the Beatles.

Zheka had a startling proposal. "With perestroika and all that, we can do anything, and I've suggested a program about the Beatles. I want you to be the host." Yuri was stunned by the responsibility of making the first-ever television program about the Beatles to be broadcast in the Soviet Union. He was only too aware that millions of fans would be waiting to pounce on any minor error or omission, ready to savage him for failing in his sacred task. He also knew the program would attract the attention of nervous TV bosses and their unpredictable political masters. He needed someone to share the burden.

Yuri found Volodya Sevitsky living in the basement of a school where he was a teacher. Sevitsky said that the Beatles had changed his life, inspiring him to learn English and to write songs. In the basement, an old military shooting gallery, he had constructed a refuge from the cultural commissars where he could study the Beatles and write his own music. He also offered a safe haven for kids to sing Beatles songs, away from official disapproval. When Yuri invited Volodya to join him in hosting the TV show, he insisted he couldn't measure up to the responsibility. Yuri asked him the name of Paul McCartney's dog. He answered instantly, "Martha." Yuri had his man.

Over the next few hours, Yuri rushed to put together the materials for the program. From his precious Beatles collection, assembled during his voyages to the West, he gathered albums, photographs, a Fab Four calendar. He was upset that he couldn't find his "little sliver," a fragment from the stage where the Beatles had played in Amsterdam.

The morning of the broadcast was a mix of nightmare and farce for Yuri. He dug out his suit, a white shirt, and a tie for the big occasion. But on the drive to the studio, his car kept breaking down, and trying to put it right, he spattered oil on his shirt and trousers. He had to go back home and change, and he arrived at the studio with less than a minute before the broadcast—to find that the recording was delayed for two hours.

At last they were called to the studio. "A historic moment," Yuri said, and Volodya took a deep breath. "Michelle" was playing from Yuri's old cassette player as they walked into the studio, and he was almost overwhelmed by the thought of all the people who had risked their education, their careers, and their happiness for the Beatles. He remembered a girl student from Minsk who had written an open letter saying: "In this filth we call a Socialist society, the

Beatles are the only thing that helps me to survive." Surely she should be presenting this program?

And then Volodya was introducing "Thirty Minutes with the Beatles," saying, "Hello dear friends, we're here with you today to talk about the work of some outstanding musicians." The recording rolled on, Yuri exploring the Beatles phenomenon, Volodya introducing videos and films and songs. As they came to an end, Volodya launched into a lament that while the rest of the world had been able to read about the Beatles and discuss their music for decades, in the Soviet Union they were still unacknowledged. Then he realized he was straying into dangerous territory and ended by bowing to "the talent and genius of the Beatles."

When it was over, they waited for Zheka, who was meeting the station bosses. As time passed, Yuri suspected there was a problem, and when she arrived she looked tense. She slipped him a box as he was leaving and asked him to keep it safe.

Final editing of the program was set for a month later, August 20, 1991. On August 19, Yuri switched on his TV to discover there were tanks on the streets of Moscow. He watched the dismaying news of the coup of hard-liners, determined to turn back the clock and abandon Gorbachev's reforms. At noon, Volodya called to tell him that the TV bosses had ordered the master tape of "Thirty Minutes with the Beatles" to be wiped. Yuri scrambled to find the box Zheka had given him. Inside, he found a copy of their program.

Within three days, the coup had collapsed. But the euphoria was short-lived, and "Thirty Minutes with the Beatles" was in limbo. The master tape had been wiped, and Yuri's cassette was all that remained. In a frantic scramble, Zheka managed to copy the cassette back onto the wiped master. But the saga wasn't over yet. The edit still had to be completed, and for three months Yuri waited for news. Finally the bosses announced that they wanted a new program, more critical of the Beatles.

Yuri was sure that "Thirty Minutes with the Beatles" would never be seen. Then, as he was about to head off for another voyage, his phone rang. The long-delayed editing of the original program was scheduled for that evening. Only later did Yuri understand what had happened. It emerged that Zheka and five other TV people had submitted their resignations over the cancelation of the Beatles program. That evening, there was news that the new Russian president, Boris Yeltsin, was about to visit Belarus. Fearing an embarrassing public rebellion by their staff, the TV bosses decided to get the program edited and broadcast as soon as possible. Unwisely, they decided to announce the broadcast. The TV station was besieged with questions from fans and worried officials. In the final two hours before the transmission, the frantic station manager changed his mind four times. At last, he gave the go-ahead and then fled.

"Thirty Minutes with the Beatles" was finally broadcast in early December 1991. I watched the copy of the tape with Yuri and Volodya, and it was obvious that almost twenty years later the program was still fresh for them. "I was really nervous," Volodya said. "I was just a school teacher. But it was a chance at last to talk to a huge audience about the Beatles music. People were amazed that it was possible." "It was a miracle," Yuri said. "There was a lot of joy when people watched it. I had the feeling not that the state lost, but we won." There were thousands of letters and phone calls asking for a repeat, but that was not to be. Hours after the broadcast, the master tape was destroyed—forever.

And just days later, at a forest hunting lodge in Belarus, the Soviet leaders put an end to the U.S.S.R.

Returning now to Minsk for a few days after making a new life in Canada over the past fifteen years, Yuri Pelyshonok still had a final surprise in store. Near the city center, we found the Beatles Café. He stared at the place as though he had seen a mirage. From outside, it looked about as rock 'n' roll as a tax office. But the canopy over the door boldly featured the Fab Four, 1964 vintage, decorated with their autographs. Yuri murmured, "unbelievable."

We went in along a corridor lined with Beatles icons—photos, paintings, albums—and came to a stylish bar and bistro. It could have been a hangout for affluent kids in Manchester. Yuri sat at a table under a giant blowup of the *Abbey Road* cover where the Fab Four marched over the street crossing one more time. Every wall and alcove was hung with Beatles stuff. "I've never seen some of these things," Yuri said. "I'm impressed." The movie of *A Hard Day's Night* played on a screen dubbed into German, and he walked across to look at a display of vintage tape recorders and radios. From the turntable of a sad little record player, he picked up a seven-inch disk with the Soviet label Melodiya. "'Lady Madonna,'" he read, "performed by a Vocal Instrumental Group." He smiled and shook his head.

Next to the bar, we found a wall crowded with comments written by visitors: BEATLES IS LOVE, BEATLES FOREVER. "This place would have been closed in a day when I was here," Yuri said, "if you were lucky." He wanted to add a comment. He wrote IN MY TIME, IT WOULD BE IMPOSSIBLE.

So it seemed that at last, after the decades when the state determined that the Beatles were as dangerous as Chernobyl, the war against the Fab Four had reached a weary compromise. The hotel pianist could play "Hey Jude," the Beatles Café could put up its posters. Could it be that Daddy had been a secret fan from the start?

25

In Red Square, it's Moscow Day 2011, and a toy train full of waving kids trundles across the cobbles where missile squadrons used to parade in front of the grim-faced Soviet leaders. Today, President Dmitry Medvedev enjoys the warm sunshine of a September morning, laughing with the leader of the Russian Orthodox Church. The spectacle of military might has been replaced by a Europop song and dance festival, staged for television and choreographed to attract tourists and new business.

Moscow Day is a kaleidoscope of the new Russia. A young soldier with a Beatles haircut belts out a disco ballad; a blonde pop diva cruises past in a blue Cadillac with tail fins as extravagant as her hairdo; a big-voiced tenor in a tuxedo shares a rock anthem with a bulky soprano; a formation of jets roars over Red Square, decorating the sky with smoke trails of blue, white, and red to celebrate Russia's national flag.

A flutter of ballet dancers in white tutus struggles to stay poised on the rough cobbles, and I see that they've swapped their ballet shoes for chunky sneakers. It feels like a metaphor for the uneasy grafting of international pop culture onto Russian traditions, and I guess I'm looking at some of the consequences of the Beatles revolution in the Soviet Union. It's not always a comfortable spectacle.

I thought back to how I felt about Red Square when I had first come here twenty-five years earlier. Walking into that huge space at midnight with snow falling, it had made me shiver—and not just because of the fierce cold. For a child of the Cold War, being in this place brought me face to face with the fearsome power that had threatened to "bury" me—in Mr. Krushchev's chilling phrase. Being here had for me the unreality of a dream, and the grip of a nightmare. Red Square was alarming, but it was also gorgeous. The spectacular stage where whole armies could march under the blood-red Kremlin walls, past the spooky mausoleum where the embalmed Lenin still brooded over his fraying revolution, was subverted by the absurd pantomime backdrop of Saint Basil's cathedral at the head of the square. The Arabian Nights fantasy of painted domes and decorated walls felt at once joyous and cruel, feeding my jumble of reactions on that first evening. It was thrilling and scary and unforgettable.

And now Moscow Day had tamed Red Square, shrinking it behind advertising hoardings and serving it up as tacky spectacle. The square was for hire, a background for commercials, a location for balloon festivals, overlooked by the windows of the great GUM department store with displays for Gucci and Vuitton and Prada. It almost made me sentimental for the old GUM as I'd first seen it in the 1980s. Back then, the window displays on Red Square had reminded me of the shops in my Yorkshire town just after the Second World War, a meager selection of frumpy dresses and plastic shoes. Even austerity Yorkshire would have rejected the dusty jars of bottled cucumbers that were a feature of GUM's window displays in the eighties. Now the glut of Western luxury baubles glowing in the Red Square windows had a hard, mocking glitter. I studied a Vuitton bag, as advertised by Mikhail Gorbachev, and then noticed that Lenin's tomb was reflected in the shop window.

I left the square behind me, feeling dejected and conflicted. Wasn't this what we hoped the end of the Cold War would bring—the messy stuff of democracy, for better or worse? I surely wasn't yearning for the ugly desperations of Soviet Moscow, but did it have to turn into this?

I walked away from Red Square and Moscow Day, negotiating a tangle of police barricades. It was a reminder that the Beatles generation had not swept away Russian admiration for a strong leader. Vladimir Putin's authoritarian rule, hounding journalists and locking up opponents, together with his tendency to be photographed riding a horse while flaunting a macho bare chest, suggested that the hippie message of "All You Need Is Love" was out of style in the Kremlin of the twenty-first century.

I went searching for a man sent by Art Troitsky to drive me to his dacha in the country outside Moscow. Art had told me he'd fallen out of love with the city, and was spending much of his time at the dacha now. "You should hook up with Arseny. He's a fan of mine, and he has a car." I could see him now, waving through the crowds, a fresh-faced young man with the crimped hair of a 1940s film star and a big smile.

"What do you say about Deep Purple?" Arseny asked as we headed out through the torrent of traffic. The Beatles' "Help" was playing on the car's CD player. It was obviously a gesture to me, as Art had told him about my Beatles history. For Arseny this was an invitation to quiz me ceaselessly about my rock 'n' roll enthusiasms. "What do you say about Led Zeppelin? What do you say about Black Sabbath?" As I knew almost nothing about Arseny's favorite bands, it was becoming a somewhat sterile conversation. But he was undeterred. He moved on to his favorite books—unknown to me—and then to his favorite Korean slasher movies—not an enthusiasm I could share, since Tom and Jerry cartoons are a bit too violent for my taste. Nothing dented Arseny's remorseless affability, or stemmed his interrogations. Convinced now that I was an irretrievable British philistine, Arseny fell back on being Troitsky's fan and enthused for a while about his hero. He moved on to his mother, who had once been a hippie and loved heavy metal, but of course loved the Beatles as well. We seemed to be lost in the interminable outskirts of Moscow.

It was a very long journey. Beyond the wilderness of shopping outlets, through small featureless towns, we came at last to Dacha-land. Ugly new houses, bloated and garish, littered the forests along the road. "Cottagezhe," I remembered they were called, in weird homage to some fantasy of an English village. We came over a hill, and a big sign in English announced SUNNYDALE DACHA PROJECT. Mercifully this didn't seem to be where Russia's rebellious rock guru was hanging out. We drove on. "What do you say about Pearl Jam?"

The birch trees hid most of the new houses out here, but Troitsky's pagoda was unmissable. Inspired, he said, by a nearby water tower, the multistory house soared into the trees. He came to meet me at the gate, and I thought he looked tired. "Come in and check out my new slacker's paradise," he said.

The first thing I spotted in the spacious living room was a cushion embroidered with the Beatles in Sergeant Pepper costumes. It looked perfectly at home in Art's hippie pad. As his new wife, Vera, cooked lunch, and his Scottie dog, Churchill, scampered around, he told me how this place was now the center of his life. "Moscow is so dirty and polluted, and the traffic is so horrible," he said, "so I work out here and try to stay away from the city as much as possible." It was a surprising shift of focus for this most urban of men, but as we talked it emerged there was more to his change of life. "I'm tangled up in a bunch of legal problems," he told me, "five separate cases at the moment." One involved a rock star who Troitsky had called the "trained poodle" of a Kremlin apparatchik. "I wouldn't be offended to be called Che Guevara's trained poodle," Art said. "Poodles are kind, intelligent dogs." He told me that he had also upset some powerful people by comments on his radio program, and now he felt the salvo of legal attacks might be orchestrated from the Kremlin. The freewheeling style of the Gorbachev years was no longer welcome, and he had the feeling he was being hounded for the decades of outspoken broadcasts and articles. "All this is affecting my health," Art said, "and now I have a really painful back problem. I'm treating it with leeches."

The quiet life in the country dacha with the leeches and the birch trees seemed to be more in tune with his post–rock 'n' roll passions. We tucked into Vera's delicious joint of lamb, and Art talked about how he was no longer interested in Britain, where I had first met him more than twenty years before. "I prefer America now, but I hate the American work ethic," he said. "These days I have a fondness for the slacker society of the old Soviet Union." Vera came in carrying their new baby and I had a feeling that the domestic cameo was drawing a line under Art's time as a renegade troublemaker. It seemed that for him the Russian rock revolution inspired by the Beatles was growing old. We talked about the current Russian rock scene, and Art said the veteran band Time Machine had become a state institution. "In fact," he said, "their leader, Andrei Makarevich, is now a cultural adviser to President Medvedev."

So Makarevich the seditious trailblazer of Soviet rock, a man whose life had been transformed by the Beatles, an underground hero who had spent years dodging the attentions of the state, had mellowed into a presidential adviser. I recalled how, in a confrontation with Art Troitsky thirty years earlier, Makarevich had insisted that the state was moving toward him. Now I wondered if there were any real victors in the fifty-year war between the Kremlin and rock 'n' roll. Perhaps both sides had settled for an exhausted stalemate— and both sides had been reshaped by the struggle.

We went for a walk up the lane, and Troitsky wanted to show me a view. We passed through a wood and came to a break in the trees where a rural panorama opened up. "See—this is a perfect Russian scene," he said, "the church, the river, the forest." It was as though he was becoming one of those aristocrats in an eighteenth-century

English painting, where the artist has been commissioned to celebrate the ownership of the landscape his patron stands on. Churchill the dog dashed around, and Vera trundled the pram. Art breathed in good Russian air, and looked content.

But it seemed he had preserved his interest in championing strange new bands. Arseny drove us back into Moscow, his interrogations mercifully muted now. Troitsky wanted me to hear his latest discovery, a Finnish band called Ville Leinonen. They were playing at the Chinatown Café, a place I remembered from a previous visit as a location for Art's birthday party. I recalled it as a gloomy warren, reminiscent of the Liverpool Cavern Club. Now it was a stylish bistro, with white umbrellas hanging from the ceiling. Troitsky introduced me to the band with my well-worn credentials as "the man who made the first film with the Beatles," and it surprised me all over again how the Fab Four connection went through these twentysomething rockers from Helsinki like an electric shock—though they can't have been born when the Beatles broke up.

They were really good, I thought, fresh and melodic and witty. They did a song that Troitsky said was a parody of Julio Iglesias, but the references eluded me. At one point they brought a blonde doll dressed in Lurex onto the stage, and it sang along with the band. Art looked like he was in for a long evening of talking and drinking, so I said my good-byes. As I was leaving the club, I spotted a poster announcing upcoming gigs. The Plastic People of the Universe were due in a couple of weeks, "presented," the poster said, "by Artemy Troitsky." Inevitable, I thought, that Troitsky would be hosting the seditious old rockers from Prague. I was sorry I'd miss them.

I was going to meet up with Art again in Vladivostok in a few days, four thousand miles to the east on the farthest edge of Russia. He had fixed for me to screen some of my music films at a festival there, as well as exhibiting a collection of photos I had taken of the Beatles and other classic rockers in the early 1960s. Before I left the club, he gave me a phone number for someone I'd been wanting to

meet for ages—a pioneer Soviet-era rock star and Beatles disciple
called Alexander Gradsky. I had been puzzled about why Troitsky
had seemed reluctant to make the introduction, but I had finally
pushed him for Gradsky's number, and at last he handed it over with
a shake of his head. "We're enemies now," Art said, "but you should
meet him."

I walked up the Moscow street where the Stilyagi used to parade in
the 1950s. Their old "Broadway" was now a string of expensive bou-
tiques and perfume outlets. It was hard to imagine those rebellious
kids braving outraged citizens on these sidewalks, which had become a kind of catwalk for affluent young women. Dodging the
flood of BMWs and Mercedes, I found the alleyway I was looking
for. I rang a bell on an unmarked steel door. After a couple of minutes, it swung open and a big man with a mass of gray hair down to
his shoulders stepped out. He saw me and waved. "Gradsky," he said.

In the hallway of his apartment, I couldn't miss the signed photographs of Gradsky with Putin, and Gradsky with Medvedev. I remembered that one of Troitsky's quarrels with him had been that he
was too close to Russia's political bosses, and they'd had some kind
of public row in a radio studio over that. We moved into a vast
kitchen, lined with glass-fronted cabinets. Gradsky's two Yorkshire
terriers, Elizabeth and Charles, skittered round our feet, and recalling Troitsky's dog Churchill, I wondered why Moscow's rock aris-
tocracy had adopted English Establishment names for their pets.

We settled down to talk at a long table, and Gradsky began by
telling me about the powerful connections that had first introduced
him to the Beatles. "My uncle was a dancer with the Moiseyev dance
troop, and he often traveled abroad. He brought me records from the
West, and I started copying Elvis Presley and the Everly Brothers. In
1960, I was just twelve when I got on a stage at Moscow University
and persuaded a visiting Polish group, the Cockroaches, to let me
sing with them." Gradsky reckoned this may have been the first-ever

rock concert in the Soviet Union. "When I was thirteen," he said, "I even made a record at one of the recording booths on Gorky Street." I relished the thought that the first-ever rock record in the Soviet Union had been made in one of those streetside booths set up to preserve fond messages from homesick soldiers.

In 1963, Gradsky's well-traveled uncle brought him the *Meet the Beatles* album. Like everyone I met from the Beatles generation, he was transfixed. "I went into a state of shock," he told me. "Everything except the Beatles became pointless." He crossed himself quickly, and the gesture looked almost apologetic.

Gradsky was a trained musician, a violinist and a singer with a three-octave range, learning to sing Schubert. But the Beatles defied his musical education. "I don't understand how they did it," he said, shaking his mane of hair. Like so many Beatles devotees, he began to compile his own book of lyrics. But his real passion was to try to be a Beatle. In 1965, with the grandson of Nobel Prize–winning novelist Mikhail Sholokhov, he put together his first group, the Slavs. It was yet another story of how the sons of privilege pioneered rock in the U.S.S.R. The Slavs were one of the earliest groups in Moscow, and in the mid-sixties they quickly became Moscow's top band.

The Slavs played at dances in colleges and schools, but Gradsky told me that the first "beat" concert in a hall with a stage was in 1966, improbably at the Ministry of Foreign Affairs. "The bands and their audiences all tried to look like the Beatles," he said. By the late sixties, he could list more than two hundred unofficial rock bands playing in Moscow. With names like Little Red Demons, Midnight Carousers, Cramps, and Bald Spots, they stood defiantly outside the boundaries of the state's Komsomol youth organization. "Hundreds of unofficial rock clubs sprung up," Gradsky said, "where young hustlers with a tape recorder and a sound system played rock music in borrowed rooms packed with sweating kids. They charged a small entrance fee, which was risky, but the odd arrest didn't cure the rock epidemic." Some bolder promoters hired local bands to play live, making thousands of rubles in a single evening—more than a worker could earn in months. "There were constant raids by Komsomol vigilantes, and equipment was regularly confiscated," Gradsky said. "Organizers were imprisoned. But rock was resistant."

Armed with his classical training, Alexander Gradsky was determined to become more adventurous. With his new band, the Jesters, he devised a rock opera based on nursery rhymes. Playing twelve instruments, he became one of the first rock musicians to sing his own songs in Russian and established a following with his blending of rock with folk-influenced Russian bard music. He became notorious for his flamboyant onstage antics, and Gradsky told me he reckoned the Jesters were Russia's first punk band. "We taught people to leave their chairs—and then we took them from a dance party to the concert hall."

"I think my real breakthrough," Gradsky said, "was doing the soundtrack for Andrei Konchalovsky's movie *Romance for Lovers* in 1973. I wrote and performed all the male vocals, and it gave me a huge audience across the Soviet Union." From the mid-seventies, he toured the country regularly, becoming a focus of the gathering Russian rock movement. "I spotted the potential of Andrei Makarevich and Time Machine very early," he said, and it struck me how incestuous the rock scene was in those years. From that point Gradsky became a very particular kind of Soviet music star, performing across a range of genres from rock to opera, traveling the world, giving a concert at Carnegie Hall, and recording with Western stars such as Liza Minnelli, John Denver, and Elton John. To confirm Gradsky's position as a grandee of Russian music, in 2000 President Putin presented him with a medal as People's Artist of Russia.

He played me some of his CDs, and it gave me a new understanding of how porous the identity of Russian rock has always been, blurring the lines between dramatic ballads, dreamy poetic laments, gritty folk songs, and soaring rock anthems. With his rich operatic tenor voice, Gradsky moved effortlessly between Freddie Mercury, Placido

Domingo, and Paul McCartney. His impeccable diction also emphasized how essential the lyrics have always been in Russian pop music. His CDs helped me to realize how "beat music" in Russia always remained more open to classical influences than in the West where, for true rock fans, the dividing line was as uncrossable as the Berlin Wall. It was one reason why Beatles ballads with their sighing violins and cellos, songs like "Michelle," "Yesterday," and "Eleanor Rigby," were embraced by millions of Soviet fans.

Finally, Gradsky played me a video of a recent concert at the Great Hall of the Moscow Conservatory. A florid conductor in a white tuxedo flourished his baton to command a huge orchestra, and Gradsky powered into a duet version of the Beatles' "Yesterday," trading the lyrics in English with a dramatic diva. It was a world away from Art Troitsky's smoky clubs and edgy rock dissidents and it wasn't hard to see how Art could have fallen out with Gradsky. "Troitsky thinks we are boring conservatives here in Moscow, while his friends in Saint Petersburg are poets." Then he added, "Poets— with their drugs and alcohol and talk." Gradsky laughed as he talked about a TV program that had brought together a group of Russian rock royalty. "They immediately began to argue, of course, and the thing almost ended in a fight."

But for all their disagreements, Alexander Gradsky and Art Troitsky shared their certainty about the impact of the Beatles in the Soviet Union. "Yes, yes, yes," Gradsky insisted, "the Beatles changed the Soviet Union. The Kremlin lost the Beatles generation, and then they lost the country."

I went back to Stas Namin's club in Gorky Park where I had started my search for the Beatles generation more than twenty years earlier. On a sunny afternoon, the place that had looked so down at heel in the winter of 1988 now appeared transformed. New paint and stylish lighting declared that the Stas Namin Center was very much in business. Gradsky had told me that he'd said to Stas years earlier,

"Why play? Why sing? You're a great organizer!" It seemed Namin had taken his advice. A plaque announced the list of companies and organizations in the Stas Namin orbit, SNC Holdings. It included a recording center, a production center, a concert agency, a model agency and fashion theater, a record company, an art gallery, a radio station, a magazine, and a TV production company. Namin had clearly become a mogul, though the band he had played for me back in 1988, Gorky Park, appeared to have become extinct.

Stas was more grizzled but as affable and unstoppable as ever in a T-shirt decorated with an evolutionary cartoon: from ape through Neanderthal to rock band, with the words SOMETHING WENT TERRIBLY WRONG. He offered me a roll call of celebrity names who had visited his center—Arnold Schwarzenegger, Frank Zappa, Pink Floyd—and told me he had been to Cuba with a Russian-American delegation including Leonardo Di Caprio. "But I'd love for you to see something we're rehearsing right now in my theater."

A dozen youngsters were milling about on the stage while a band ran through a spirited version of "All You Need Is Love." We sat in the stalls, and Namin told me about the show. "It's a musical I've written about how the Beatles helped to destroy the Soviet Union, and it's really based on my own experiences back in the sixties."

The cast began to rehearse a scene, and Stas whispered an outline of what was going on. "A group of students who love the Beatles have got together in secret to sing some of their songs when the head of military training bursts in and orders them to stop singing forbidden music." I watched as the scene played out between the bullying commissar and the protesting students, and the simple fable with its cartoon characters still got to me. The reenactment of the officious brutality handed out to a bunch of kids for singing songs felt all too convincing, and it reminded me of that KGB squad who had gone to Sasha Lipnitsky's dacha to snuff out his little concert. The surreal stupidity of the assault on pop music was somehow perfectly encapsulated in this modest fantasy. "I'll kick you all out into the subways," the commissar was ranting. "This is music about love," a student was protesting, "music that will change the world!"

Then the scene became a fairy tale. The students persuaded the commissar to listen as they sang the Beatles' "Because." Inevitably, he was charmed and won over, going on his way to the accompaniment of "All You Need Is Love." Only in fairy land.

After the rehearsal, Namin wanted me to see a video. "This is another thing we're doing at the center," he said, "the Beatles in India concert." He told me he was, like all good hippies, a devotee of George Harrison and his passion for Indian spiritualism. He had offered his theater in Gorky Park to the Moscow Krishna Temple for a concert of Beatles music.

He slipped in a CD and I watched an extraordinary spectacle. A man in a shimmering blue turban and Indian sherwani jacket was performing George's "Here Comes the Sun." The song had been refashioned as a swaying hypnotic anthem, punctuated by cries and invocations, but the real shock was the troupe of dancers swarming around the singer. Women in searing pinks and greens, with fantastic headdresses modeled on the spires of Indian temples, gyrated; a man with a lion-head mask and a waistcoat decorated with exotic birds, yellow and blue and pink, twirled ceremonial swords, which flashed in the pale Moscow sunshine.

"Why don't you go and talk to Yuri Parshikov at the Vedic Cultural Center?" Namin suggested. "He's the Hare Krishna guy who arranged the Indian Beatles concert here." I usually cross the street to avoid Hare Krishna processions, and I've always found their insistent brand of chanting uncomfortable and cloying. I'm an inveterate rationalist and skeptic, so I was surprised to find myself touched by the joyous performance I had just been watching on the video. "That would be interesting," I said. ˙

I trekked out into the Moscow suburbs, losing my way in a tangle of muddy lanes. Finally, I found the Vedic center, a featureless modern building that offered no hint of transcendence. Yuri was a cheerful, round-faced young man with circular spectacles, and he welcomed me with a vegetarian Krishna cake. I thought it tasted like balsa wood and strawberry jam.

We chatted in front of the shrine, a bizarre clutter of gods and cows and old gurus. "The Beatles really gave humanity something," Yuri said. "They changed people to look for something higher—not to live life like a vegetable." He said he was going to India soon for his annual visit to the birthplace of Krishna—"just chanting the holy names and wandering around." It sounded wonderfully relaxing, a bit like Art Troitsky's dream of slacker's nirvana. I liked this gentle man, even though his tangle of gods and gurus eluded me. And he said something about the Beatles that I hadn't heard on my travels, and it seemed right. "Their music was filled with some kind of fresh-ness, maybe something childish. An open heart."

26

All along the road into Vladivostok, the trees were shrouded in gray dust. A vast road-building scheme went on for mile after mile, turning the landscape into a dead wilderness, which reminded me of images beamed back from the surface of Mars. Maybe that had to do with my sense of having fallen off the edge of the planet arriving here at the farthest limit of Russia, seven times zones east of Moscow. I had wanted to see Vladivostok for years because it had always seemed so impossibly remote, out here on the edge of the Sea of Japan, beyond North Korea, beyond Beijing. Of course that was the pull of the place, that sense of existing on the margins of imagination. I remembered the old maps where medieval cartographers marked an unknown land with the warning "Here be dragons." And now I had arrived at last in Vladivostok, where the warning "Here be tigers" was a reality. I had heard that a tiger had been spotted not long ago prowling through the outskirts of the city, wandering in from the endless forests of Primorye. Wild tigers? Stalinist gulags? Gigantic nuclear tests? This place had it all.

I peered through the brown curtains of the ancient Soviet bus. No sign of tigers—just more Martian wilderness scattered with earth-moving machines, tractors and diggers standing idle while gangs of workmen sat around smoking. It was as though out here on the edge of everything, the huge country had finally exhausted itself.

I had come to Vladivostok to find if there was anyone left of the Soviet Beatles generation here, four thousand miles from Saint Petersburg—from where Kolya Vasin had felt he could almost see Liverpool. Was there anyone who still remembered and cared? I knew the city had been a closed military base until the 1990s, one of a scatter of places across the Soviet Union sealed off from the outside world for decades by Stalin's paranoia and by military secrecy. Nuclear bases and bomb factories had always been prime candidates for lockdown, usually shut away behind sinister science-fiction names like Arzamas 16 or Chelyabinsk 45. As "non-places," they never appeared on maps or railway timetables. Still, for the insulated citizens of the closed cities, there were compensations. I had seen something of those privileges when I filmed with Vladimir Pozner inside Russia's biggest missile base, near Saratov on the Volga. The city of Svetly was shut away behind checkpoints and barbed wire; but life was dramatically better than in the ramshackle village just outside the fence. The villagers of Tatishchevo lived in crumbling wooden shacks and pumped their water from muddy wells. Inside the base was an alternative universe where people enjoyed comfortable apartments and schools that would have been envied in Moscow. We filmed a naming celebration for new babies, with twirling teenage ballroom dancers and champagne.

Vladivostok earned its closed status as headquarters of the Russian Pacific Fleet, based in the city's vast Golden Horn Bay. When Russia grabbed the place more than a century ago, ahead of envious Western powers, it was claimed that the bay could shelter all of Europe's navies. Everything about the city felt exotic, the ultimate destination in Russia's Wild East. In the 1960s, when the Beatles generation on the other edge of Russia were beginning to tune in, it was still a two- or three-week rail journey from Moscow to Vladivo-stok on the Trans-Siberian Railway. I wanted to know if the Beatles message had made it across the continent, how it had could have found its way through the fences, or whether the Fab Four were now as rare here as those tigers.

We passed a garishly colored statue of a tiger, and I saw a horse running loose in the midst of traffic. Through the veil of my jet lag after the seven-hour flight from Moscow, everything seemed wild and edgy. At last the old bus rattled into the city, wheezing up the switchback hills overlooking the harbor that have reminded some visitors of San Francisco—Vladivostok's twin city. To me it looked more like Liverpool—if Stalin had been in charge of the town plan-ning. Gray tower blocks littered the hillsides, and the place still had the brooding feel of the closed city.

But things were clearly stirring. The streets were alive with young women, teetering along on daringly high heels and squeezed into microskirts that emphasized legs as long and slender as the cattle-herding women I'd filmed in East Africa. The city seemed to be under siege from battalions of construction cranes, and a gigantic new suspension bridge was poised to throw itself over a bay. The bus juddered to a halt near a colossal statue of heroic soldiers. "That's the memorial to the fighters for Soviet power in the Far East," my driver said. Clearly the old Soviet empire still had some fans here. But to-night at least it looked as though the heroic fighters would have to share the stage with a rock concert. A huge open-air stage was being set up in the harbor square, and guitar riffs were roaring across the waterfront as roadies assembled their rock paraphernalia.

I jumped down from the bus. A blonde woman with no-nonsense spectacles bore down on me, trailed by an impish man sporting a pigtail. This had to be Natalya and Andrei, the moving spirits of the Pacific Meridian Film Festival. "You must come see photo gallery," Natalya commanded. The exhibition of rock 'n' roll photographs I had taken in the early sixties was due to open in a couple of days, and Natalya wanted me to see the venue. The State Philharmonic Hall was an imposing building, commanding the waterfront with a fine prerevolutionary panache. In a window, I spotted a familiar photo of John Lennon—a picture I had taken almost fifty years earlier. It was now the centerpiece of a poster for my exhibition "Rock Icons." Seeing it here on the other side of the world was disorienting, like a hallucination fed by jet lag.

I followed Natalya and Andrei up a grand stairway to the gallery, an attractive room overlooking the harbor. It was a good place for the photos of the lads from Liverpool to find a berth. I would be hanging the pictures tomorrow in frames sent from Moscow, and Art Troitsky would introduce the opening the day after that. But would anyone come, I wondered? And then as I was leaving the gallery, a guy came up to shake my hand. "I am Beatle man," he said.

I had only recently rediscovered my rock photographs, and the show in Vladivostok would be the first time I had put them together for an exhibition. Bringing them all the way from England, nestled between the shirts and underpants in my suitcase, had made me revisit the time, almost fifty years before, when I had taken the pictures. Could it possibly have been so long ago? I could still see those afternoons in the Manchester TV studios when I was a kid with a camera. The Beatles, the Stones, Little Richard, and Jerry Lee Lewis came to record shows in the studios where I was a trainee director, finding my feet in the routines of nightly magazine programs. As the sixties began to lift off, an extraordinary parade of people who would soon become rock royalty passed through the studios to plug their latest records. The Beach Boys, Simon and Garfunkel, the Kinks, the Hollies, and countless others came and went, most of them without causing much of a stir. The Rolling Stones did upset one producer, who declared that their hair was unacceptably long for a family program and tried to have them ejected. Crisis talks ensued, hair was preserved, and the Stones did their thing.

My boyhood passion for photography had recently been rekindled by a new single-lens reflex camera, and from time to time I wandered into the studios where the visiting rock folk were performing to grab pictures. Following that first filming with the Beatles in August 1962, I had renewed the acquaintance when they came to perform "Please Please Me" in January 1963. Over the following year they returned regularly to the Manchester studio, and when they came to perform "I Should Have Known Better" in October 1964, I grabbed a single roll of film, exchanged a few words with the boys, and moved around the studio snapping a couple dozen shots as they rehearsed the song. I finished the roll of film, and then went back to working in another studio on a program about the history of cycling. Over the next few months, I looked in on other rock people with my camera and took a few more rolls of film. And then, unaccountably, I lost my rock photos.

Where the hell were they? Why didn't I take hundreds more pictures? How could I have been so casual about having a front-row seat as the giants of 1960s rock 'n' roll paraded past my camera? From time to time I kept looking, but after a while I reckoned that between office juggling and house moves, they must have slipped through the cracks in my life. That was how it was, after all, with making documentaries. I would be consumingly involved with a project for a few weeks or months—guerrilla war in Africa, earthquake in Peru, nomadic tribes in Ethiopia, jazz in New Orleans—and then one night the film would be broadcast, and the next morning it was gone. All those intense relationships, the war criminals, the saints, the film crews, the never-ending cycle of engaging and moving on. I took thousands of photos wherever I went, but I kept remembering the missing rock photos. Where were they? Were they any good? Might they be worth a fortune?

And then, not long ago, I had found them. I opened a drawer and there they were, shut away in a plain envelope. I peered at the shadowy images preserved on negatives—John Lennon, Paul McCartney, Mick Jagger, Little Richard, Jerry Lee Lewis. They had slumbered in my drawer over the decades, like pharaohs snoozing in their tombs. I was ecstatic. I hunted down a man who could print the negatives, a rare craftsman in an age where digital cameras had made black-and-white negatives as irrelevant as typewriters and carbon paper. In a London basement, I watched as Peter Guest—who prints Linda McCartney's archive—coaxed life back into my old negatives. The Fab Four swam up out of the developing bath, youngsters again on the verge of everything.

I told Art Troitsky about the photographs, and I could see that even the "Jesus of Cool" was intrigued. "Why don't you do an exhibition?" he said. "Bring the photos to the Pacific Meridian Festival and I'll host the opening." Now I was in Vladivostok, looking at a poster for "Rock Icons."

The tops of the harbor cranes were vanishing into a sea mist as the rock concert blasted out from the stage. It looked like a concert anywhere; a buxom girl and a strutting man with a medallion were projected on a huge screen, firing an anonymous anthem at the crowd gathered round the heroic statue. Now I just needed to sleep. The distant uproar of the concert drifted through my hotel window as I pulled the curtains shut.

Next morning, at the Hyundai—the only remotely international hotel in Vladivostok—they were gearing up to be the focus of the film festival. In the lobby, a gang of youngsters in blue-and-white striped T-shirts were busy laying out leaflets and checking guest lists. They resembled a jolly yachting crew, radiating can-do energy, and they were mostly, I gathered, volunteers from the university. I met up with Vasilisa, a friendly young woman with impeccable English who said she was going to be my guide. She was nineteen, she loved the Beatles, and she said she was studying Chinese—"Like many of my friends." It gave me an intriguing tilt on things, being in a place that looked out on the world from the very edge of my mental map. For Vasilisa and her friends, China was as close as Paris was for me at home in England. "Many girls drive to China to buy clothes," she said. "It's so much cheaper." She said girls also popped into China to look for husbands.

I was still feeling bleary, and the breakfast room of the Hyundai, swathed in shades of brown like the rest of the hotel, didn't exactly encourage guests to greet the day with a smile. Glum waitresses dispensed lukewarm sausages, and it seemed that the limited charms of post-Soviet hospitality were being tested out here in Vladivostok. Festival delegates peered into their coffee, and I spotted a handsome Frenchman carrying his own bread to a table. "I brought it from Paris," he said. "I have been here before." He lifted his eyes to the ceiling.

One way and another, my life has been choreographed for decades by these documentary festivals. If it's November, it must be Amsterdam; January is Biarritz, in April doc migrants trek to São Paulo, May is Tel Aviv—and so the year winds on. It's a resolutely un-Hollywood circuit, populated mainly by poverty-stricken doc folk desperate to screen some film they have mortgaged their babies to make, and to beg funding for their next venture about the plight of tribal people in the rain forests. The style is more anoraks and backpacks than designer dresses and shades. I found that meeting up with the same supplicants touting the same films year after year was increasingly dispiriting, and I had jumped off the merry-go-round some time ago. Vladivostok promised something new. It was too far away for even the most intrepid documentary gypsy, and anyway they had offered to show my photographs. I couldn't say no.

Natalya and Andrei had a crowded schedule of events arranged for me. On a morning when the sun was smudged by the inevitable dust, we drove out along a switchback of vertiginous streets to an interview at Radio Lemma. It looked like radio stations everywhere: dying plants on collapsing shelves, ashtrays piled with cigarette butts. The torrent of questions about the Beatles suggested that the boys were still big in Vladivostok. "What do you say about George?" "Do you think Paul is really dead? His bare feet on the Abbey Road cover surely prove it." "What was John Lennon really like?" The questions were translated by an elegant woman called Larissa whose card told me she was "a Professor Coordinator for Cross-Cultural Projects." She said she had been a Beatles fan since she was a girl. I was still feeling drowsy, but one phone-in caller grabbed my attention. He was disappointed by the films in the festival program. "Can't we have more films of violence and humiliation?" he asked. The radio show's hostess put her head in her hands.

I had asked to meet some local Beatles fans, and Andrei, the festival organizer with the pigtail, evidently had a hotline to the local Fab community. "No problem finding Beatlemen," he said; and the next morning he delivered an authentic fan. A quiet man with steel-rimmed spectacles in a white Honda sedan came to pick me up at the hotel. "Vladimir Studenkov," he murmured as we powered up another dizzying hill. At the end of a wordless journey, we got out of the car. We were high above the city, and my companion introduced a spectacular panorama with a wave of his arm. It was as though this mild man was somehow claiming ownership of the city. Feeling unsteady, and about to topple over the balustrade into the huge space with its tangle of half-completed roads and bridges crammed up against the vast harbor, I tried to understand why I'd been brought here. To talk about the Beatles? To enjoy the view? As we stood there, Vladimir and I and the spectacle of Vladivostok, behind us there was a burst of laughter. I looked up and saw a bride in a white dress with her brand-new husband. They were standing at the foot of a towering statue, a monkish-looking figure in a long robe. "It's a monument to Saint Cyril," Vladimir said, "the man who devised the Russian alphabet." I guessed this must be the local version of the Yuri Gagarin statue in Moscow, a shrine where newly married couples dedicate their wedding to a hero. It all heightened the sense I often have in Russia, where I'm unsure of what's really happening.

"So Vladimir," I ventured at last, "tell me about you and the

Beatles." It was the trigger he was waiting for. "I grew up in a town about two hundred miles from here," he began, and I tried to imagine how remote that must have been when he was a boy, growing up in a place where wild tigers were much easier to find than Beatles records. "It was a closed military town like Vladivostok," he went on, "but I had heard a Beatles song recorded by a soldier from a military radio." It had been hard for privileged kids in Moscow and Leningrad to track down information about this hypnotic new music. Hunting for the Beatles from Komsomolsk, where Vladimir lived on the limits of the Soviet Wild East, must have been like searching for a new constellation with toy binoculars. But he had the unstoppable dedication of the convert. "I found an old copy of a music magazine from Czechoslovakia, *Melodiya* it was called, and it told me something about the Beatles." That source disappeared after the Soviet invasion of Czechoslovakia in 1968, but by then Vladimir had found other ways to fuel his passion.

He looked out over the city toward the bay, sparkling now in a splash of sun. "I wanted to record Beatles music from the Japanese radio I could pick up, but I couldn't find any reel-to-reel tapes." Again, the Soviet military came to the rescue of a rock-starved teenager. "I got hold of army audio tapes. They were big, as wide as a book, so I sliced them into thin strips that I could use in my reel-to-reel tape recorder." As so often on my journey, I was staggered by the ingenuity and pioneering determination of the Beatles generation.

Vladimir Studenkov's memories were interrupted by a shouted greeting, and a rangy man with the bristling gray hair of a startled badger strode toward us, introducing himself before he arrived. "Alexander Gorodny," he yelled, and then crushed my hand in a fierce grip. I spotted his Frank Zappa T-shirt, but he was already urging us toward an immaculate building that looked like an outstation of a Disney theme park. Cherry-red roofs and turrets gave the place the look of a child's fantasy castle. "My gallery," Gorodny announced. At last I began to understand why I had been brought to this place with

Gorodny's castle high over the city. The Beatles connection was still mysterious.

A shiny brass plaque announced that we had reached ARTETAGE, and along with Vladimir I followed the two-tone shoes of our unstoppable host as he galloped up several flights of gleaming white stairs. Leading the way, Gorodny gave us a running commentary about the gallery. "Artists in Vladivostok felt isolated in Soviet times, but they adapted in the same way jazz and rock music adapted. When Gorbachev arrived, they dragged their work out of storage, full of hope." He reached the top of the stairs and paused at the door of a huge room lined with paintings. "But we all had a feeling of lost possibilities."

He moved on. "We'll look at the pictures later. Come into my office, and let's talk about the Beatles and rock 'n' roll." With a child's abandon, he hauled up his Zappa T-shirt to reveal a Rolling Stones tattoo on his shoulder—the inevitable lascivious-mouth-and-lolling-tongue logo. On the wall, a photograph of Jimi Hendrix smiled down approvingly.

From a cupboard, Gorodny hauled down a pile of books, each beautifully bound in blue denim. "This is how I kept the faith in Soviet times," he said. As he turned the pages, I saw an exquisite record of rock 'n' roll history. He was clearly a remarkable draftsman, and he had drawn perfect copies of scores of classic album covers: the Beatles' *Abbey Road*, of course, and *Sgt. Pepper*, the Who, Pink Floyd, the Doors, King Crimson, T. Rex, Jethro Tull, Stones, Stones, Stones. It put me in mind of Kolya Vasin's archive in Saint Petersburg, but where Kolya had amassed a collage of clippings and memorabilia, Gorodny had labored to create a handmade memorial to decades of forbidden Western rock. The precision and detail had the obsessive quality of a monkish scribe.

"How on earth did you find all these albums to copy when they were illegal?" I asked, "and Vladivostok was so remote and closed to all outsiders?" Gorodny seemed lost in his memories as he turned another page and found a naked body on which he had replaced all the acupuncture points with names of rock bands. The Beatles were the heart. "Well, that's interesting," he said. "Remember, Vladivostok is a huge port city, so we always had an endless traffic of ships and sailors bringing in new things. We often got news before they did in Leningrad, and I remember we knew Janis Joplin was dead before kids in Moscow." It was another reminder that my mental map was skewed. Vladivostok was wildly remote from my European perspective; but the huge port connected the city to the outside world. Of course it was how the port of Liverpool became a gateway for the black American music that had fired up the Beatles' love of rock 'n' roll.

Still, Alexander Gorodny had his battles. "In the sixties, I had red shoes and long hair, so they sent me off to the army. I was forbidden to go outside the Soviet Union." While he was in the army, two of his precious books were stolen. After his military service, he became a sailor and spent much of his time in foreign ports collecting rock albums. On his visits home, he would tape the records for his friends and the virus claimed more victims. "In 1969," he said, "I found myself in London and I was determined to be at the Rolling Stones' free concert in Hyde Park." I remember it well, because I was there for that mass gathering of the 1960s tribes—a quarter of a million mods and rockers and hippies. That Hyde Park concert, when Mick Jagger released ten thousand butterflies and recited a Shelley poem in memory of Brian Jones who had just died, became lodged in the collective 1960s memory. It was cherished as the last good moment before the hippie dream collapsed—and those butterflies devastated every green plant within miles. "My ship got orders to sail, so I missed the concert," Alexander said, "and it still upsets me now more than forty years later." I told him I had filmed that Hyde Park concert, and I would be screening the film here in Vladivostok. He grabbed my hand.

Vladimir Studenkov had been quiet for a while. Now he said,

"The Beatles spoke to the Russian soul." Alexander Gorodny echoed the thought I had heard in Moscow. "If such wonderful music is forbidden, we knew there must be something wrong with our country." Then he smiled. He opened another of his books. "Now those times are like a bad dream." He found the page he was looking for. "Alice Cooper came here," he said, and there was a photo of Alexander with Alice. Remembering Cooper's stage show featuring guillotines, electric chairs, and boa constrictors, I couldn't imagine what had brought the outrageous grandfather of heavy metal to Vladivostok. But I also recalled that Alice was a huge golf fan, so maybe there was a special course somewhere out here where he could fight a tiger for his lost ball.

We went into the gallery, a handsome space lit up with sunlight cascading through a glass roof. There were dozens of paintings on the walls, and Alexander was visibly proud of the collection. "These were all done by artists from this region before perestroika, when it could still be dangerous to speak out," he said. There were startling images, mixing anti-Communist jokes and religious icons with blasphemous portraits of Lenin. I remembered what Gorodny had said about "lost possibilities," and how artists had been compelled to adapt like rock fans. Art Troitsky had said that the Soviet Union had vanished like fog in the morning; but looking around the gallery I could see some of the costs of that long struggle to resist the dictates of the commissars who insisted that artists should be "engineers of the human soul."

I walked back to his car with Vladmir Studenkov. He told me that he now spent much of his time making digital copies of his huge rock collection and swapping them with friends across Russia. I wondered if he had ever traveled in the past beyond his isolated home in Komsomolsk—a town built by idealistic young pioneers in the early 1930s with the slogan "Subjugating Time and Overcoming Adversities." "Were you able to be in Red Square when Paul McCartney played there?" I asked him—and then wished I hadn't. He looked upset. "No," he said, "but I saw the concert on TV." He looked out over the city. "I cried." He put his hand on my arm and it was clear he wanted to say something more. "The Beatles were like bread for us."

Documentary festivals soon morph into self-absorbed communes with their own territories and rituals. This time, the Hyundai was the gathering place. For me, breakfast meant meeting up with a bleary Art Troitsky, climbing out of yet another late-night bash with local movers and shakers. He was hanging an exhibition of his collection of paintings in a Vladivostok gallery, and he told me he was calling the show Still Farther East. He unfurled a poster that featured one of the paintings: a highly colored portrait of a black woman in a pink shawl with a white dog sprouting yellow wings. I thought it looked perfectly Art. The elegant Frenchman who transported his bread from Paris was a breakfast regular, and I gathered he was preparing the way for film star Vincent Perez who, like me, was presenting an exhibition of his photographs at the festival. Half of Vincent's photos were stuck in Moscow customs, so his front man was spending most his days trying to get them out. He was, I thought, enviably relaxed—but then he mentioned that his wife was a stratospherically rich wine heiress.

And so the days rolled by in a benign daze of screenings and openings. For me there was the curious experience of being some kind of second-hand celebrity. My Beatles connection made me the target of autograph hunters and groups of Fab fans who lined up to be photographed with "the man who filmed the Beatles a long time ago." I felt as much of a fraud as I had when I was asked for my autograph in the sixties by an insistent but deluded man outside the TV studio in Manchester. I signed "Yours sincerely, George Harrison." I had the hair for it in those days.

One of the festival volunteers told me she had caught the Beatles virus from her mother. She brought her mum over to say hello.

Mum had stories about how Beatles albums used to flood off the boats arriving in the harbor. "But you had to be careful," she said. "You could be punished copying them and passing them around."

The festival's nightly rendezvous was the Hyundai's rooftop bar. A robotic band played nonstop bossa nova, waitresses who seemed traumatized by some recent tragedy served ruinously expensive drinks, statuesque hookers drifted by. I met the French film star Perez, who was smart and charming. He had entrancing stories about how he had inherited Carla Bruni from Mick Jagger as his girlfriend, and then had passed her on to Nicolas Sarkozy. I felt I had slipped through a time warp into 1967, where Paul McCartney might turn up with Jane Asher and Marianne Faithfull would drop by with Mick.

Art Troitsky's opening was hot and claustrophobic. Hundreds of people glanced at the paintings and then moved on hoping for a glimpse of the famous Troitsky. Television cameras twirled, cell-phone cameras flashed. I fought my way outside and found Perez, relaxing with a drink. We watched as Art emerged, burdened by a huge bouquet. "What a star!" Vincent said.

I walked up the blue carpet, feeling I had slipped into a fantasy. The official opening of the Pacific Meridian Film Festival was clearly aiming for the full Oscar-night glitz. Anorexic women and tanned men in tuxedos and dark glasses were welcomed to the carpet by a thunderous announcer. Crowds of spectators cheered and blitzed their cell-phone flashes at every new arrival. And now it was my turn to run the gauntlet of the celeb-hungry crowd. They can have had no idea who I was, but they cheered and flashed anyway. I approached the receiving line, an unsmiling troop of navy men in pressed white uniforms, and then the real stars of the evening, the governor of Primorye Province, broad-shouldered and command-ing, together with his first lady, a former actress. I had been advised that the festival was really her toy, and she looked radiant in her gold ball gown and big diamonds. She offered her cheek to Art Troitsky for a fond kiss. Somewhere, a military band was playing "Yesterday." At the head of the carpet, I was interviewed for television by a pretty girl who also had no idea who I was. It was all preposterous, and hugely enjoyable.

I joined the throng in a hot holding area, sipping warm sweet champagne.

This was all much more fun, I thought, than the regular festivals of my experience where people got together for grave conversations about the problems of fund-raising, or the whims of BBC executives. And there wasn't an anorak or a backpack to be seen.

I gathered we were awaiting the arrival of a real celebrity. I had been startled to discover that Liza Minnelli was to join us for a screening of *Cabaret*. It has always been one of my favorite films, but it felt a very long way from home here. Minnelli had been recruited for the festival by a man who had caught my eye prowling through various events for days now. Rock Brynner was an unmissable figure, a tiny man perpetually welded to his fedora hat, and much given to regaling everyone in sight with his stories. Since his father was Yul Brynner, they were sometimes interesting stories. Yul Brynner had been born in Vladivostok and his house in the city was a place of pilgrimage. But Yul had moved out for Hollywood, and the star of *The King and I* and *The Magnificent Seven* had provided his son with A-list acquaintances. I had overheard Rock Brynner telling someone that as a boy, he used to babysit Salvador Dalí's ocelot, and that had impressed me mightily. After tending to the ocelot, and its unpredictable owner, I guessed that persuading his friend Liza Minnelli to circle the planet and come to Vladivostok would have been a breeze.

And here she was, that utterly familiar face being shepherded through the crowd by Brynner. She walked a little stiffly now, but she dispensed her smiles with the effortless warmth and confidence of a true star. I wasn't entirely sure that the celebrity hunters here knew who Liza Minnelli was either.

In the impressive auditorium, the opening entertainment began. High-energy dancers, imported from Moscow, dashed through a gauche routine about moviemaking; a pair of comedians, also imported from Moscow, seemed to baffle the audience, plowing on for minutes without generating a single laugh. Alongside me, I noticed Art Troitsky was deeply asleep. The opening ceremony came to a climax as a procession of freakishly tall girls walked onto the stage. Like a parody of a game show, they struggled to balance bulky glass awards on wobbly-looking plinths. I fought to stifle a huge sneeze.

The screening of *Cabaret* began. To my disbelief, Minnelli's magical songs were completely drowned by a gravel-voiced Russian translation of the lyrics. On my Beatles wanderings, I had often been told that Russian popular music placed a high priority on the lyrics, but this was too much. I groped my way to an exit.

The governor's reception was a strangely muted affair after the Hollywood pastiche of the festival opening. About a half-hour out of the city, the official mansion was a charmless white office block. It was dark now, and guests stumbled around in the gloom harvesting hot dogs and canapés from platters displayed in small plastic tents. The governnor's first lady passed by with a throng of acolytes, her jewelry sparkling in the gloom. Folk groups played on a distant stage. The beams from green lasers flickered in the trees. I talked to a nice young Englishman called Stravinsky who bashfully admitted he was a direct descendant of the great composer, and said he was here to conduct the Vladivostok Symphony Orchestra. "We need a lot of rehearsal," he said. He promised he'd come to my photo exhibition the next day, and I had a memory of how his illustrious ancestor once went to hear Charlie Parker in New York. Parker had spotted the great Stravinsky and mischievously inserted a quote from *The Rite of Spring* into his solo.

Art Troitsky went on the stage to sing something lugubrious with an anonymous band. Still trying to throw off the remains of my jet lag, I was ready to call it a day. As I was making my way to the gate an insistent woman wanted to interrogate me about the Beatles. "What do you say about John Lennon?"

From the window of the gallery where people were gathering for my photo exhibition, I watched an old man with an accordion. He wore a jaunty naval hat, and alongside his seat he had opened a case with a colorful poster inside the lid. I could just see the words FOLK SONGS and a few scattered coins. It was a timeless Russian scene, with nothing to place it in the twenty-first century. I turned back into the gallery and my two dozen rock photos on the walls felt weirdly out of place. Little Richard strutting his stuff on top of a piano; Jerry Lee Lewis raving into a microphone, mobbed by leather-clad rockers; Mick Jagger, impossibly young, sharing a song with Brian Jones; and the Beatles, larking in a TV studio. I felt responsible for dragging them around the world, and I wondered what kind of welcome they'd find here.

There was quite a crowd gathering now, peering at the photos, copying them on their cell phones, setting up video cameras. My new Beatles chums Alexander Gorodny and Vladimir Studenkov gave me a wave. Alex Stravinsky was here with his Russian wife. I was dragged off to be photographed with elderly Beatles fans, lobbied to sign autographs by matrons with purple hair and youths wearing Beatles T-shirts. Gorodny pushed through the crowd. "I brought you something," he said, and handed over a copy of the album Paul McCartney had made for fans in Russia. The "golden disk" that had been converted into cars by Yuri Pelyushonok and his shipmates had clearly made it all the way to Vladivostok. Like Pelyushonok, Gorodny felt a personal connection with the record. On the back, after his name he had drawn a peace sign.

Soon there was a queue of people clutching scraps of paper, gazing at me with that hungry look of fans anywhere, eager for a brief contact with this man who had met the Beatles long, long ago. For a moment, I had a glimpse of how stifling it must have been for the

Fab Four, shut inside a bubble of neediness and adoration. Now the interviewers were gathering, with their tape recorders and video crews. For me, the struggle to find something new to say to the repeating litany of questions—"What was Paul McCartney like?" "What do you say about Mick Jagger?"—began to induce a mild panic. There was a burst of shouting, and through the crowd I saw Art Troitsky, who was a real celebrity here, grappling with a woman wearing a John Lennon cap and brandishing a camera. It was time to declare the exhibition open.

Troitsky freed himself from his insistent fan and came across to join me. "Poyekhaly," he said, quoting Yuri Gagarin's breezy words before he blasted off into history: "Let's go!" I was happy to follow Gagarin's lead for my own tiny liftoff. Art was the perfect launch controller for my exhibition, funny, informative, concise. I thought he looked surprisingly bright, as he told me he'd been singing at the governor's reception until two thirty in the morning. I was well aware that his support added a lot to the occasion and to the interest in the pictures. There was applause, and then the autograph hunters swooped again. I felt like Brian in *Monty Python's Life of Brian*, pursued by thousands of supplicants who are convinced he's Jesus. But I felt this was not the place to employ Brian's unforgettable response to his baying followers: "I say unto you—fuck off!"

A chubby round-faced man with circular spectacles had been hovering for a while, and now he needed to ask me a question. "Do you think I look like John Lennon?" he said, flashing a confident smile. "Everyone says I do." I looked at the man, lost for words.

27

As I approached the end of my time in Vladivostok, I was also ending my journey to explore how the Beatles had rocked the Kremlin. A search that had begun for me thirty years earlier, when the Soviet Union had seemed frozen and unchangeable, was winding to a close here on the remote edge of a country transformed beyond imagining.

I spent a few hours wandering the city from the old Chinese quarter to the soaring new bridges across the harbor. Exploring the tracks behind the featureless apartment blocks, I came upon ancient wooden houses marooned amid vegetable plots, and I felt I was tracking the story of the place, getting a sense of the pell-mell changes that were tearing up historic Vladivostok as they were refashioning Russia itself in the early twenty-first century.

Over the final few days in Vladivostok, I screened five of my films, and tried to answer a torrent of questions. A woman veiled in black net pursued me bearing a photograph of a pretty boy with a guitar. "My son is so talented," she said, "you must take him to London and introduce him to record producers." I felt a bit like John Lennon when he was asked to lay his hands on wheelchair fans and make them walk again. The autograph hunters kept up their hunt, and I

was asked to smile for countless photos alongside people whose mo-
tives eluded me. I found myself growing fond of this place a very
long way from home.

On my last day, I went back to my photo exhibition. It was quiet
now, just an elderly man carrying a plastic bag who was gazing at
the Beatles pictures in a kind of rapture. Out on the street, the old
guy with the accordion and the naval cap was playing his folk songs.
I found a chair and sat down in front of the Beatles pictures.

It had all begun for me with those kids playing in a cellar in Liverpool. Like millions of others across the world, I had followed the
extraordinary blossoming of their music across the sixties, and the
story always had the special personal ingredient of that first encounter. Again, like most of my generation, I had lamented the ending of
the Beatles, and from time to time had become entangled with the
continuing story—the deaths of John and George, the resolute
grumpiness of Ringo, the unstoppable epic of Paul—as the music
somehow refused to fade and became a soundtrack of our lives.

The Beatles had become bound up with my gathering obsession
with Russia. As I followed the Gorbachev revolution and the collapse
of the Soviet Union, I had been astonished to discover how often the
Beatles were part of the story. Tracking that story from Moscow and
Saint Petersburg to Kiev and Minsk, and finding it was still being
told here in Vladivostok, confirmed what I had come to realize along
the way. The Beatles had done something remarkable here.

But how had it happened? How had Art Troitsky's "monster state"
been shifted by a few three-minute songs? As I had traveled through
the Soviet Union in its final years, I had witnessed some of the forces
pushing for change. There was the final loss of faith in the utopian
Soviet project and its dream of making a new society; there was the
unavoidable recognition that the vast networks of central planning
were exhausted and could never deliver a better life for citizens who
were becoming more aware than ever of the outside world after Gorbachev's tentative liberations. And as a disenchanted commentator

observed, trying to mix totalitarian control with a bit of democracy was "like trying to fry snowballs." The melting of monumental state systems left them more vulnerable than ever to the seditious impact of the rock 'n' roll generation.

Above all, there was the huge frustration of millions of young people who understood their lives were defined and constrained by an old ideology and a frozen bureaucracy. In Belarus, I had seen how in the twenty-first century an entire state was still shut away from the world by its rulers, and it gave me a vivid snapshot of how it had been for the Beatles generation in the U.S.S.R. At the same time, the kids were finding their own escape routes. Seva Gakkel had told me in Saint Petersburg, "I belonged to the Beatles world." In a society where politics was dangerous and new ideas were seen as threatening, culture was embraced as the only way to pursue change. Andrei Tropillo, the man who made millions of Beatles records available to Soviet citizens, put it simply. "This is what the Beatles did. They opened the door to Western culture, and that produced a cultural revolution that destroyed the Soviet Union."

I remembered how many of the people I had met felt sure that their lives had been changed by these four young men they had never been allowed to see. Andrei Makarevich had been inspired to become a rock musician, and so had Stas Namin and Boris Grebenshikov and Alexander Gradsky. In a real sense, the explosion of rock music in the Soviet Union had been ignited by contact with the Beatles via crackling illicit radio stations and with the crazy improvisations of records on bones. And as Nikita in Kiev put it, "The Soviet Communist Party was strangled by our tape recordings." Hearing about those homemade guitars and vandalized telephones, I had felt the unstoppable force that had powered the Beatles generation.

Most fundamental of all was the way the Beatles phenomenon seemed to have shifted something inside the heads and guts of that generation. I was made to understand how visceral that shift was felt to be. Time and again people talked about being "freed from fear," about the Beatles having "killed the slave inside them." As Boris Grebenshikov put it, "The Beatles started to change the way people think, the way people feel." Time and again, people I met insisted on making a direct connection between the impact of the Beatles and the collapse of totalitarianism. Art Troitsky declared, "They alienated a whole generation from their Communist motherland, and prepared Soviet kids for different human values. The message we took was 'we're free even though we live behind the Iron Curtain.'" And Vladimir Pozner, the Soviet journalist and propagandist who had spent decades making truth into good news, put it directly. "The system was built on belief and fear. The Beatles helped people to overcome the fear—and they showed that the belief was actually stupid."

At the end of my journey, it still seemed extraordinary. I'm a confirmed agnostic about most things, and John Lennon's song could be my mantra: "I don't believe in magic / Don't believe in Bible / Don't believe in Jesus"—and, like Lennon, I don't believe in mantras. Of course John had ended his list "I don't believe in Beatles." And I had struggled to believe this story of how the Beatles had rocked the Kremlin. Fifty-year-old pop songs by a group of lads from an enemy country, who were banned and derided—had they really shifted a superpower? As improbable, surely, as the notion that culture can force change? As naïve as the slogan "all you need is love"; as Utopian as the song "Imagine."

The old guy with the plastic bag who had been gazing at my photographs came and introduced himself. "Viktor Alexandrov," he said. "I'm an engineer and historian—and a musician. I used to have this band." He unfurled a poster. It showed a group of youngsters, decked out in full Sergeant Pepper gear. Three guys, two girls smiled out at me, a youthful Viktor in the middle. "That was us," he said. "We always loved the Beatles."

CODA

In February 2012, a feminist punk collective called Pussy Riot became the latest recruits in the battle between popular music and the Russian state. The improbable battleground was the monumental Cathedral of Christ the Savior in central Moscow, not far from the Kremlin. The original cathedral had been destroyed by Stalin, and the lavish replacement was built in the 1990s. From a distance it looks impressive, a vast edifice topped with huge golden domes. Up close, it's a kitschy Putinesque fantasy, and for the political pop activists of Pussy Riot, it had an obvious appeal. They had launched their mischievous assaults on Russian establishment targets eighteen months earlier, staging their brief unannounced performances in carefully chosen locations. The group mounted their attack on the excesses of the fashion industry in an expensive clothing store, and then startled diners at an expensive restaurant by delivering a song about the indulgences of lavish eating.

Pussy Riot chose the Cathedral of Christ the Savior to focus on their ultimate target, Vladimir Putin. Masked in their trademark fluorescent balaclavas, they began to deliver their punk prayer beseeching "Holy Mother, Blessed Virgin" to "chase Putin out." Within seconds, police grabbed the women and bundled them out of the cathedral. It seemed to be the end of the protest.

Then, in the days after the performance, three members of the Pussy Riot collective were tracked down and arrested by police. Following his reelection as Russian president in May 2012, during a speech signaling an impending political crackdown, Putin called for harsh punishment of the Pussy Riot Three, as the arrested women had become known. The Patriarch of Moscow and All Russia condemned the performance as blasphemous, saying, "The devil has mocked all of us." The women were held for months facing charges of "hooliganism motivated by religious hatred," which carried a threat of seven-year sentences. At a time when Putin was bearing down on all areas of opposition, including the shutting of more than a thousand websites, the detention of Pussy Riot was seen as part of the biggest drive since the Soviet era to silence government critics.

A gathering chorus of Russia's cultural elite called for the release of Pussy Riot. Some twenty-five thousand people signed a letter of protest, and benefit concerts were held from Prague to Warsaw. Sting, Pete Townshend, and Yoko Ono lent their support. One of the leaders of the campaign to free the women was Art Troitsky.

I met up again with Troitsky in the summer of 2012 when he was lecturing at Middlebury College in Vermont. He was somber about the implications of the Pussy Riot affair. "This couldn't have happened, even in Brezhnev's time," he told me. "It's a reminder that Russia is still a hundred-percent medieval system ruled from the top." But he insisted that while the attack on Pussy Riot was a throwback to Stalin's rule over Russian culture, Russian citizens were different now. "People from the Beatles generation who want to live normally are aware of other countries, and they know things don't have to be this way."

I recalled a video I had seen recently of a flash mob gathering in Moscow in which hundreds of youngsters had come together for a thrillingly choreographed version of "Puttin' on the Ritz"—rebranded as "Putin on the Ritz." It had happened at about the same time as the Pussy Riot performance in the Cathedral of Christ the Savior, and the joyous energy of those kids dancing in the flash mob on a raw winter's day confirmed Troitsky's belief that the children and grandchildren of the Beatles generation are determined to defy the Kremlin's latest crackdown and insist on a "normal life."

Art Troitsky, mellow in Vermont, July 2012.

Talking in the benign sunshine of a Vermont summer afternoon, Troitsky recalled the anti-Putin demonstrations of the Moscow winter. "I was on crutches after a foot accident, but I was beaten to the ground by police," he said. Now he also told me how the campaign for the imprisoned Pussy Riot women was gathering strength. "As Putin has banned 'gatherings,' it would not be realistic to stage a concert in our police state," he said. Writers and artists have arranged protest walks, attended by thousands, and Art had been asked to arrange musicians' walks. "I told them that musicians don't walk. So we decided to set up an Internet project asking musicians who support honest elections, law reform, and the Pussy Riot women to donate one track of original music. So far, we've received more than three hundred tracks."

The protesters against Putin have chosen the color white as their banner, often pinning a white ribbon to their coats. Putin has called the ribbons "condoms." In response, Troitsky told me he had addressed a recent demonstration dressed in a white rabbit costume. "I cut off the ears so I looked like a rebellious condom."

But the three women remained in jail, refusing to speak to authorities, even to confirm that they had taken part in the performance at the cathedral. In late July 2012, trial proceedings began in a Moscow district court surrounded by riot police facing protesters in the pouring rain. The Pussy Riot Three were paraded in court each day, closely guarded in a glass cage. In early August, they made their defiant final statements. One of the defendants, Maria Alyokhina, compared the trial to the repression of culture under Stalin.

Performing in Moscow during the trial, Madonna declared her support for the women by wearing a balaclava and displaying the words *Pussy Riot* on her back. "I pray for their freedom," she said. Russia's deputy premier branded Madonna "a slut."

Finally on August 17, 2012, the Pussy Riot women were found guilty of hooliganism and inciting religious hatred. They were sentenced to two years in a penal colony, sparking violent arrests in Moscow and demonstrations of support in dozens of cities around the world.

Meanwhile, the tracks continue to pour in to Art Troitsky's music project to support Pussy Riot. Soon enough he was able to fill four or five CDs. He had decided on a title: "The White Album." "After all," he said, "the original Beatles record with that title contained

'Revolution 1,' 'Revolution 9,' and 'Back in the U.S.S.R.' And since white is the color of our protest movement, that feels perfect." Paul McCartney sent a letter to the Pussy Riot Three urging them to "stay strong." And Troitsky asked McCartney to send a song for the new "White Album"—to rock the Kremlin one more time.

ACKNOWLEDGMENTS

My journeys in search of the extraordinary story of the Beatles in the old U.S.S.R., the new Russia, Ukraine, and Belarus have been made possible over the years by the generous advice and support of many people in Russia and the former Soviet Union.

My sincere thanks to the people who guided me and introduced me to the Beatles generation:

Kolya Vasin, Yuri Pelyushonok, Stas Namin, Sasha Lipnitsky, Andrei Makarevich, Boris Grebenshikov, Vladimir Matietsky, Vova Katzman, Sergei Ivanov, Svetlana Kunitsina, Masha Keder, Masha Oleneva, Alexander Gradsky, Andrei Tropillo, Igor Salnikov, Seva Gakkel, Maxim Kapitanovsky, Mikhail Safonov, and Yoko Ono.

My special thanks also for good conversation and fresh insights to Reggie Nadelson, Vladimir Pozner, and the late Jo Durden Smith.

Several earlier accounts have helped my understanding of the rich and sometimes bizarre story of popular music in the Soviet Union, and its importance in promoting change. I would like to acknowledge in particular:

Back in the USSR: The True Story of Rock in Russia by Artemy Troitsky; two books by Yuri Pelyushonok, *Strings for a Beatle Bass: The Beatles Generation in the USSR* and *Through the Eyes of a Cockroach*; the Ottawa Beatles Site (beatles.ncf.ca); "Rock on Russian Bones" by Kolya Vasin; *Red and Hot: The Fate of Jazz in the Soviet Union 1917–1991* by S. Frederick Starr; and *Rock Around the Bloc: A History of Rock Music in Eastern Europe and the Soviet Union, 1954–1988* by Timothy W. Ryback.

INDEX

NOTE: Page numbers in *italics* indicate a photograph.

A Note on the Author

LESLIE WOODHEAD OBE is one of Britain's most distinguished documentary filmmakers and made the first-ever film of the Beatles, in 1962. His films have won many international awards, including recognition by the Emmys and Peabodys in America and by BAFTA and the Royal Television Society in the United Kingdom. He is the author of two books, *My Life as a Spy* and *A Box Full of Spirits*. He lives in Cheshire.